Editorial by Sophie Cunningham

I kept a diary in 1975, through my first year of high school. I retain a particular fondness for my entry of 11 November: 'Today the Prime Minister of Australia was sacked. Mum and Dad say it's the end of democracy as we know it. Janice and I smoked a menthol cigarette.' At the time, of course, I was unaware of the Whitlam government's culpable actions regarding Indonesia's imminent invasion of East Timor, which took place a few weeks after Whitlam's sacking. His government had, however, already been made aware of the death of five Australian-based journalists in East Timor, and accepted the Suharto government's version of the stories that the Balibo Five were (variously) blown up in a house or caught in crossfire during battle. That culpability was passed, like a baton, from Whitlam to Fraser, to Hawke, to Keating and then to John Howard. It was Howard who finally supported East Timor's Declaration of Independence on 20 May 1999, though his government's refusal to put Australian troops on the ground for the referendum of 20 August allowed the Indonesians—in violent and graceless defeat—to kill around 1400 (more) Timorese, forcibly move 300,000 East Timorese into West Timor, and destroy some 90 per cent of East Timor's buildings and infrastructure, thus condemning it to several more generations of struggle. Australian troops finally went into East Timor in September 1999.

It is a strange feeling when one's childhood makes the shift from recent past to history. Things blur. It becomes harder to separate personal memory from media memory. Perhaps that's why Generation Jones kids (I'm one, apparently) are described as having 'a certain unrequited, jonesing quality'. It seems we're that 'large anonymous generation . . . Jonesers were given huge expectations as children in the 1960s, and then confronted with a different reality as they came of age in the 1970s'. But I digress. At the time of the initial invasion I was allowed to watch an hour of television a day—but news and current affairs shows were not included in that quota so I watched a lot of those. I can't remember if I'm so familiar with the footage of Greg Shackleton's reports from East Timor because I saw them at the time, or later, in the wake of media coverage of his disappearance—along with that of four colleagues—on 16 October 1975. Nonetheless my familiarity with the look and feel of that kind of footage made my response to Robert Connolly's film *Balibo* particularly visceral and I was surprised by the extent to which the story of the Balibo Five felt deeply personal. I also felt a deep shame. As Connolly said in my interview with him (p. 151), 'there's every reason for that shame to be part of our own national story'.

Shame is a word that was much used when I was growing up, and 'Shame Fraser, shame' was often chanted at demonstrations in the seventies. But shame strikes me as an emotion, like guilt, that is difficult to convert into any kind of meaningful outcome. It's an emotion that I felt most recently when watching the extraordinary *Four Corners* report on 8 June about an Aboriginal elder who died after being transported hundreds of kilometres and for four hours in a metal van in temperatures in the mid-forties. He suffered third-degree burns sitting on the metal floor of the van. The fact that people employed by a government agency can still perpetrate violence this gross against our indigenous population beggars belief. It would seem our current Prime Minister's moving and public shame back on 12 February 2008—'We apologise for the laws and policies of successive Parliaments and governments that have inflicted profound grief, suffering and loss on these our fellow Australians'—has not made a difference.

One of the things that is extraordinary about the story of both the Balibo Five and Roger East (the journalist who was assassinated on the docks of Dili soon after uncovering the details of their death) is that the shame their story provoked, the ramifications of those murders, contributed to East Timor's eventual independence. The tenth anniversary of Independence was celebrated on 30 August 2009. It is in solidarity with that anniversary that *Meanjin* is publishing the interview with Robert Connolly and an essay on the deaths at Balibo by Sian Prior that reminds us just how important memory, and remembering, are.

EDITOR
Sophie Cunningham

POETRY EDITOR
Judith Beveridge

DESIGN & PRODUCTION
Chase & Galley

COVER & SECTION ILLUSTRATIONS
Jon Paton. All illustrations are funded by the
Copyright Agency Limited (CAL)

NEWSREEL ILLUSTRATIONS
Oslo Davis

COPYEDITOR
Richard McGregor

PROOFREADERS
Natalie Book, Richard McGregor and Ian See

OFFICE MANAGER
Mary Kennedy

EDITORIAL ASSISTANT
Jessica Au

WEBSITE DESIGNER
Barking Sparrows

INTERNS
Bella Li, Daniel Mackay and Ian See

ADVISORY BOARD
Louise Adler, Laura Carroll, Kate Darian-Smith,
Mark Davis, Ken Gelder, Deb Verhoeven, Chris
Wallace-Crabbe, Michael Webster, Angela Woods

FOUNDING EDITOR
Clem Christesen (1911–2003; editor 1940–74)
Meanjin was founded in 1940. The name,
pronounced mee-*an*-jin, is derived from an
Aboriginal word for the spike on which Brisbane
sits. The magazine moved to Melbourne in 1945
at the invitation of the University of Melbourne.
The University has continued to be *Meanjin*'s
principal sponsor. In 2008 *Meanjin* became an
imprint of Melbourne University Publishing Ltd.

SUBSCRIPTIONS
Contact the *Meanjin* office, or subscribe online
at our website.

WHERE TO FIND US
Postal address: *Meanjin*, 187 Grattan Street,
Carlton, Victoria 3053 Australia
Telephone: (+61 3) 9342 0317
Fax: (+61 3) 9342 0399
Email: meanjin@unimelb.edu.au
Website: www.meanjin.com.au
Twitter: twitter.com/Meanjin
Facebook: www.facebook.com/pages/Meanjin-
Quarterly/49183750265?ref=ts

CONTRIBUTIONS
Unsolicited articles and stories are considered.
A style guide will be found on our website. Mini-
mum payment to contributors is $50 for poems,
$100 for prose. Copyright of each piece belongs to
the author; copyright of the collection belongs to
Meanjin. Republication is permitted on request to
author and editor. Published contributions by aca-
demics are refereed on request. See our website
for details. The views expressed by authors are
not necessarily those of the editor or publishers.

CORRECTIONS (AND APOLOGIES)
In Adrienne Eberhard's essay 'Sickness and the
Art of Healing' published in *Meanjin* 68: 1, the
last two sentences of the first paragraph are not
hers. The confusion occurred during typesetting.
In Rachel Buchanan's essay 'Len Lye and Me'
published in *Meanjin* 68: 2, the image on page
24 should be accompanied by the caption:
'Installation view of Len Lye: *Five Fountains and
a Firebush*, Govett-Brewster Art Gallery, New
Plymouth, 7 December 2007 – 24 February 2008.
Image courtesy Len Lye Foundation, Govett-
Brewster Art Gallery'. Equally, the caption for the
image on page 26 should read: 'Film still from
Rhythm (1957, 16mm, black & white, sound). Image
permission Len Lye Foundation, courtesy Govett-
Brewster Art Gallery, New Zealand Film Archive'.

PRODUCTION
Typeset in a variety of faces designed by
Hoefler & Frere-Jones
Printed and bound by BPA Print Group
Distributed by Pan Macmillan
Print Post Approved PP341403 0002
AU ISSN 0025-6293

○CONTRIBUTORS○

MEERA ATKINSON (P 94)
is a Sydney-based writer. Her short fiction, essays, articles and poetry have appeared in many publications including *Griffith Review*, *Heat*, Salon.com and *Best Australian Stories 2007*. Her website is meera.atkinson.googlepages.com.

GEORGIA BLAIN (P 183)
has published four novels and a memoir, *Births Deaths Marriages*. Her essays and short stories have been published in numerous journals both here and overseas and her first novel, *Closed For Winter*, was made into a feature film.

CAROLINE CADDY (P 218)
has eight books of poetry to her name. Her books have won the WA Week Prize, the NBC Banjo Award and the Wesley Michel Wright Prize for Poetry. She lives in Western Australia.

MARY CALLAHAN (P 32)
is a Melbourne designer who has won many awards for her book designs for a range of Australian literary titles, including *Gould's Book of Fish*. *Nick Cave* Stories led to her first-ever encounter with a rock star.

JUSTIN CLEMENS (P 38)
has written extensively on contemporary Australian art. His criticism has appeared in various publications. His recent books include *Black River* (re.press, 2007), illustrated by Helen Johnson, *The Mundiad* (Black Inc., 2004). His latest book is *Villain* (2009), published by Hunter Publishers. He teaches at the University of Melbourne.

OSLO DAVIS (P 6)
is a Melbourne illustrator and cartoonist.

DAN DISNEY (P 221)
is completing a PhD at the University of Melbourne and is a managing co-editor with Five Islands Press.

STEPHEN EDGAR (P 222)
lives in Sydney. He has published seven collections of poetry, the most recent being *History of the Day* (Black Pepper, 2009). In 2006 he was awarded the Philip Hodgins Memorial Medal for Literature.

BEN ELTHAM (P 52)
writes about Australian politics, arts and culture for a number of publications and blogs, including Mess+Noise, *Artlink*, *Arena*, *Crikey*, *Larvatus Prodeo* and the *Courier-Mail*. He is the national affairs correspondent for New Matilda and a fellow of the Centre for Policy Development.

KATE FIELDING (P 125)
develops innovative spaces for telling underrepresented histories. She has filled several research and public history roles including, currently, the Warburton Arts Project based in remote Western Australia.

BEN FOX (P 125)
is a performer, designer and community cultural development worker. He is currently the Artistic Director of Warburton Youth Arts, Western Australia. His website is benfox.com.au.

CAROLYN FRASER (P 20)
is a Melbourne-based writer and letterpress printer. Her artist books are in national and international collections, including the State Library of Victoria, the New York Public Library, Yale University and the Library of Congress. She writes a blog under the nom de plume girlprinter and has a studio in the Nicholas Building.

MARITA HASTINGS (P 232)
is a NSW writer. In 2008 she won the Emerging Poet Award in the Inverawe Nature Poetry Competition, and this year won a Northern Rivers Writers' Centre residential mentorship, funded by Arts NSW.

CAROL JENKINS (P 16)
is a Sydney writer whose work has appeared in *Island*, *HEAT*, *Southerly*, *Cordite* and *Antipodes*. Her first book of poetry, *Fishing in the Devonian*, was published in early 2009 by Puncher & Wattmann. In 2007 she established River Road Press, which produces audio CDs of Australian poetry.

SUSAN JOHNSON'S (P 164)
sixth novel is *Life in Seven Mistakes* (Heinemann). 'How to Cook a Family' is taken from the abandoned prologue. 'Writing a novel is partly a process of elimination. The idea is to end up with a book that resembles Forster's "incalculability of life" as closely as possible.'

ELMO KEEP (P 76)
is a writer interested in music, film and new media theory. She has taught writing for the web at the University of Technology. Gene Simmons of KISS once spat water at her during a press conference. She lives and works in Sydney.

JOHN KINSELLA'S (P 223)
most recent volume of poetry is *Shades of the Sublime and Beautiful* (Fremantle Press and Picador, 2008). His *Divine Comedy: Journeys through a Regional Geography* was published in September 2008 (QUP and WW Norton).

MATTHEW KLUGMAN (P 67)
is a lecturer in Sports Studies at Victoria University and a Fellow of the Centre for Ageing, Rehabilitation, Exercise and Sports Science at Victoria University. His book *Passion Play: Love, Hope and Heartbreak at the Footy* has just been published by Hunter Publishers.

MICHELLE LEBER (P 216)
is a Melbourne poet. She has been a guest at local poetry readings, festivals and community functions. Her work has appeared in the *Age*, literary journals, ecology bulletins, high school texts and on trains.

CAROLINE LEE (P 200)
is a writer and performer. She won the 2005 A.B. Natoli Prize for her short story 'the yo-yo' and has had stories published in the *Sleepers Almanac* and *Visible Ink*. The first draft of her novel *Stripped* was completed with the assistance of the 2005 Marion Eldridge Award for Emerging Women Writers. She can be contacted via her website, carolinelee.com.au.

ROBERTA LOWING (P 224)
recently completed her Master of Letters at Sydney University. Her work has appeared in journals such

as *Blue Dog* and *Overland*. She organises the monthly PoetryUnLimitedPress Poetry Readings & Open Microphone Competition in Glebe, Sydney.

SHANE MCCAULEY (P 225)
was born in England but has lived in Western Australia for most of his life. He has published five books of poetry, most recently *Glassmaker* (Sunline Press, 2005). He was awarded the 2008 Max Harris Poetry Award and edited the anthology of WA poets *Amber Contains the Sun*.

BRIAN MCFARLANE (P 103)
is an adjunct associate professor at Monash University, and visiting professor at the University of Hull. His latest book is *Michael Winterbottom* (Manchester UP, co-authored with Deane Williams), and his *Encyclopedia of British Film* (Methuen) has recently appeared in its third edition.

MAGGIE MACKELLAR (P 117)
is a writer and academic. She holds the 2008–09 Peter Blazey Fellowship for her manuscript, which is forthcoming with Random House in 2010. She has published two books, *Core of My Heart My Country* (2004) and *Strangers in a Foreign Land* (2008).

MARK MORDUE (P 81)
is a writer, editor and journalist. He is the author of the travel book *Dastgah: Diary of a Headtrip* (2001). Mark was also guest co-editor of *Meanjin* on Rock'n'Roll (no. 3, 2006). He is completing a novel for his MA in Writing at UTS. His website is markmordue.com.

RUBY MURRAY (P 168)
was born in 1983. She is the winner of the 2009 Alan Marshall Short Story Award and an academic researcher with a background in environmental politics and deliberative democratic theory. Ruby is based in Melbourne.

PIERZ NEWTON-JOHN (P 177)
is a web developer and writer based in Melbourne. His stories have been published widely in Australia. He won the Alan Marshall Short Story Award in 2008 and the Boroondara Literary Award in 2006.

MANDY ORD (P 125)
is a Melbourne-based cartoonist and illustrator. She has self-published her comic stories, and her work has also appeared in a broad cross-section of local and international anthologies. Her first graphic novel, *Rooftops*, was published by Finlay Lloyd in 2008.

JON PATON (COVER AND DIVIDER PAGES)
is inspired by Japanese and traditional American tattoo art, brooding landscapes and music. His illustration work has appeared in *Rolling Stone*, *Business Review Weekly* and *Sneaker Freaker* magazine.

JILLIAN PATTINSON (P 226)
is a Melbourne writer whose poems have been published in Australian journals, *Antipodes* and various anthologies. She is currently working on her first poetry collection.

MIKE POTTENGER (P 13)
is researching corruption and organised crime as a PhD candidate in the Faculty of Arts at the University of Melbourne. He also teaches in the Faculty of Economics and Commerce there.

SIAN PRIOR (P 59)
has been a journalist and broadcaster for nineteen years. She travelled to East Timor in 2004, 2005 and 2009 to research freelance stories for print and radio. Her website is sianprior.com.

TIM RICHARDS (PP 16, 195)
should be not confused with other Melbourne writers using the same name—he wrote the bizarre football column *Endgames* for the *Age* in the late 1990s.

PEPI RONALDS (P 15)
is a freelance writer with a background in media and the arts. She works at the web design firm Reactive. She likes to spend the rest of her time exploring the everyday things that make up our lives. Her website is pepironalds.com.

PETER ROSE'S (P 227)
latest collection is *Rattus Rattus: New and Selected Poems* (Salt, 2005). He edited the *Best Australian Poems 2008* (Black Inc.) and is the current editor of *Australian Book Review*.

MARIA TAKOLANDER (P 219)
is the author of a chapbook of poems, *Narcissism* (Whitmore Press, 2005), and a full-length poetry collection, *Ghostly Subjects* (Salt Publishing, 2009). She is a lecturer at Deakin University in Geelong.

SAM TWYFORD-MOORE (P 10)
is the co-editor of *Cutwater*, a new literary anthology. His nonfiction efforts have been published in *Meanjin* and the *Big Issue*. He is currently working on a novel, *The Surfer's Guide to Good Fiction*.

ROD USHER (P 228)
lives in Extremadura, Spain, with his wife Angela Gutiérrez. He is a former literary editor of the *Age* and senior writer for the European edition of *Time* magazine. His books include the novels *A Man of Marbles* and *Florid States*, and a volume of poetry, *Smiling Treason*.

CHRIS WALLACE-CRABBE'S (P 230)
most recent books of verse include *The Universe Looks Down* (2005) and *Telling a Hawk from a Handsaw* (2008). He chairs the newly established Australian Poetry Centre in St Kilda.

RACHAEL WEAVER (P 143)
is a research fellow in Literary Studies at the University of Melbourne.

MICHAEL WINKLER (P 111)
is a writer living in Melbourne. His work has appeared in many journals and anthologies including *Overland* and *Sunset* (Penguin).

MARIA ZAJKOWSKI (P 231)
lives in Melbourne. She facilitates the creative writing group at the Port Melbourne Neighbourhood House and is also a community development worker. Her poems have appeared in journals in Australia, New Zealand, the United States and online.

Rent Me!

Some FOR LEASE boards you may have missed.

PURE APARTMENT PORN

Dream on, sunshine—this baby costs a veritable mint! Has a weekly rent equal to that of a late model Ford Festiva. It's what Madonna could afford, had her last three albums sold. Use the Wi Fi, central heating or touch-free taps and we take your bond. The brass floors are ornamental, *so keep off!* With balcony views of Susan Renouf's teeth.

THAT'S ABOUT THE SIZE OF IT!

Agoraphobics will be climbing over themselves to get in! Our genius architects have crunched 2LDK into something akin to South Vietnam's Cu Chi tunnels. No need for furniture! Ideal for a slim, single, friendless contortionist. Like a prison cell, with rent!
(Previous tenant, a labrador breeder, asphyxiated.)

'HONEY. DID YOU HEAR SOMETHING?'

This extremely affordable, spacious, clean modern place is a noise sponge. And there's noise-a-plenty about! Upstairs, steel capped shoe-wearing neighbours rumba on particle-board floors. Old insomniac over the way spot-welds corrugated iron with a rotary vane compressor. Old lady in number six has oboe lessons via Skype with her teacher in Brussels. And the second you hit the hay someone, somewhere, cranks up frickin' New Zealand dub.

GET BACK TO NATURE!

Connect uncomfortably with the elements in this pitifully insulated 'bungalow'. Neglected by a never-seen lazy landlord (*you want something fixed, the rent goes up!*), this one-room shack backs on to the aluminium smelter's car park. Fifties high-pile carpet is now a fraying mess, and the water pressure relies on the tide. As featured in *Today Tonight's* exposé on that guy who abandoned those greyhounds.

OSLO

SAM TWYFORD-MOORE

IT AIN'T BEIRUT: BALTIMORE ON THE WIRE

NEWSREEL ILLUSTRATIONS BY OSLO DAVIS

NEARLY A YEAR AFTER ITS FIFTH AND final season finished screening in the United States, you could find the first four seasons of the HBO-produced television series *The Wire* on DVD at the popular retail franchise JB Hi-Fi for under fifteen dollars each; a thirteen-episode series for less than you'd pay for most thirty-minute CDs. If you went out and purchased the discounted discs you could then watch thirteen hours of Barack Obama's favourite TV show. Obama admitted his love for the show early in the Democratic primaries (citing the gay criminal-with-a-code-of-ethics Omar Little as his favourite character). At the same time, Hilary Clinton gave her support to the sentimental medical soap *Grey's Anatomy*. Obama made the wiser choice and in making it he wasn't just courting the votes of Baltimore or wider Maryland, or that of *The Wire*'s co-creator David Simon, though he eventually won over all three.

The Wire is committed to dealing with the realities of living and working in a decaying American city. Whether Obama saw a little of himself in the characters is open to speculation; he may have identified with the calm authority of Lieutenant Cedric Daniels or with the political idealism of Democrat mayoral candidate Tommy Carcetti. Carcetti had his work cut out for him, as a white man running for mayor in a city with a majority black population. Carcetti is Obama inverted, but they were both striving for the same thing: a chance for real political change.

In her lecture 'Speaking in Tongues', delivered at the New York Public Library, Zadie Smith credited Obama with being not only able to speak for people, but also to speak them, mimicking their speech through an 'enviable facility for dialogue'. Obama, according to Smith, can do the 'black old lady from the South Side, white Harvard nerds, black Columbia nerds, activist women, churchmen, security guards' and so on. This ability to enact a plurality and multiplicity of voices—put to good use in Obama's memoir Dreams from My Father—is seen also in the writing of Wire co-creators, former crime reporter David Simon and ex-cop, ex-teacher Ed Burns. Language is central to the perceived authenticity of the show. Sydney Morning Herald TV critic Greg Hassall confessed to Simon that he had to watch the show with the subtitles on to keep up with the dialogue. British newspaper the Independent provided readers with a liftout Wire glossary when the series was screened for the first time on the BBC; essentials included Burner (disposable mobile phone), Mope (police term for a drug dealer) and the Package (consignment of drugs). This devotion to the naturalism of street-speak apparently comes from the journalistic background of many of The Wire's writers. However, the show had only two recurring black writers—Joy Lusco and David Mills—who, between them, wrote only five individual episodes of the sixty-episode run. By comparison, Simon and Burns contributed thirty episodes over the five seasons.

The first two seasons of The Wire did not deviate from the genre of police procedural—centring on a Major Crimes Unit and the drug dealers they are targeting—that Simon had already explored in his 'nonfiction' novel Homicide: A Year on the Killing Streets and its television adaptation. In the third season of the show, however, Simon and Burns recruited more writers: the crime novelists Richard Price and Dennis Lehane, along with former Baltimore Sun editor and political reporter William F. Zorzi (playing veteran newspaperman Bill Zorzi, a version of himself, in the fifth sea-

son). This signalled the widening scope of the show. Location scouts went further out into Baltimore to find suitable backdrops to scenes; new, more elaborate sets were built. Police procedural extended to 'urban procedural'. Characters such as Carcetti were introduced and their ambitions and machinations became as central to the show as the cops and criminals. The Wire was compared to the nineteenth-century novel: it was doing for Baltimore what Dickens had done for the London of Bleak House. Richard Price described The Wire as the 'Russian novel of an HBO series'. The Wire differs from network programming like CSI in not offering stand-alone episodes and leaving most of the plot open-ended. The episodes of each season serve the same function as chapters in a novel: they tell one long narrative, one step at a time. This approach won much praise from critics, but the ratings remained low.

Whether it was the intention of co-creators Simon and Ed Burns or not, The Wire has become the go-to guide for Baltimore on film—and it was press the city could have done without. Simon talked about having outstayed his welcome with The Wire, coming after Homicide and another HBO book-to-television adaptation, The Corner. Baltimore native John Waters, a kitsch filmmaker known for offending locals with his depraved depictions of his hometown and a fan of The Wire, told a public radio broadcaster in April 2009 that the governor of Maryland had 'really hated [The Wire], thought it made Baltimore look bad. I told him I've seen maps in Japan that people have of the worst corner in Baltimore.' Simon felt Baltimore wasn't that bad. As he put it to Salon.com in 2002, talking about the dangers of researching on the streets of Baltimore, 'it ain't Beirut'. The graffito 'Body-more, Murderland' was grafted onto T-shirts as a slogan and sold for profit. Baltimore benefited from the production being based in the city. Former Republican governor Robert Ehrlich eventually appeared in a cameo on the show, along with a number of real-life Baltimore figures including former mayors and drug barons.

The Wire doesn't speak only for Baltimore though. Halfway through watching the fourth season of the series, I had an hour-long meeting with my disability employment network officer. We talked about the series in relation to her work environment and clients. I outlined the focus of the fourth season. It is set in a state school, where both Roland 'Prez' Pryzblewski and Howard 'Bunny' Colvin—good police turned great teachers—come to grips with the education system. (Prez and Bunny are the characters easiest to warm to, partly thanks to the parental roles they adopt; in Colvin's case thanks to the gentle performance by Robert Wisdom.) I summed up Colvin's experience—he was recruited by an academic to test out a socialisation program for troubled students—by explaining that Colvin had stressed that he couldn't reach kids over a certain age, that by sixteen their lives were already being lived in accordance with the rules of the game. In talking about *The Wire*, we were not talking about television, we weren't talking characters or scripts, acting or direction, we were talking about issues and policy and our broader experiences. A conversation based on a television show can spin off into a social-welfare agenda; a friend who now works for Justice Health had watched all six seasons of prison drama *Oz* and partly credited the series with the insight needed for the job. It is a testament to *The Wire* that it provided similar insight for Barack Obama, *Wire*-devotee-cum-President of the United States.

DAN BAUM'S #NEWYORKER-FAIL

The idea is this: be employed to churn out 30,000 words per annum as a staff reporter by one of America's most prestigious and sought-after publications, be

fired three years later and then twitter about the experience around the time your book gets released. At least that's what journalist Dan Baum did earlier this year, taking full advantage of the micro-blogging site to provide a bite-sized account of his time at the *New Yorker*.

'People often ask why I left the New Yorker,' read the first few tweets. 'After all, I had a staff writer job. Isn't that the best job in journalism? Yes. Nobody leaves a New Yorker job voluntarily. I was fired. And over the next few days, I'll tell that story here, in 140 [c]haracter chunks.' And so he does, from his initial elation on being employed, to his disappointment as six of his stories are killed, and his bitter personality clash with editor David Remnick, which Baum cites as the main reason for his eventual sacking. The twitterfeed also yields some interesting, albeit biased, insights into the inner workings of the much lauded magazine. Baum explains that staff writers are employed under contract, which means that they do not receive health insurance and the contracts are up for renewal every year. He also tells followers that 'the office itself is a little creepy. It's not exactly like being in a library; it's more like being in a hospital room where somebody is dying . . . There's a weird tension to the place.' This observation may be a vague salute to Tom Wolfe, who in 1965 wrote an outlandish profile on then *New Yorker* editor William Shawn, entitled 'Tiny mummies! The true story of the ruler of 43rd Street's land of the walking dead'. In true new-journalism style, Wolfe wrote a spectacular parody of the magazine that cast Shawn as a funeral director presiding over a staff of ghoulish undead. Wolfe's article caused quite an uproar when it was

published by the *New York Herald Tribune*, leading to a flurry of angry letters from Muriel Spark, E.B. White, Walter Lippmann and even the reclusive J.D. Salinger. Baum's twitterfeed has likewise caused a stir. *New Yorker* staff writer Susan Orlean retaliated with this tweet: 'Dissing your boss? Whining abt story credits? Writing stories that aren't good enough to run? Seeming to dislike the mag itself? Hmmm.' Baum hit back and a brief online scrap-fight ensued (at least as much of a scrap as can be had with a limit of 140 characters).

Regardless of this digital finger-pointing, the interesting thing about Baum's exercise here is that it demonstrates yet another incarnation of Twitter as a new media form. No longer just to do with social networking, Twitter is an aspect of self-promotion and public exposure. When asked why he chose to write on Twitter instead of selling his story to, say, another magazine, Baum replied that he was 'intrigued by the idea of micro-serialisation'. 'This takes the form to a ridiculously atomized state,' he said on Rumpus.com. 'My story is of interest to media types, who also seem to be . . . tuned into Twitter, so form fit function.' There was a little more to it than that though. Baum was fired in 2007, so why did he wait two years to write about the experience? Perhaps it had something to do with the release of his book, *Nine Lives: Death and Life in New Orleans*. By twittering on the inner workings of his former employer, Baum has managed to create a significant amount of interest in both himself and his work. Baum's followers on Twitter now number more than 2400 (not bad by any standards) and *Nine Lives* gets the benefit of an extended shelf life. For those interested in reading Baum's story in full, the

feed has been reproduced on his website: danbaum.com.
JESSICA AU

MIKE POTTENGER

ROBBIN' HOOD

Earlier this year Dr Julian Luxford of the University of St Andrews in Scotland discovered a note in the margin of a medieval history book which claimed that Robin Hood had plagued England with 'continuous robberies', suggesting the man may not have been as saintly as he has been portrayed in folklore. I wasn't surprised. I'd had my own doubts about the legging-clad menace. Though I had long suspected something wasn't quite right, it wasn't until I read a book by Diego Gambetta about organised crime in Sicily

that it hit me. Hood was no grand hero; a cursory glance at what we know of him from pop culture and lore reveals his sinister roots as a medieval Mafioso, and he and his band of Merry Men were organised criminals.

ROBBING FROM THE RICH To run a powerful and profitable criminal organisation like the Mafia, at least some of the members need to have the capacity and willingness to use or threaten violence. To assert power as a group outside the laws of the state and acting as an alternative to (or even substitute for) state authority requires being able to challenge the state's theoretical monopoly on force. To survive and operate outside the law while robbing from the rich, the Merry Men relied upon their mastery of swords, bows and staves. Criminal organisations also have exclusive membership, often granted only after candidates have proven themselves. For a would-be Mafioso this may involve specific tasks and ceremonies, with a need to prove oneself capable of violence. It was only after a one-on-one fight with Hood that Little John joined the crew.

Once formed, such an organisation deploys its capacity for violence as a means to many profitable ends, including intimidation and extortion. These are the very tactics Hood used to steal from the rich: cornering lords and noblemen on the dark paths of Sherwood to demand payment if they wished to pass safely. The Sicilian Mafia used sophisticated techniques such as allowing strangers to be taken advantage of by local businessmen, but the principle remains the same. Both the Mafia and the Merry Men realised that using violence is quite costly and sometimes risky. Where possible, Mafiosi prefer to establish

and trade on (or extort with) a *reputation* for violence. What better way to establish such a reputation than to win the local archery tournament, sending a clear message that you are not to be trifled with? To affirm your power you then need access to and preferably control of the flow of money and information. This can be a tricky business, so in Sicily Mafiosi would concentrate their power in very specific geographical areas that they could dominate. Sherwood Forest, anyone?

Gambetta observed that Mafiosi in Sicily had an interest in helping locals and offering genuine protection to those who would pay. For a fee, for example, they could safeguard a business from defaulting clients. Less an act of benevolence than a business strategy, this allowed the Mafia to strip clients of their cash in substantial but tolerable doses, rather than overfishing their main source of profits. Fleece strangers in one go, but keep your fellow citizens alive and well enough to continue providing you with a steady stream of income. Surely this wasn't Hood's caper? In addition to extorting cash from rich travellers, he might also have protected his fellow citizens from injustices inflicted by the Sheriff, such as suffocating taxes, but he didn't charge them for it, did he? In Sicily, at least the Mafia took direct payment for protection. In Sherwood, the Merry Men would steal funds and take what they liked before returning whatever was left over: they had to fund their operation somehow. As the people would be glad to get even something back, they were unlikely to complain if they thought it was too little. We may know that Hood gave to the poor, but we don't know how much he kept for himself as a charge for services rendered.

GIVING TO THE POOR Handing out

handfuls of cash is also part of a sound Mafia business strategy. Making charitable donations helps endear the organisation to the public, makes people more willing to tolerate them and less likely to report the organisation to the police (this charitable carrot was, of course, balanced by the threat of a large stickful of violent reprisal). Such methods ultimately help legitimise their power. Hood frequently gave money to the poor, but I suspect the stories gloss over the fact that he did it to shore up his legitimacy and to counter any complaints about his extensive coercive power. And let's not forget the Mafia's tendency to pay bribes to buy the favour of public officials. An early story of Hood tries to present the decision to give some cash to a knight who is down on his luck as kind and selfless. I imagine Hood saw that this man was likely to have some influence in a feudal political system, and hoped to have the knight in his pocket.

In Hood's case, even if the means were nefarious, surely the ends were noble? The stories would have us believe that Prince John, or at least the Sheriff acting on his behalf, ruled with an iron fist. Surely a Mafia-style organisation set in opposition to such tyranny, while not ideal, is preferable to an autocratic state? The Sicilian Mafia, like many criminal organisations, took up the mantle of opposing tyranny when it opposed Mussolini's autocratic power; although this won them increased support and popularity in postwar Italy, there's every reason to believe it was done more in response to the threat Mussolini posed to their power. In this case, as in Sherwood, people began to regard their domination by a criminal gang as a necessary evil or tolerable second-best to an inefficient and/or autocratic

state. Nonetheless, the Mafia and the Merry Men were illegal organisations looking after their own interests first and foremost.

Finally, then, don't all the good stories about Hood outweigh the one bad sidenote Dr Luxford found? Don't forget that Mafiosi are also much celebrated in their way, not least their repeated idealisation and immortalisation on the silver screen; antiheros can be celebrated and feared too. Perhaps most disturbing in the case of Robin Hood is what we *don't* know about him. Experts such as Dr Luxford will tell you that there is very little written evidence of Robin Hood ever having existed. It seems that the Merry Men, like the Mafia, placed great importance on keeping a low profile and maintaining secrecy. Who knows what sinister acts may have been carried out by a gang of thugs? I imagine that at the very least it would have included the odd horse's head in the Sheriff's bed.

WOODY WORDS, TINNY WORDS

In the old Monty Python sketch, Graham Chapman and Eric Idle play an aristocratic husband and wife who like lovely 'woody words' such as 'gorn' and 'sausage' but have a hysterical disdain for dreadful 'tinny words' such as 'litterbin'

and 'newspaper'. As it turns out, this skit may have reflected a general truth. Visualthesaurus.com has produced a list of the most hated and most loved words as ranked by users—the most popular being words such as 'eclectic', 'Schadenfreude' and 'perspicacious', and the least favourite being phrases such as 'vomit', 'ointment' and 'slacks'. The most loved word is, unsurprisingly, 'love'.

The reasons for this are varied, but the deciding factor seems to be a sensory reaction to the interplay of semantics and sound. A dash of onomatopoeia also helps swing the verdict either way. Certain words such as 'serendipity' and 'grace' have a kind of feel-good appeal, whereas 'crud', 'pus' and 'nostril' blend inelegant consonants with unflattering images. Overuse also contributes to a healthy aversion—words such as 'whatever', 'awesome' and 'like', which have been exhausted by a generation of slack-jawed teenagers, have recently fallen out of favour. Institutional and administrative jargon such as 'perfunctorily' and 'appropriate' are equally disliked. The most despised word by far is 'moist', which even has its own Facebook hate group: 'possibly the worst word in the English dictionary', ranted one member, while another described it as a 'sick, repugnant word' (perhaps they should join forces with the Comic Sans haters and form one supergroup?). Many people also have their own particular phonetic ticks. '"Succulent" ranks for me among the most disgusting of English words,' wrote one user. 'Just hearing the word spoken makes me a bit nauseated.'

'These deep-seated sentiments about words are very often inexplicable,' writes Visualthesaurus's Ben Zimmer. 'Sometimes our perspective on language isn't exactly rational: we love some words and absolutely despise other ones.' Whatever the reason, there is clearly a lot of loathing out there. Perhaps users should take a leaf out of Monty Python's book and start saying their favourite woody phrases to cheer themselves up in the manner of Graham Chapman's effusive 'caribou gorn'.

JA

PEPI RONALDS

THE HAND THAT SIGNED THE TITLE PAGE

I admit to feeling a little pasty and my pulse is certainly working overtime. But self-control is paramount at this moment and I call in all of the public speaking tips I've ever heard. Deep breaths. Rehearse and refine your lines. Remember to add emphasis and inflection. Be confident. Finally, the person before me steps aside and my cue arrives. It's my first book-signing event and I am face-to-face with one of my intellectual heroes, author Robert Hughes.

'I, I'm sure you always hear this,' I stammer in a disembodied voice, 'but I just wanted to say that I've found your work very inspiring.' Hughes signs my book with a flourish, looks up at me with a wry smile and says, 'Funnily enough, one never tires of hearing that.'

The moment is etched into my copy of *American Visions* with boxy print and confident black ink. Hughes has even taken the time to include my name (and spell it correctly). The book is like a treasure—brightly coloured and tangible, it somehow links the academic to the personal. So why do we like signed books?

'There's something unique and magical about having a book signed by the author when he's present,' Hai Nguyen, founder of authorstrack.com, tells me in a trawling Bostonian accent. 'I don't think anything could replace that moment when you see them and you're kind of star struck.'

'It brings the book to life and the writer to life,' says Emily Harms, marketing manager at Readings. 'A lot of people like [them].' That's why we see autographed books piled high in store displays and listed on places like eBay. But if you thought an ample autograph creates an ample bank account, think again. It's an urban myth that signed books are worth more—the signer has to be a prize-winner or close to death's door (either side) for that.

Psychologists have been working on a number of theories to explain our attachments to things like signed books. They've even coined a phrase for it, which is originally borrowed from philosophy: *essentialism*. Did you have a teddy, a blanket or (as in my case) a stuffed parrot called Stuffy that you held dear as a child? Not just something that you were fond of, but something that despite its inanimateness you felt had a personality—an *essence*—all of its own? Bruce Hood, director and psychologist at the Bristol Cognitive Development Centre, and author of the

recently released book *Super-Sense: Why We Believe in the Unbelievable*, thinks that these early 'attachment objects' could explain our fondness for physical connections with people we identify with.

Essentialism is a predominantly Western phenomenon. Hood speculates that the desire for memorabilia could be unleashed at an early age. 'In Japan and countries like that, children sleep with their mothers well into late childhood. Whereas in the West we move our children in the first or second year to sleeping separately.' This seemingly simple separation may cause a significant change in our perception of mass produced and inanimate objects. Children soon 'self-soothe', Hood explains, by attaching themselves 'to whatever is in the crib—typically a blanket or a soft toy'. Of course we grow out of those objects. However, the blanket (or Stuffy) prompts a connection between objects and people we identify with. Perhaps that's why the punters who were lined up to have their books signed at last year's Melbourne Writers' Festival were nursing them like babes in arms. 'Objects take on an emotional significance,' says Hood. (Just consider your average wedding ring.) Nguyen confirms this desire for the essence of something in his book collection: 'Most of the time I attend the events and get the signed books myself—so that I know it's actually authentic.'

Publishers are also well aware of the attraction we have to signed books. They organise the events and it is rumoured that they pay people with 'nice handwriting' to forge autographs in the books of high-profile (and time-poor) authors. Others have held online book-signing events: you receive an email containing the author's signature. Yet despite a dedicated following among readers and publishers, nothing threatens the essentialist tendencies of the fraternity more than, well, there being no books.

The International Digital Publishing Forum's statistics of wholesale ebook sales indicate a graph that trends upwards—just like my heart does when I look at my signed copy of *American Visions*. Early ebook readers are of limited appeal (they seem nothing more than glorified PDF displays), but manufacturers will soon overcome such limitations. At that point even luddites (among whom I count myself) will have to admit that reading an ebook of say, *American Visions*, might be better, if different in a not-so-bad way. Though I wouldn't be able to hold, turn and smell the pages, I would be able to drill down to view high-resolution images, and even enjoy video and audio components. I could download the book in a fraction of the time it would take me to go to the bookstore, for a fraction of the cost and—it must be noted—carry it at a fraction of the weight.

'Physical media is so last year,' comments Dan Goldman in an article about Amazon's ebook reader, the Kindle (allyinsider.com). 'Everyone is going to have [an ebook reader] in the not too distant future.' Certainly if you consider the pressure printing and distribution costs put on publishers (as well as the environment), there is a compelling case for the ebook. Hood is not too worried that the pleasure of a book-signing session will dissolve. 'If we still have this burning urge to make connections with people we'll simply transfer that to different objects. Whilst the medium might change, I think the human nature won't.'

A service provided by vir-

tualbooksigning.net confirms this notion. Here you can sit on *your* couch and watch your favourite author sign a copy of the book from *their* couch. And then? The website states that 'in a few days your book will arrive at your doorstep'.

As a book-launching author-to-be, Hood has given some thought to his book-signing events. 'I'm actually going to use some of my own blood in my signature,' he quips. 'That's about as essential as you can get.'

TIM RICHARDS

THE FINAL SERIES

These philosophical encounters are based on overheard fragments of a long conversation between two Collingwood supporters on an interminably delayed Sandringham train.

FIRST QUALIFYING FINAL
MCG 7 SEPTEMBER
COLLINGWOOD VERSUS DESCARTES

'Heath . . . Heathy Shaw . . . He just should'na done it. You can't think like that and be thought of as a thinker.'
Won

SECOND PRELIMINARY FINAL
MCG 21 SEPTEMBER
COLLINGWOOD VERSUS WITTGENSTEIN

'Fuckers can whinge all they like. No way was that arse. Every time a bloke kicks the pill, he's got some kind of goal, and if his kick goes through the goal, you can't say that's not what he meant.'
Won

GRAND FINAL
MCG 28 SEPTEMBER
COLLINGWOOD VERSUS PETER SINGER

'*You know who I blame?* . . . Josh Fuckin' Fraser. He had the chance to nail that fuckin' animal. If you don't nail 'em when you've got the chance, they're gunna come back to kill ya.'
Lost

CAROL JENKINS

THE ART OF LISTENING

As a form of literacy, listening might be considered an impostor. Its orphan status in the curriculum is both parodied and applauded in the last, unfinished Dr Seuss book, *Hurrah for Diffendoofer Day* (1998), where, in Diffendoofer School, 'Miss Bobble teaches listening . . . Miss Fribble teaches laughing'. While it is often assumed we can all listen if we want to, how good are our ears as critics? As a culture, have our collective listening skills been dumbed down so that most of the time we merely hear things without taking the trouble to listen to the complex and the subtle? Is listening too much like hard work, and what would Miss Bobble say about all this?

Comprehension of the spoken word takes more active memory work than reading. When we were an oral culture, listening was the important first step in transferring knowledge. Both fiction and nonfiction used poetry, with its sound prompts to memory, to provide the framework for storytelling—rhyme and repetition were added to the mainstays of narrative and image to make a sticky neural fixing agent. Remnants of this persist: 'Thirty days have September, April . . .' still works for me. Yet while there has been a resurgence of listening (audiobooks are claiming more and more shelf space in bookstores), listening to poetry can be more demanding than listening to prose. One of the key differences between prose and poetry is that all the little wheels in a poem—the spoken word—are liable to work on each other in various ways, so when it comes to listening to the poem the job is to hear the interaction of sound patterns as you work out what the condensing lens of the form is conveying directly, metaphorically and culturally. The reward sought by the reader is the transformative moment of empathetic understanding and revelation, where a set of mirror neurons inside your head are convincing you that you might well be the poem's narrator.

As a publisher of audio CDs of Australian poetry, listening accounts for a great part of what I do. Listening is a great help in finding new work, recording and editing poems for accuracy, sorting out bumps, distortions, plosives, fade-outs, slurs, background noise, mouth noises (don't ask) and breath. But how do people read their work? Audiences have a range of one-liners to put down a poor reader—I've heard readings described as having the aural drive of a washing machine and a voice likened to cheap china falling on cement—but when we hear something well read we pay little attention to why or how this is so.

In March this year, the UK Poetry Archive's co-director and then-British Poet Laureate Andrew Motion announced the inclusion of five Australian poets—Judith Beveridge, Peter Boyle, joanne burns, Stephen Edgar and Vivian Smith in their impressive online archive of audio poetry (poetryarchive. org), saying: 'It has always been our intention to make the Poetry Archive as widely representative as possible of poetry in English, and these latest additions, by very distinguished Australian poets, are an ornament to the site. We're proud and grateful to have them, and the wider world will be grateful too.' Each poet's profile included a critical appraisal of their opus, and as part of that it fell to me to contribute a sentence or two on how they read their work. While there is a long and sophisticated history of music criticism and of literary criticism, the cupboard with the commentary on reading is not well stocked. But as Andrew Motion asked for a sentence or two it seemed I should oblige.

Commentary on how a poem is read is a tricky, but by no means impossible, task. Although this aspect is not often dealt with in any detail in poetry reviews, I set out to get some understanding of how a poet's speech works. Back to Miss Bobble. How a poet reads their own work is akin to their DNA, only more personal. Reading could be classed as the writer's art phenotype; it lets the astute listener in to see how the poet wears their poem. The poem is a kind of aural clothing and, in reading, the poet is your dresser—showing you how the sleeves fit, for example, or those little syntactical shifts so you can get into their shoes and walk around. They give you a guided tour of this architecture of words, opening surprising doors and nuances of meaning. The different spin that can be put on a single word will not be underestimated by anyone with teenage children or friends who have been told 'whatever' in four different ways.

What can be said of these selected recordings? Some things about the reading reflect the work itself. Beveridge's reading of her poems, for example, has a flawless tempo that shows the rhythmic structure that supports her writing. Her voice has a gentle diplomacy and a concision that naturally enhance those parallel qualities of intimacy and clarity that define her poetics. In Stephen Edgar's CD *Photography for Beginners*, a selection of his poems ranging over his last twelve years in print, his reading is characterised by clarity and expressiveness, accompanied at times by an understated sense of humour. Interestingly joanne burns, for me, sets up a theatre of words, easing listeners into a satisfying space between following her and cogitating on where they might possibly go.

How a poem reads is the litmus test for some and extraneous for others, but without privileging either page or sound it is worthwhile to listen for yourself. Miss Bobble will be proud of you.

IN COLOUR

NOTES ON PROVENANCE; OR, TOM ROSS'S TOOTH

CAROLYN FRASER

PHOTOS BY DARREN JAMES

1. Massillon, Ohio. Pop. 31,325. Lost on my way to visit Mrs Georgia Ross, I stop in at a random haberdashery store downtown to ask directions. Discover that the woman behind the counter went to high school with Mrs Ross, possibly forty-five years ago. Mrs Ross's living room is white; white carpet, white couch. Awkward in not-so-clean work boots, I sit forward on my seat as we sip iced tea. Mrs Ross offers homemade cookies. There is a photograph of Tom Ross on a side table.

A narrow passage leads down to the basement. This was Tom's space: an 8 x 12 Chandler & Price platen press, a 26" cutter, boxes of yellowing envelopes, tied-up type, tackle boxes full of spacing. Dirt encrusts everything. We negotiate over the cutter, which will need to be lifted up and out the narrow staircase in parts. I buy the Kelsey Excelsior—a toy press—out of sentiment, not need. Most else, Mrs Ross is anxious to be rid of for free: the highly coveted 1923 *American Type Founders Specimen Book and Catalogue*; a glass-fronted eraser display case; a box of miscellanea: old-style quoins, promotional flyers for long-gone printing suppliers. She keeps an ink cabinet for a grandson, away at the time in the service, thinking he may or may not be interested.

There is more than one box of Megill gauge pins. The boxes are lovely; the pins, in my opinion, near useless. In one, I find a wadded-up tissue. Inside, a yellowed old molar, filled more than once, carefully wrapped up and stuffed away. Was he busy downstairs, printing on his own time after work, after dinner? The tooth, source of much bother, finally wrenches completely free, but Tom's downstairs, and a quick swill of coffee easily washes away the taste of blood in his mouth. No need to go upstairs. He wraps it up, stuffs it in a little blue box, gets back to the press.

2. When I remember my time fossicking for letterpress equipment in the Midwest, mostly I remember being cold. In Indianapolis, on a Thanksgiving weekend one November, I visited Dave Churchman's warehouse, known as the Boutique de Junque. Dave's place is cold. A large wood stove heated a disappointingly narrow radius in one room; Dave's wife Charlene sat close to it. My memory is of a warren of rooms but it's possible that the Boutique de Junque might be a single span broken into smaller room-like spaces by towering walls of type cabinets and cases. It is the kind of place in which a GPS could come in handy.

I bought my font of Kingspor Bros Orplid here in 30 & 48 point. Designed by Hans Bohn in 1929, Orplid is a distinct display face with a 3D shadow, hardly an all-rounder. After employing it on a calling card for my friend Emily, I sent Dave a note with one of the cards. He wrote back that he was pleased to receive it as he had not previously believed it possible to use Orplid even halfway decently. He told me I'd proved him wrong.

3. Best you get down here ASAP, Roy Lang Jnr advised. Stone Printing Co. was the last printing plant in downtown Cleveland; on the sixth floor of a building on the west side, down near the Flats. Most companies moved to the suburbs long ago, or, at the very least, out of the heart of downtown. Stone's was the last. Roy's guys were shifting an

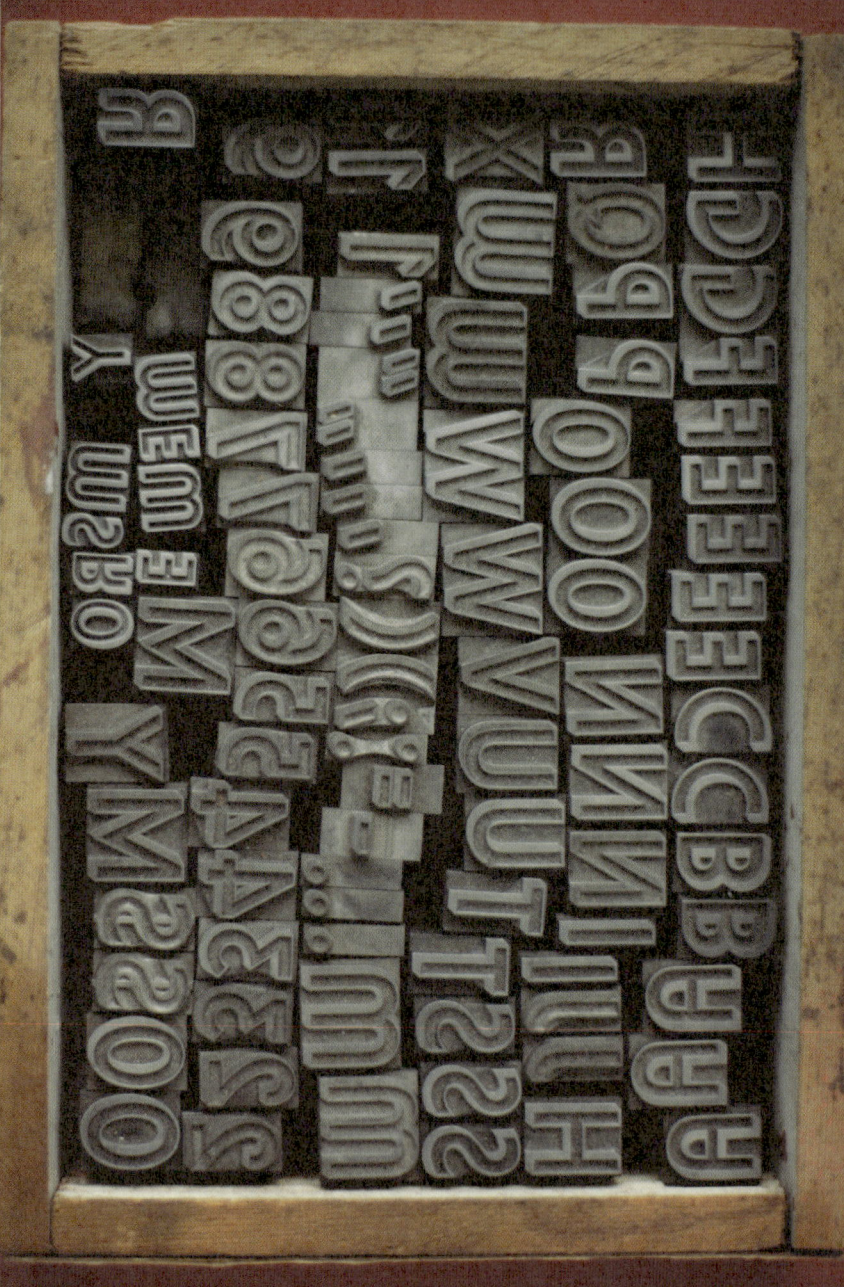

enormous four-colour offset press, but he'd noticed some bits and pieces about that he thought would be of interest, and the boss didn't mind me poking about. There was a miterer, used to cut mitred corners into cast rule for borders and forms. There was a room filled with cans of dried-out ink, and some abandoned powder-coated steel flat files. There was a complete illustrated *Webster's Dictionary* (second edition) with only its cover slightly adrift; a glass glue bottle with screw cap and spout; some cast-iron jogging wedges, perfect for weights; and a replacement blade for a Hammond Trim-O-Saw, a machine I didn't own but hoped I might one day.

There was a large room that might have been partitioned once: desks and filing cabinets floated about unmoored. The filing cabinets were as valuable to me as recovered sunken treasure: file after file of promotional material for type foundries, ink companies, paper mills, machinery manufacturers and a manual for the Trim-O-Saw. I came to realise that Stone had acquired at least one other business over time: the W.H. Kull Co. of 1278 West 9th Street, and that Cleveland was rich with printing-supply houses with names like Art Roth and the venerable-sounding Caxton. Here were the paper records of an era of sales calls, of follow-up letters on embossed letterhead, of hand-signed Christmas cards. In a manual for the Universal Mono-Tabular Broach, the company writes that ' . . . the installation of this equipment in your plant, we trust, will be the beginning of a very pleasant business relationship between us. May it grow closer as the years pass.' Like an archaeologist or a thief, I took anything vaguely interesting.

This was what remained. The company would continue on, but none of this was required any more. These names typed onto envelopes: these people were dead. These labour-saving devices: machines long obsolete. In a desk drawer, I found a pair of reading glasses, ketchup packets and, neatly folded, the front page of the *Plain Dealer*, 12 September 2001: the twin towers of the World Trade Center in flames.

4. Harry D. Bubb, 7197 Valley View Road, Hudson, Ohio. It was once the pleasant lot of the hobby printer to produce his own custom stationery, and I am in possession of quite a few galleys of standing type in which names and addresses are set in metal type and tied securely with printer's string. Harry Bubb's is one. Bubb was a member of the Rowfant Club, a private, men's-only bibliophile club in Cleveland. Housed in the oldest continually occupied house in the city, the club is secretive about its activities. In 2000, a member of the club contacted me about a press and printing equipment in the basement. On my first visit, I entered through the back door into the kitchen. Staff were preparing lunch. In the basement, an ancient club member was typing catalogue records on a manual typewriter. In a far corner there was an 8 x 12 Chandler & Price Platen, a non-motorised Vandercook SP-15, a double steel type cabinet and a single wooden standing frame. It was all mine for the taking, bar the Vandercook and a complete run of Stephenson & Blake–cast Caslon. Thus began months of negotiations, which ended badly but for two things: Harry Bubb's double-wide steel cabinet and the chance to see inside the house.

It was much as you'd imagine any grand Victorian house, all brocade and burnished wood, but with more books than you'd normally encounter and a stuffed woodchuck on the mantel. On second thoughts, perhaps the taxidermy shouldn't have been so unexpected, but it surprised me, as did the hundreds of candlesticks about the place. The woodchuck, stuffed in an attacking rampant position, is referred to by Rowfant members by its classical name—*Arctomys monax*—and is the club's mascot and symbol. Every Rowfant member has his own candlestick and uses it to reserve his place at the dinner table.

Harry Bubb's address forme is set in a serif face; however, much of the typefaces in his double cabinet are mid-century-style sans serif advertising faces: Venus Extended, Spartan Black, Hellenic Wide. There are a couple of cases of wood type and a font of 96-point Century Schoolbook. There is a perpetual calendar, a two-colour Christmas border of holly leaves and berries, and a font of arrows with sans serif numerals inside. In addition, there is a case of copper photoengravings, and small cuts featuring candlesticks. The engravings are of groups of men outside a handsome house, men on a picnic, and of lavishly furnished nineteenth-century rooms. In one, there is a stuffed woodchuck on the mantel.

The shelves in the library at the Rowfant Club are filled with candlesticks topped with snuffers. Presumably, somewhere among them is Harry Bubb's, moved into the library when he died. He'd no longer be needing it to mark his place at the table.

5. For a brief moment in the nineteenth century, handsetting type was a wildly popular sport. According to historian Walker Rumble, its most brilliant exponents—known as Swifts—were capable of amazing feats of speed and accuracy: on 19 February 1870, George Arensberg, 'The Velocipede', set 2064 ems of solid Minion type in a single hour in an era in which 700 ems was considered average. This peculiar interlude was part unconscious celebration of the primacy of the human hand, part exuberant defiance in the face of encroaching automation. It is perhaps the true mark of a craftsman that he values and is protective of his tools, and in the printing office no other tool engenders this protective impulse so much as that held by the compositor towards his composing stick.

The composing stick, made up of bed, rail, knee and clamp, is a true extension of the human hand, allowing individual letters of type to be held in place and to measure as the compositor forms words, sentences, paragraphs. Nineteenth-century printing giant Theodore Low De Vinne, known for his advances in productivity and cost efficiency, conceded that 'expert compositors own their own sticks and rules, and will use no other. They get used to their size, weight and feeling, and say that they can do more work with them than with other sticks and rules apparently as good.' This loyalty is in the pursuit of craft, an implicit partnership between man and stick in service of the work.

Which is why it's so galling that none of my sticks have matching knees, or that the micrometer ('probably the greatest single advance in stick history') seems faulty, or that my favourite stick was inadvertently left behind in Cleveland. A good craftsman never lends nor blames her tools, but it's impossible for me not to look longingly at page 943 of the 1923 *ATF Specimen Book and Catalogue*, wishing I could order a stick brand-new.

Instead, I make do with a Rouse Standard Job Stick (serial number E5522). The sound of type dropping into the stick is of rhythmic, small, quiet clicks; there is pleasure in spacing out a line evenly, thinking about the space between a final *w* and a beginning *v*. My hand reaches for a letter, feels for the nick, places it next to the letter that came before. My fingers know the difference between 10 and 12 point, the thickness of a brass as compared to a copper. The stick lies in my palm, my thumb resting on the lines as they grow. I am lucky in this instance to be right-handed, left-handed sticks being as elusive as unicorns. Sometimes, at this speed, I'll see something in my writing that I want to change. Printers call this 'writing in the stick'.

I have another favourite stick, though it remains ornamental. A Buckeye stick, made by Chandler & Price and named after Ohio's state tree, it was a gift from Eric May when I first established Idlewild Press in Cleveland in 2000. (It sits on display next to Eric's old Ohio licence plate—LTRPRES.) Noel Riefel gave me my copy of Martin K. Speckter's *Disquisition on the Composing Stick* (The Typophiles, Inc., New York, 1971). In it, Speckter writes that the relationship between a printer and his composing stick is

> *an intimacy transcending that of almost any other graphic arts implement. The printer's press, no matter how small, is too large, too heavy, too ponderous to evoke personal sentiment. Pieces of type, although they may be admired for the beauty of their forms and the perfection with which they perform their intended functions, exist in too huge abundance to be loved; one may derive pleasure from the beach, but who can cherish each grain of sand?*

6. Sometime soon after it came into my possession, I asked Fritz Klinke to check the Vandercook archives for my press's original-owner record. An SP-15, serial number 27441, it was shipped on 9 February 1968 to the Evangel Press in Nappanee, Indiana. The Vandercook was always a proof press, and presses of this era were used primarily to produce camera-ready art for offset. They're not usually as bashed around as production presses and allow the small-press printer to produce precise, albeit slow, work. My copy of the original index card shows optional equipment shipped with the machine: Type 'A' Form Rollers; Power Ink Distribution and Automatic Washup; Special .968' Bed with Galley Thickness Bed Plate; Curved Plastic Cover for Inking System; Steel Paper Cabinet; and a Positive Lockup Bar. The press was inspected by J. Hlavin and stamped with his name.

I bought the press from Asa Peavy, my friend and one-time boss in San Francisco. He was either upgrading to a table-top Albion and a German-built Asburn, or throwing in the towel, I can't remember which. He is a talented, though ambivalent, printer. I arranged to ship the press to Cleveland, Ohio, by road, not realising at the time that it would pass right by its original home in Nappanee, a tiny town in northern Indiana, about halfway between Chicago and Cleveland. Later, I'd ship it by rail to Los Angeles and by freighter to Melbourne, Australia. The Evangel Press still exists and, as the name suggests, prints Christian texts for the Evangelical, Wesleyan and Anabaptist traditions.

When I bought my Chandler & Price 10 x 15 New Series Platen for $500 from Roy Lang Snr it was coated in grime: the good, greasy kind. With almost no rust, its ink disk shiny and unpitted, it took hours of scrubbing with a toothbrush to reveal the name Chandler & Price on the plate between the roller frames, longer still before I could read the serial number engraved onto the bed. Number C68046, built in 1925 no more than a mile from my studio at West 72nd and St Clair. The press still has its ink fountain and counter, and a Kimble motor, most likely original to the press. There was a tympan sheet still held tight under the bails, imprinted with the name and address of a local print shop. Curious, I look up the name in the yellow pages: it still exists. When I call, the man answering says, yes, the press had belonged to his father. He was neither surprised nor interested in my call. I cut the address from the tympan, stored it safely, then lost it. I don't remember the name.

Uncrated, the Chandler & Price weighs 500 kilos. The Nicholas Building, also built in 1925, has a relatively small goods lift accessible off Flinders Lane. The lift is rated to 680 kilos. Arriving early on the day of the move, we find the lane blocked by a truck sucking out waste oil from the Kentucky Fried Chicken shop. The smell is nauseating; overpowering. I say to Darren, one of my moving blokes, boy, that must be the worst job ever, and he says, no, it's not. You plug it in and go get a coffee and the paper.

Peter Horne, the boss, assures me that there won't be much buggerisation, and there isn't, until the last crate of the day. It makes it into the lift with a little clearance either side and Darren squeezed in front. This is our mistake. Darren is not a small man, perhaps 150 kilos. Perhaps had it not been the last crate of the day, I might have made the calculation in time, but didn't. It's subtle; a sudden jerk, then halt. Nothing. The grills are opened, slammed shut, the lever tried again. Nothing. The lift is broken: 500 kilos of press and 150 kilos of person inside.

7. In the 1920s, nearly a quarter of all commercial printing in the United States was done in New York. Businesses that had previously congregated in lower Manhattan moved north to be closer to the newly opened Holland Tunnel, dominating Hudson and Varick streets. The typesetters and photoengravers moved further north still, into the Flatiron District. In the 1990s, evidence of this population was still visible in signage painted on upper-level windowpanes, and small cards beside buzzers. It was as if progress at street level happened at a much faster rate than that happening on the upper floors. Looking up, it might be 1925; straight ahead, most definitely 1996.

Esquire Photoengraving was at 4 West 22nd Street. The building's lobby was unremarkable, the lift standard Otis-built. But when it opened onto the third floor, you were in a different world, one that had shrunk to a few rooms, now strangely empty. I was shy, and new to printing, and never got to know any of the three elderly men who worked there, or what exactly they did. I'd drop off art to be made into type-high magnesium plates, and would come back days, maybe a week later to pick up the completed items. At the time, I knew I was seeing something rare. I wished I had the courage to ask if I could take photographs, but didn't. Instead, I took a friend with me one time so that she could see it for herself, and so I'd have a witness if I ever needed to corroborate my memory.

The rooms, at least the ones I saw, were bare but for a table in the front room around which the men sat, and a proof press out the back. I remember it being dark inside; the space might have been illuminated by bare bulbs. The plates, when delivered, were wrapped in newspaper; the proofs were sloppy and smudged. But it was the walls that were remarkable: completely papered, découpage-style, with girlie pictures, none all that recent. Time, and cheap paper, had faded many but they weren't mute: cartoon-style speech bubbles were carefully cut out and glued to the images so that the girls

were talking to each other, to the three old guys, to us. I wish I could remember what they were saying, but even at the time, most of it was incomprehensible to anyone without thirty years tenure in the place: all in-jokes and innuendo. What remains in memory is a work of art, a smutty monument to friendship, and a hell of a lot of free time on the job. Sometime in the mid 2000s I went back to see if Esquire was still there. It was a hairdressing salon. The lift opened onto a bright, shiny space, all mirrors and polished floors. Esquire Photoengraving was gone.

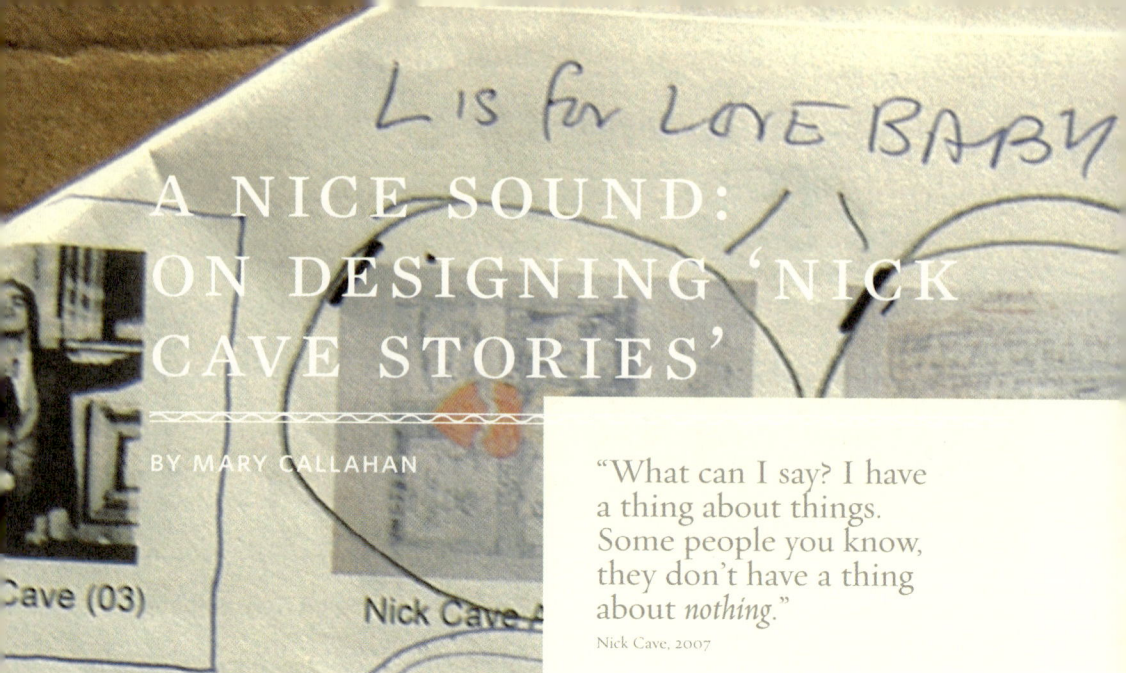

A NICE SOUND: ON DESIGNING 'NICK CAVE STORIES'

BY MARY CALLAHAN

> "What can I say? I have a thing about things. Some people you know, they don't have a thing about *nothing*."
>
> Nick Cave, 2007

I find it difficult to throw out what's left after a book like this has finished in production. Untidy stacks of paper that should be cleared away become a record of each day of a book's making. I was keen to use as endpapers the pages of thumbnails that were my reference list of the objects we had to shoot. Referencing the production of the book was deemed too 'tricky'. Perhaps I push it too much sometimes. I guess I was getting too close to stripping away the artifice that most books uphold. They exist to lead you to another world and immerse you in their subject. Maybe I'm trying to undermine that somehow.

old english font

with brackets

no more

③

Notebook known as 'Sacred and Profane'. 1985

on tour 7

IMG_0355

IMG_0364

The wrong font

I enjoy pairing together unlikely things—using typography and layout to tease out more readings, and open up other contexts for words. This quote I thought needed space—it was placed early in the pages—a nice entry into the 'things' that follow, yet at the same time it is heavy (or is it light?) with the irony of much of Cave's writing. White space lent a wry gravitas to the quote—it's just plain funny. It's the same laconic wit that has him write 'THE END' on a holy card on the first page of the notebook pictured.

Requiem, the serif font chosen for the book, gives the quote the air of a proverb. Sometimes the right font can make a personality appear on the page. It's laid out range left, at the top of the page, a list, workmanlike—not centred and precious—but the font is elegant and classical. Mix a straightforward placement with a font that fights against it somehow, and sometimes you get a nice sound.

Nick Cave Stories, published by the Victorian Arts Centre Trust in association with Nick Cave: The Exhibition, the Arts Centre Gallery, Melbourne, 2007.

Collection photography in Nick Cave Stories by Dan Magree

The Bad Seeds were in Manchester on tour. It was
there that Cave 'rescued' the 'Kylie' shoulder bag now
in the Collection and was photographed by Peter
Milne trailing it around the world on tour.

A Nick Cave story would not be complete without
talking about him as the embodiment of 'dapperness'.
For over 25 years his beloved bespoke suits have been
made by Sam Arkus of Berwick Street, London, and
one of them now resides—Cave would say meaning-
lessly—in the Collection along with a pair of his
favourite stylish brown slip-on shoes. It seems that
Nick Cave has always worn business suits, playfully
toying with our preconceptions of rock stardom.
He then subverts this by appearing in T-shirts embla-
zoned with visual messages such as 'Smith & Wesson
Handguns'.

Love has many meanings for Nick Cave.

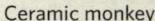

Ceramic monkey

There was no valid reason to feature this more insignificant piece from the Nick Cave collection. There were pages and pages from Cave's notebooks and journals clamouring for a space on the page, but the photographer and I championed its cause.

A cheap ceramic souvenir from Gibraltar given to Cave, it became a minor celebrity during our intense two-day photo shoot. The monkey had its own photo session, requiring a whole new set-up to the other objects in the collection. For what reason did we give it this attention?

And while laying out the pages, wrestling with too many images and too few pages, I always kept a spare page aside for the monkey.

I'm not sure what Nick Cave actually thought about its inclusion—I sensed he was quietly amused as he watched us trying to wield the 'things' from his elusive and poetic oeuvre into some kind of coherent order that a book of this nature usually demands.

To me, the monkey's irrelevance spoke volumes.

Souvenir of Gibraltar monkey given to Nick Cave by Martyn P. Casey

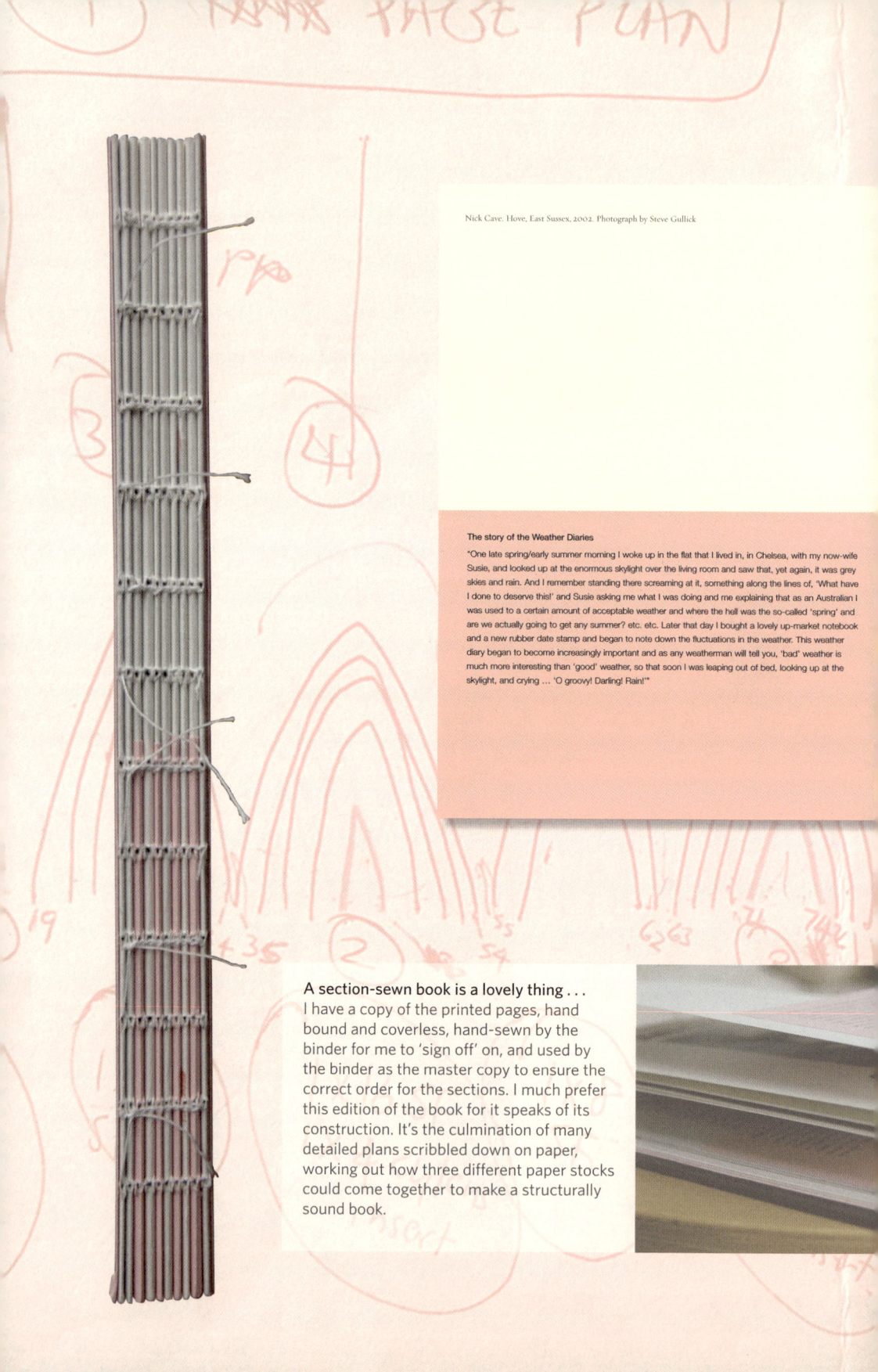

The story of the Weather Diaries

"One late spring/early summer morning I woke up in the flat that I lived in, in Chelsea, with my now-wife Susie, and looked up at the enormous skylight over the living room and saw that, yet again, it was grey skies and rain. And I remember standing there screaming at it, something along the lines of, 'What have I done to deserve this!' and Susie asking me what I was doing and me explaining that as an Australian I was used to a certain amount of acceptable weather and where the hell was the so-called 'spring' and are we actually going to get any summer? etc. Later that day I bought a lovely up-market notebook and a new rubber date stamp and began to note down the fluctuations in the weather. This weather diary began to become increasingly important and as any weatherman will tell you, 'bad' weather is much more interesting than 'good' weather, so that soon I was leaping out of bed, looking up at the skylight, and crying … 'O groovy! Darling! Rain!'"

A section-sewn book is a lovely thing . . .

I have a copy of the printed pages, hand bound and coverless, hand-sewn by the binder for me to 'sign off' on, and used by the binder as the master copy to ensure the correct order for the sections. I much prefer this edition of the book for it speaks of its construction. It's the culmination of many detailed plans scribbled down on paper, working out how three different paper stocks could come together to make a structurally sound book.

Pink slips

The book was coming together nicely, if not frantically. We'd been through the pages with Nick and he seemed happy. Several days later I got a call from the author telling me Nick had written short paragraphs on some of his 'things' that featured in the book.

I'm pretty good at keeping myself open to new ideas as a book is coming together. I can be accommodating, bending and yielding to the outside forces that are my clients. Very often it's the last-minute inclusion that can be the missing piece that you'd been looking for to lock in the design.

Also, *I* am guilty of being unwilling to pin myself down to a design until the last minute.

But this was ridiculous.

I was pushed to come up with how to get these musings into what were basically finished pages. The author thought it important to keep his voice separate to those of the other contributors. So I went with a practical idea of sprinkling slips of paper throughout the pages. Choosing deliberately gaudy cheap pink office paper, I began to enjoy disrupting the smugness of the expensive paper.

Becoming known as the 'pink slips', they came to fit in nicely with Cave's practice of bringing the mundane and the poetic together. He has a 'thing' about office supplies. His weather diaries are written in office diaries, each day stamped with a rubber date stamp. I hoped for the pink slips to look like they'd been stolen from the same grey steel stationery cabinet beside the tearoom.

MYTH, ABJECTION, OTHERNESS: CONTEMPORARY AUSTRALIAN ART

CAL/*MEANJIN* ESSAY BY JUSTIN CLEMENS

A few years ago, the curator Russell Storer remarked to me: 'People often ask me what's going on now in art, and all I can honestly say is—everything!' Unhelpful as it may be for anyone attempting a survey of the field, even the most glancing acquaintance with contemporary Australian art would confirm the truth of Storer's observation.

To enter any of the contemporary art galleries in any of Australia's major cities is to be confronted by a dizzying array of works. In one, you might find a recognisable yet abstracted horse's skull, slightly larger than life-size, riveted together from pale aluminium and named *Colt*, its folded blank teeth at once comforting and menacing, the shadows of its sockets sucking in the idle glance. A few flights of stairs will have you entering to a sequence of large photographs of a young indigenous Australian dressed in an absurd tartan costume with an outrageous false beard, acting out the myth of Isaac and Abraham in a lush European forest. In one photo he stands, arms crossed, by a log against which an axe has been propped; in another, he cowers beneath a luminous parody of a humpy. At the back of a large public gallery, a gargantuan gleaming assemblage of spotlights and speakers like adult Meccano—entirely dominating the large white exhibition space—sporadically erupts with a blinding and deafening violence. In yet another art space, quiet ambient sounds recorded in Iceland and in New York issue from a series of small speakers nestled in the joints of an angular construction of wooden struts, the whole crowned by imageless rectangular cool colour projections above. Another short walk and a lift ride up a few floors will get you into a small darkened room with a looped split-screen projection that splices scenes from the original 1980s *Miami Vice* TV show on the left, together with scenes from the movie remake on the right.[1]

This sort of range doesn't happen only between galleries, but also within the same gallery space. There's a promiscuous commingling of painting, photography, video and installation, among other productions, depicting all manner of events, and concocted from a mind-blowing range of materials. The range of influences, directions, relationships and ambitions is extraordinary. In fact, you don't even have to enter a gallery to see art, since art's long since taken itself out of such spaces, into real and virtual universes such as inner-urban backstreets and outer-suburban housing estates and real-time immersive dig-

1 This is a telescopic diary entry from an afternoon visit to several Melbourne galleries. The works described are, in order: Alexander Knox, *Colt*, at Murray White Room; Christian Thompson, *Lost Together*, at Gallery Gabrielle Pizzi; Marco Fusinato, *Aetheric Plexus*, at 'New 09', ACCA; Geoff Robinson, *North*, at Gertrude Contemporary Art Spaces; and Damiano Bertoli, *Continuous Moment: Bad Infinity*, at The Narrows.

Christian Thompson, *Isaac*, 2008, 100 x 100 cm, c-type print, edition of 5. Courtesy of the artist and Gallery Gabrielle Pizzi, Melbourne.

ital environments such as Second Life. Even more disturbingly, art's long taken itself beyond being linked to the senses of sight and sound.

It is not just that we live in a world in which lots of different people are doing lots of different things and showing them in lots of different places to lots of different audiences with lots of different kinds of evaluative procedures (although that's of course true). This drive to divergent multiplicity is essential to the practice of contemporary art, and not just an external happenstance. Also, Australian contemporary art is, for a number of reasons, an epicentre of this kind of thing—and all the more exemplary for hardly being recognised at all.

It is impossible to be impartial when speaking about art. This isn't just a question of quantity or of quality (though it is that too), but implicates the production and forms of address of art itself. In one of my favourite sequences of art criticism, Johann von Goethe speaks of his shifting appreciation of Michelangelo vis-à-vis Raphael. After a return to the Sistine Chapel, his diary entry of 2 December 1786 reads:

> After being dilated and spoiled by Michelangelo's great forms, my eye took no pleasure in the ingenious frivolities of Raphael's arabesques, and his Biblical stories, beautiful as they are, do not stand up against Michelangelo's. What a joy it would give me if I could see the works of both more frequently and compare them at leisure without prejudice, for one's initial reactions are bound to be one-sided . . .

Goethe, still meditating on the problem, goes back to it in July the following year:

> First it was Raphael I preferred, then it was Michelangelo. One can only conclude that man is such a limited creature that, though his soul may be open to greatness, he never acquires the capacity to recognise and appreciate equally, different kinds of greatness.[2]

2 Johann von Goethe, *Italian Journey*, Penguin, Harmondsworth, 1970, pp. 147, 371.

One master crowds out the others. For Goethe to say this is one thing: today the situation is all the more fraught, precisely because so much of contemporary art puts into question the possibility of judgement itself—as it simultaneously puts into question the notions of 'genius', 'greatness', 'authority', 'technical accomplishment' and so on. Even if we stick to the very restricted Euro-US art-historical twentieth century of Marcel Duchamp, Kasimir Malevich, Jasper Johns, Yves Klein, Piero Manzoni, Joseph Beuys, Andy Warhol and all the crazy groupuscules from the Futurists, the Dadaists and the Surrealists to the Situationists and beyond, it's hard to deny that art has become, as the Australian poet John Forbes once remarked to me, 'totally ontological'.

Basically, this means that art today is at once more material and more theoretical than ever before. More material, because not only are any and all materials now available to the world of art—from mud and hair to the most up-to-date products of our technophile civilisation—but also because what 'materials' are, what 'materiality' is, becomes an important question in its own right. This is also one of the reasons art is now more theoretical than ever before. Confronted by a piece of contemporary art, you are prompted to ask questions about every level of decision that the work incarnates: its materials, placement, creator, forms, allusions and so on. The onus is on the viewer to interpret these as decisions on the artist's part; more precisely, one can seldom be sure that any element of a contemporary artwork hasn't been freighted with significance, however obscure.

3 Thierry de Duve, 'Five Remarks on Aesthetic Judgment', *Umbr(a)*, no. 1, 1999, p. 20. Elsewhere, de Duve points out that the injunction of contemporary art is something like 'Do whatever!' The paradox is this: absolutely anything ('whatever') can be denominated and received as 'art' but, precisely because anything whatever can be art, nothing is able to be 'art' absolutely; the act and judgement can also always be reversed, be held to have failed. See his *Kant after Duchamp*, MIT Press, Cambridge, Mass., 1996.

4 de Duve, 'Five Remarks', p. 21.

This means that art is also obsessed with the now—and no longer with 'the new'. What's *new* presumes there's an *old*, a clear temporal progression, but contemporary art—as opposed to 'modern art'—is situational, not historical. Modern art thought of itself as 'modern' precisely in regard to what *preceded* it; contemporary art, by contrast, doesn't seem to care when or where anything came from, just so long as it can be put to use *here and now*. Contemporary art is in an intense discussion with its own very specific situation, and not with linear history. As the art historian Thierry de Duve notes, 'the word "art" is not a concept, but a collection of examples—different for everyone'.[3] This has the further consequence that 'all feelings are authorized by modern art'.[4] Art is no longer a clarified institution nor principle, nor any particular set of forms or techniques or attitudes or practices—at precisely the same moment the art world itself has become a hyper-organised, global corporate system.

Lest anybody think this is just a deleterious failure of people to realise that there's still an essence to art, to good art, and all this confusion is the miserable claptrap of degenerate know-nothings, the argument is actually as rigorous as it gets. In mathematics, it is certainly possible to confirm that a particular object has a property—but there is no way to count as a whole all the objects with this property. One can still identify works of art—but there is no over-arching consistency to 'art' itself. De Duve again: 'Everything which is today considered to be a masterpiece of modernity . . . was exposed to judgments of the "this isn't art, this isn't painting, this isn't music, this isn't literature" sort. Such judgments have to my mind all the structure of a negation, if only because pronouncing something to be non-art is already a way of substantiating the fact that the object in question is a candidate for art.'[5] Art now often takes this paradoxical gap between singular and universal as a crucial theme: if you can *definitely* adjudge that *this* is art, then it's definitely not.

5 de Duve, 'Five Remarks', p. 21.

Take the output and career of one of Australia's most successful and controversial painters, Juan Davila. The Chilean-born Davila migrated to Melbourne in 1974, and immediately set about producing an astonishing sequence of post-surrealist works, invariably scandalous in their content and effects. Typically deploying a garish, disjunctive palette, in which baby-shit yellows are smeared by dank vermilions, and spattered blues are streaked with dark chocolate browns, Davila draws on an encyclopaedic range of imagery and techniques—high art, low porn, Australian media icons, Chilean folk heroes, popular cartoons and psychoanalytic operations—to present freakish, enigmatic and compelling scenes. In *Crocodile Dundee* (1988), a degenerate lifesaver grimaces while sodomising the eponymous Crocodile Dundee, who is simultaneously being fellated by an aggressive black-eyed lizard against a backdrop of indeterminate smears, scores and scratches, a clumsily rendered group of faces, Parliament House in Canberra and other objects. The 1991 *Portrait of Bungaree* depicts a hallucinatory winged version of Bungaree with a nursling

Juan Davila, *At War*, 2002, 60 x 50 cm, oil on canvas. © Juan Davila, courtesy Kalli Rolfe Contemporary Art.

ancient in his arms, and stabbing his own gigantic bandaged erection with one supernumerary claw. Bungaree teeters on a swollen sciapod foot, his other leg a stump poised over a demented little wallaby, while diverse insignia proliferate on and around his patchwork body like the snaky coils of the Medusa. In *At War* (2002), a pallid, sad-faced nude half-draped in a cloth stamped with the emblem of the Red Cross sits, legs crossed, beneath the legend in large red capitals 'Arselickers' war is over', the date 'May 2003' in much smaller dark capitals, and, in black cursive script below, 'Australia Defeated in Middle East'.

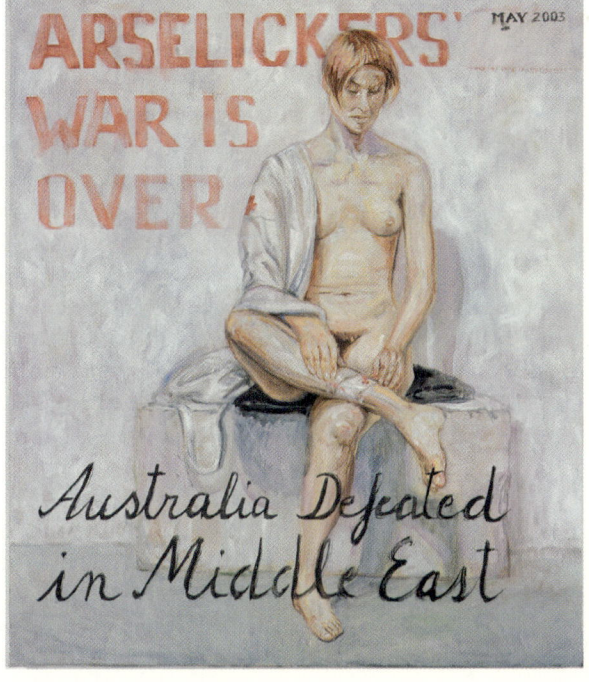

You can immediately see why Davila's work was one of the bugbears of Fred Nile's Festival of Light, as it is still of conservative art critics and variegated state representatives. In 1994, Davila's painting *The Liberator Simón*

Bolívar caused an intercontinental scandal when shown at the Hayward Gallery in London. As the *Independent* newspaper reported it, 'Venezuela, Colombia and Ecuador have all protested to the Chilean government over the painting . . . Two of the countries' ambassadors asked Chile yesterday why it was financing what the Colombian ambassador called "gutter art".'[6] As Davila asserts, 'Pornography transferred to painting permits two things: the showing of what has never been represented, and the debasing of the idea of high art by bringing popular materials to it.'[7] It's not just the injection of pornography and popular imagery into high art that's at stake, though; Davila's animus is particularly directed against the narcissistic ideals of nationalist iconography, whose foundations in real murder and mutilation he ceaselessly seeks to reveal through his own virtual transgressions.

So Davila's assault on the image of the body is explicitly connected with issues of disavowed colonial invasion on the one hand, and the unleashing of repressed psychosexual desires on the other. What makes Davila contemporary is not so much the shock value of the works themselves as his voracious mutability, his relentless sampling of radically heterogenous images and texts and techniques, and his unforgiving affirmation of the powers of expression. Davila's practice is still primarily painting—but directed by an extraordinary attentiveness to its deformation, the significance of assemblage and installation, to its possibilities for articulating otherwise unspeakable desires and acts.

Something similar is at work in another painter whose life, work and ambitions, at first glance, couldn't be further from Davila. Whereas Davila manifestly engages with transcultural, translingual and transsexual themes, Philip Hunter is local, focused and non-figurative. Yet both artists are untethering the foundations of Australian myth-making. For years, Hunter has been obsessively painting the Victorian landscape, returning again and again to the *Central Districts, Day Plains* and *Ghost Paddocks* of the Wimmera. From the late 1990s he has developed a signature style that presents the Wimmera as a hallucinatory environment in which sinuous, luminous lines pulse and interweave across a surface punctured with bursts of darkness and irregular clouds of earth. In *Lines in the Dirt* (2006), a thin red horizon line divides the canvas almost in two: the pale sky above ripples slowly with streaks and swathes of scratched-out clouds modulating to a near-imperceptible blur of blue; the earth itself ripples, shimmers, swirls, composed of a complex composition of dots, jagged lines, rifts, holes and opacities in colours that range from blood-red to ochre to jet. As the architect Peter Corrigan puts it in his introduction to a recent Hunter catalogue: 'It is the unexpected sense of isolation, the deep iridescent effects of light and the sense of presences lurking in the shadows that incline us toward a metaphysical quality in this art.'[8] In Hunter's paintings, personal memories are mashed together with a virtuosic technique influenced as much by indigenous motifs as by Rubens and Turner.

The metaphysical quality of Hunter's paintings at least partially derives from his abiding commitment to the landscape genre itself, long after the industrial mechanisation of the Australian farmland, the concomitant depopulation of rural areas, the struggle for indigenous land rights, and environmental degradation have stripped landscape of its traditional justifications. If there is an anachronistic art form today, it is landscape painting. From the point of

6 *Independent*, 12 August 1994, p. 1. The ill-tempered if influential British critic Peter Fuller, speaking in the mid 1980s about some of the recent success stories of Australian art, including Davila himself and Mike Parr, one of Australia's great performance artists, expressed the view that: 'Like Davila's, Parr's work is simply too unpleasant to describe in any detail': *The Australian Scapegoat: Towards an Antipodean Aesthetic*, University of Western Australia Press, 1986, p. 27.

7 Quoted in Sebastian Smee, 'Burning down the house', *Weekend Australian*, 30 September – 1 October 2006, p. 19.

8 Peter Corrigan, 'The Line of Light', in *Lines in the Dirt*, Tim Olsen Gallery, Sydney, 2008, np.

Philip Hunter, *Lines in the Dirt*, 121 x 107 cm, oil on canvas. Image © and courtesy of the artist.

view of much contemporary art, landscape painting is the very exemplar of what has to be superseded: old, boring and politically compromised. Paradoxically, this means such painting—now freed from the burden of having any serious pretensions to being either central or contemporary—continues to experiment and extend itself. Techniques of representation and presentation worked out in landscape painting often reappear, overlooked and unacknowledged, in self-consciously up-to-the-minute multimedia installations. It's not just, as Australian artist Janet Burchill said to me in a different context, that 'so much painting today is about the death of painting' (which is true). It's that, as Hunter stated in a 2001 Radio National interview with Julie Copeland: 'It's not for me so much a question of its (painting's) relevancy, or its position in some hierarchy of mediums that are appropriate for contemporary arts practice. What I think is much more important is that painting can actually give you another angle, a view on the world that is different to a filmic experience, a photographic experience, an installation or sound experience.'[9] On the one hand, this is a kind of re-uptake of a great modernist principle: each of the arts explores what it and only it can do. On the other, it's a postmodernist statement about the shattering and democratisation of media: art isn't given hierarchically, but through singular experiences.

9 Philip Hunter, quoted in Ashley Crawford, *Wimmera: The Work of Philip Hunter*, Thames & Hudson, Melbourne, 2002, p. 25.

By contrast, A Constructed World (ACW) is unapologetically postmodern in its promiscuous use of media and its unforgiving assault on the artist–audience division—though its members too are in pursuit of singular experiences. ACW comprises two itinerant Australian artists, Geoff Lowe (who began his career as a painter) and Jacqueline Riva. Lowe and Riva work together, but not simply as individuals, nor simply as a couple, nor simply as collaborators. They are peripatetic, constantly on the move from Melbourne to New York to Turin to Paris to Bordeaux to Singapore, and their work often takes transformations of movement as its object. Acw typically intervenes in the spaces of existing structures (sometimes official art-sites, sometimes not), erecting transient extra- or subconstructions that de- and re-regionalise those spaces, and which affect the sorts of movements that can be made within them—whether those movements are 'physical' or 'abstract'. As one young Australian artist remarked to me, ACW 'has to be conceived not so much as a type but as a vast geodesic network constantly striving to globalise itself'. Acw's transient installations use a wide range of domestic or familiar materials (crinkly blue plastic tarpaulins, for instance), and often resemble shonky versions of a range of structures (gazebos or toolsheds, for instance). These constructions often have no clear purpose or too many possible purposes, but encourage a kind of stupefaction: you often don't quite know what to do with them, how to look at or move through or talk about them.

A Constructed World, 'Hobbes Opera Part 1, 7 Nation Army', 2008, performance, CAPC Museum of Contemporary Art, Bordeaux. Image courtesy of A Constructed World.

A recent ACW work is titled *Help Yourself*, a double-video piece dedicated to masturbation. On one screen, a sequence of images shifts past, including advertising for Elle Macpherson underwear, the elegant model's elongated hand twitching immobilised above her lingerie-slick cunt; classical high-art images, the holy mother's careful fingers encircling the infant Jesus' little prick

like a shell nestling its kernel; a scene from a Warhol flick, in which an anonymous hand tenderly cuffs and jerks off a cock clad in a white sheet like Casper
the Friendly Ghost; a cut from a porno flick of a chick on a nice plump bed,
knees up and spread, fingering herself diligently for the gaze of some diegetic
character off-camera; and so on. The voice-over is extracted from an interview
between Lowe and a well-known English psychoanalyst. The psychoanalyst
speaks of how difficult it is for parents to acknowledge their children's mastur-
batory habits; of the centrality that discussions of masturbation played in the
Wednesday evenings Sigmund Freud hosted in the early, heady days of psychoanalysis, attended primarily by overeducated and overdressed bourgeois
gentlemen smoking cigars; of the problem of accounting for what the French
psychoanalyst Jacques Lacan called 'the idiot's enjoyment'. This discussion is
interrupted by another voice-over by Riva. Another video in the same space
restaged a day in the life of Samuel Pepys, the great seventeenth-century
English diarist, who records his own encounters with pornography and masturbation in a way that is at once prurient and moralistic. Pepys has to burn
the book that excites him too much, becoming an exemplary case of the para-
doxes of exhibitionistic self-censorship.

An attempt to extend collaborative forms of creative practice and reception is at the heart of ACW's work, whether between Lowe and Riva themselves,
or with other artists, writers, even random gallery-goers: art practice as a kind
of estranging conviviality. Over the past decade or so, ACW has enthusiastically
set up and participated in all sorts of vehicles, including the 1990s *Artfan* (with
reviews by, in Lowe's words, 'people-who-said-they-didn't-know-about-art')
and the blog *Speech* <http://speech2012.blogspot.com>. Part of ACW's point is
to enable—without determining—new forms of interaction with art, as well as
new kinds of dialogues about what art might be and do.

Such dialogues can even happen inadvertently, as in the recent Australian
media frenzy over the allegedly paedophiliac aspects of Bill Henson's photographs—a frenzy that implicated Kevin Rudd, actor Cate Blanchett, the NSW
police and an enormous number of other interested parties, some high art,
some committed activists, some from the general public. Given the uproar,
Henson's photographs hardly need any further introduction. They are impec-
cably shot, technically outstanding and deeply semiotically nourished; Henson
likes to place naked teen bodies in inky environments, suffusing his images
with a hyper-aestheticised post-Romantic melancholia. Of course, he does
a lot else too—beautiful shots of the Paris Opera and high-contrast, monu-
mental landscapes—but the loneliness and loss of adolescence have become
a kind of signature subject. This, indeed, turned out to be the problem: complaints about the email invitation to the opening of Henson's May 2008 show
sparked a police investigation. Rudd himself declared the photographs 'absolutely revolting' (although the Classification Board later gave them a PG rating),
while Malcolm Turnbull, leader of the Opposition, admitted to owning two
Hensons—both, apparently, entirely nubile-free.

When this sort of thing hits the mass media, even the excessive virtuosity
of such images comes to be interpreted simultaneously in radically different
frames: are these works in which the sadness and solitude of young people
are given an extraordinary aesthetic freighting, or simply horrid images to be

10 David Marr, 'Panic and Censor', *Monthly*, December 2008 – January 2009, p. 14. See also Marr's book *The Henson Case*, Text, Melbourne, 2008, and his spot on SlowTV, <http://www.themonthly.com.au/tm/node/1268>.

11 Rex Butler, 'Bill Henson: The Letter Returns', *Broadsheet*, vol. 37, no. 4, 2008, p. 277. It might also be helpful to recall here, as does Jennifer Friedlander in a related context, that 'The modern notion of the child emerged around the same time as the invention of photography, and from the start, nude children have figured prominently as photographic subjects', *Feminine Look: Sexuation, Spectatorship, Subversion*, State University of New York, Albany, 2008, p. 93.

damned and obliterated, and their maker punished? The low tenor of the discussion could hardly endear the government–media apparatus to anybody. As David Marr noted: 'Though the Henson row is probably the biggest art controversy in half a century, the nation's art minister had nothing to say. No politicians were game to stand up to the child-protection lobby and say the obvious: this panic was way out of hand.'[10] Unfortunately, Marr contributes to the problem to the extent that Henson's project becomes nothing more than another opportunity for lamenting the vitiation of solid liberal-democratic values. The best account of the furore was given by Rex Butler, who points out that 'it was those who complained about the photos who provided them with their best reading, not insofar as they objected to them and tried to silence them, but like any good analyst, they listened to them and let them speak'.[11] As Butler points out, Henson's work is fundamentally of the same order as humanitarian victim publicity, with its quasi-biological alibi (adolescence as a period of transition between child and adult) and its sensationalist appeal.

There is no such covert complicity with the demands of culturally dominant elites in the work of Tracey Moffatt, which ranges across photography, art and music videos, and film. Moffatt is in command of a special kind of blank postmodern irony, in which the generic components of identity—personal, cultural, racial—are deconstructed with a rigorously camp seriousness. In her early photographic sequence *Something More* (1989), the artist herself, dolled up in a foxy red dress criss-crossed by black roses, escapes a pastiche outback shack inhabited by a rough hard-drinking bloke in a blue singlet and a slutty smoking blonde, pursued by a couple of kids in shorts and a cartoonish coolie complete with a long black queue. The sequence concludes with a shot of the artist splayed face down on the asphalt, her dress pulled up to her hips and her legs akimbo, while a road arrow informs us that we are still 300 miles from Brisbane. In *Under the Sign of Scorpio* (2005), Moffatt once again dresses herself up, this time as a series of famous women ranging from the suicidal American poet Anne Sexton and indigenous poet Oodgeroo Noonuccal to the Rhodesian–British novelist Doris Lessing and Hillary R. Clinton. These images are barely representational at all—you'd only know the putative subject because the name is scrawled on the image in white—and generate garish melodrama from the isolation of an arbitrary but fateful trait. All these women were born, like Moffatt herself, 'under the sign of Scorpio'. This strategy of overtly kitschy identification is itself a kind of meta-identification, sampling the processes of such artists as Cindy Sherman, whose famous *The Complete Untitled Film Stills* depict the chameleonic Sherman dressed up as a variety of B-grade actresses. All this hyper-reflexive postmodernity, however, is bound to place by specific local affiliations: in the early 1960s, at the age of three, Moffatt was given up for adoption by her Aboriginal mother to a white Brisbane family.

As Geoff Lowe recently remarked to Jacqueline Riva and me about Moffatt's achievement, 'She really turned the sock inside out.' In response to our blank stares, Lowe immediately added, 'I'm trying to make a topological point here.' His point was this: in the 1990s Moffatt transformed the possibilities for Australian artists abroad, as much as her work transformed the possi-

bilities for local artists, indigenous and
non-indigenous. Moffatt's films have
been shown at the Cannes festival; her
works have been collected by MOMA
in New York and the Tate in London;
she remains one of Australia's most
successful contemporary artists internationally. Moffatt reputedly used to
announce to New Yorkers that in Australia she was as 'big as Madonna'.

As Babar the Elephant says to his
kids when they freak out over parodies
of Munch's *The Scream* and Picasso's
Les Demoiselles d'Avignon at the grand
opening of the Celesteville Museum of Art:

Tracey Moffatt, *Something More 5*, 1989, 98 x 127 cm, from the series of 9 images, Cibachrome. Courtesy of the artist and Roslyn Oxley9 Gallery, Sydney.

> 'Doesn't it have to be old to be in a gallery?' asked Alexander.
> 'Doesn't it have to be pretty?' asked Flora.
> 'It doesn't "have to be" or mean anything,' said Babar. 'There are no rules to tell us what art is.'[12]

When middlebrow children's books are
on the way to being pretty much right
about contemporary art, something
really serious has to have happened. In
the place of 'art', what we get instead
is 'culture'. And we get it everywhere:
museums, galleries, art schools, uni-
versities, the media and their assorted
personnel blare endlessly about survey shows, representation, art today,
culture today, cultural studies today,
Australia today, good financial planning, how to strengthen industry links
and maximise audiences.

Tracey Moffatt, *Louise Brooks*, 2005, 43.2 x 58.4 cm, from the series *Under the Sign of Scorpio*, archival pigment ink on acid-free rag paper. Courtesy of the artist and Roslyn Oxley9 Gallery, Sydney.

One of the great things about the contemporary Australian art market,
however, is that it's not tied so directly to these exigencies as many other
so-called cultural fields. In the literary marketplace, the economy is very differently distributed and regionalised, and products, being inherently multiple
('books', 'magazines', 'texts'), have very different modes, places, temporalities
and personnel. But in the weirdly constituted global-feudal-democratic-cap-
italist artzone, you don't have to sustain any particular type of narrative in
order to make some kind of living. The point is just to do something that makes
a difference—no matter how you do it—and the omnivorous desperation of
the contemporary art world to get something that's absolutely 'now' drives its
minions ever onwards with the whip of possibility.

This structural desperation affects every level of the art world, not just the
artists themselves. Art criticism in this country is at once more ecumenical

12 Laurent de Brun-
hoff, *Babar's Gallery
(Closed Mondays)*,
Abrams Books, New
York and London,
2003, pp. 34–5.

and highbrow—and, goddamn it, much more diverse and exciting—than its literary counterpart. You only have to read a couple of lines by Ted Colless or Philip Brophy to get a jolt, not to mention the writings of artists such as Stuart Ringholt. This is of course partially because there's just a lot more cash, glamour and power flowing about the art market, but also because its desperation tends to corrode almost all inherited prejudices. At its limit, this means curators, critics, artists, gallerists and even buyers start mouthing recondite philosophical concepts. You can pick up two-bit catalogue essays from any gallery these days, with authors expatiating endlessly about Zen Buddhism, Marcel Proust, G.W.F. Hegel, Plato, Glenn Gould and their relation to *this* work. Even if the references are misunderstood, the point is that the contemporary art world is in some ways genuinely adventurous and risk-taking—at least compared to the aggressive timidity of the local literary marketplace—and even more so since it's not averse to genuinely intellectual protest.

The young Australian artist Bianca Hester relates a recent conversation she had with the visiting Italian curator Francesco Stocchi about what had most struck him about the local scene. Stocchi reported 'that Melbourne (and Sydney) artists in particular seem to "do everything" '. As Hester continues: 'And he's totally right. Artists here do way more than make "art" in any simplified kind of way. They write, work in collectives, teach, develop exhibition strategies, curate, open their own spaces, generate publications—thereby engaging most aspects of art production, presentation and distribution.'[13] How is it that Australia has become such a vital place for contemporary art, and without anybody really recognising it?

One of the ironies of being a postcolonial and perhaps post-European settlement is that, although the cultural cringe is supposedly behind us, long-established communication channels to Otherness are still gaping wide. As a result, Australian artists perhaps have an easier time than artists from such old centres as New York, London or Tokyo in having a direct line to elsewhere. Contemporary Australian artists can be especially attentive to what's going on in Slovenia and Thailand and Chile. And, given that Australia is a wealthy, heavily suburbanised and highly educated country, an enormous number of people are ready to try their hand at one or another role in the zone of art, all able to survive if not succeed. Moreover, since the key institutions that regulate the passage from the

13 Bianca Hester, 'Enabling Restraints', in Kate Daw and Vikki McInnes (eds), *Bureau*, vca Margaret Lawrence Gallery, Melbourne, 2008, p. 18.

Elizabeth Newman, *Untitled*, 2009, 150 x 100 cm, fabric on pine ply. Courtesy of the artist and Neon Parc Gallery, Melbourne.

outside to the inside of the art world are today so well organised and regulated—the varied magazines, ranging from blogs such as *the art life* through *un Magazine*, *Eyeline*, *Photofile*, *Art World*, *Australian Art Collector* and *Art & Australia*; the exclusive private galleries in Paddington in Sydney or Flinders Lane in Melbourne; major public galleries such as the NGV, NGA, AGNSW; dedicated contemporary art spaces such as the Brisbane Institute of Modern Art, Perth Institute of Contemporary Arts or the Australian Centre of Contemporary Art; university galleries such as Monash University Museum of Art or the Ian Potter Museum of Art; periodic festivals such as the Biennale of Sydney—the competition is intense. (Of course, the people making the least money out of all of this tend to be the artists, though this quasi-marginality can still generate some symbolic capital.) Despite these efforts, however, local art remains 'Post-Provincial, Still Peripheral' (as Anthony Gardner titles his contribution to the forthcoming *Cambridge Companion to Australian Art*).

Yet contemporary Australian art has real power, often performed with a violent, sometimes noxious hilarity. Take Richard Bell's various *boutades*, including the now-notorious 'Bell's Theorem', which proposes 'Aboriginal Art—it's a White Thing'; Brook Andrew's large post-Warholian screen-print series, which blows up an old anthropological photograph of an Aboriginal couple fucking in the desert sand, the man on top turning to the camera and grinning like a loon; Ash Keating dumping ten tonnes of rubbish outside the Penrith Civic Centre; the wooden text pieces of Emily Floyd, with titles such as *Permaculture Crossed with Feminist Science Fiction*; Patricia Piccinini's abject genetic mutations, with their small white children fondling smug, hairy, fleshy obscenities; or Elizabeth Newman's minimalist cut-out felt hangings and fluorescent tubes tacked onto plywood boards.

To invoke the French literary critic Maurice Blanchot's remarks on Emily Brontë, art 'is not civic duty; it is precarious, abyssal exposure to what lies at the edge of human experience'.[14] If this brief survey can risk any generalisations about Australian art, it is that this art, perhaps more consistently and frantically than that of other places, assaults nationalistic iconography in an attempt to unhinge the myth from the place. To do so, it deploys every medium and technique available, typically generating effects of distortion, ugliness, abjection. The average Australian artist makes a lot more work in a lot of different ways than, say, a European counterpart. This assault on iconography is primarily fuelled by a keen attention to otherness, to the foreign. For Australian artists, Australia is to be remade by its very unmaking. The savage and memorable events they create give us an Australia more true and more strange.

14 Leslie Hill, '"Affirmation without Precedent": Maurice Blanchot and Criticism Today', in Leslie Hill et al. (eds), *After Blanchot: Literature, Criticism, Philosophy*, University of Delaware Press, Cranbury, 2005, p. 69.

ESSAYS

THE CURIOUS SIGNIFICANCE OF TRIPLE J

BEN ELTHAM

IT'S ABOUT EIGHT O'CLOCK ON a Thursday morning in May and triple j's breakfast team are hard at work. Robbie Buck, Marieke Hardy and Lindsay McDougall (The Doctor) are interviewing Hilltop Hoods in preparation for their trip to Sale in regional Victoria for triple j's One Night Stand concert the following Saturday.

But despite the talent gathered together in the ABC studio in Ultimo, the Hilltop Hoods interview of 28 May 2009 was not a particularly noteworthy piece of radio. McDougall and Hardy riffed with Suffa and Pressure, Hilltop Hoods rappers, about the resemblance of their microphones to phalluses; Hardy made a joke about 'brewer's droop', while Buck tried to draw the conversation back to Hilltop Hoods' headline performance at triple j's One Night Stand in Sale. About the best that could be said for the interview was that it was diverting, perhaps mildly amusing.

This is the sort of moment on triple j[1] that so annoys certain musicians and fans. It gives rise to the fear that triple j, supposedly a national youth public radio network with a licence to support and 'unearth' new Australian contemporary music, is simply a simulacrum of commercial FM stations, with a format and a music playlist not markedly dissimilar to national commercial networks such as Nova.

Is this the best we can expect of a taxpayer-funded national youth radio network? What exactly is the role of triple j, and is the network fulfilling it? Is triple j too commercial, or not commercial enough? Does it rotate too many songs, or does it play too much weird stuff that has resulted in the flight of its core audience of 18- to 24-year-olds? Is the network a national juggernaut that makes and breaks artists with impunity, or is it a relic of a bygone era, before the advent of the internet, when radio was the key way to listen to new music?

This essay attempts to answer some of these questions. In researching it, I spoke to musicians, music industry executives and radio people from across the sector, including triple j's music director Richard Kingsmill and other staff at the broadcaster. What emerges is a picture of a network that, for all its significance, is in many ways misunderstood. Triple j is a keystone of contemporary Australian culture and a kind of strange hybrid that sits in an uncomfortable middle ground between its commercial and community radio cousins. Indeed, the level and intensity of criticism the network attracts is a sign of the network's importance.

[1] triple j insists on being name-checked without any capitals. Like Australian rock band silverchair or the mobile phone company 3, the network's small 't' and 'j' is a conscious marketing decision and reflects a particular world view that takes brand identity seriously. Triple j's marketing staff will vet press releases and posters for this punctuation to ensure the network's brand identity is maintained.

In late 2007 two Australian musicians, Ben McCarthy and Keir Nuttall, started a Facebook group entitled 'Split JJJ into Two Competing Stations—Save the Oz Music Industry!' Their idea was simple: create a second station alongside the existing model of triple j in the manner of BBC Radio 2 in the United Kingdom. The group's manifesto does a good job of explaining what many Australian musicians find objectionable about triple j: 'Initially, the fact that it was a government entity (therefore not subject to commercial pressures) meant that it could provide an opportunity for diverse and obscure music that would never have a chance on commercial radio to be heard nationally,' the group's page records. But '[triple j] has strayed from this charter, and is now behaving like its commercial rivals i.e. it excludes variety and diversity in the name of building its own brand,' the page continues. 'Currently the only effective outlet for new artists is run like a typical government department.'

The Facebook group grew slowly until early 2009, was covered in the mainstream media and briefly gained some traction with Facebook members before dwindling into the sort of semi-obscurity that describes the majority of Facebook campaigns. It boasted 2765 members by the start of June 2009. 'As the discussion unfolded, some people pointed out that "split jjj" wasn't a very practical idea and I came to agree,' Nuttall explained to me in an email. 'Lots of smart people joined the group and it really showed me what a complex issue the whole thing is and that I am not the kind of person who could be a lobbyist,' he added.

But the Facebook group—Nuttall insists 'it never became a proper campaign'—generated a lot of interest in Australia's relatively small and highly connected music industry, arguably far more than it warranted. This was partly because it dared to say the sort of things that can be heard over a pint of beer at any Australian rock music venue on any given night: that triple j was too commercial or, alternatively, that triple j had lost 'the kids' to Nova by not being commercial enough; that triple j played too much hip-hop; that triple j won't play your band if Richard Kingsmill doesn't like your haircut; that triple j has abandoned its glory days of the nineties.

Some of these criticisms make no sense. At one level, the message-board chatter about triple j on websites such as Mess+Noise reveals nothing more than the prejudices of those writing it; a lot of the criticism of triple j is from people who no longer listen to the network or identify with its goals.

But many musicians have thoughtful and good-willed criticisms to make. Nuttall, for instance, is an award-winning songwriter and musician who writes and performs with Kate Miller-Heidke, one of Australia's most talented emerging pop stars. He thinks a key problem is triple j's 'centralised playlist, which is all about nurturing triple j's corporate identity rather than reflecting the community around it . . . Do Kings of Leon or Lily Allen need high rotation on taxpayer-funded broadcasting?' he asks, pointing out that US band Kings of Leon are the most-played act on triple j. 'This is not enhancing Australian culture and community, it is just positioning the triple j brand.'

Ben Butcher, a Melbourne musician, shares some of these concerns. Butcher has been in a number of bands that have received varying levels of support from triple j, including the highly regarded Baseball; he thinks triple j is Sydney-centric and finds it frustrating the network isn't closer in nature to community stations.

'When I hear bands like Phoenix, Kings of Leon and Bloc Party being constantly played, I can't help but think that old Sydney people are running the station, second guessing what the kids like . . .' he wrote in an email.

But many in the industry have a different view. One of the most insightful is Stephen Green, the programmer for the Queensland music industry conference Big Sound and an executive for digital radio services company D-star. Green worked as a radio 'plugger' for eight years in the 2000s and has detailed inside knowledge of the process of FM radio programming.

Like most Australian music fans, I didn't know how a particular song makes it onto playlists on Australian radio. Green patiently explained the process to me in a long phone interview. The basics are disarmingly simple:

> Basically the plugger has a meeting with a music director, brings in music and plays it . . . They're relatively informal, most stations will do them once a week, in Sydney meetings are generally held on a Tuesday, everyone has their fifteen minutes or half an hour and they go in and pitch what they've got. Generally you don't go all out and do Powerpoints [sic], it's about getting music directors to listen to it. If you're sitting in front of them you know it's being done.

Green told me that triple j pluggers meetings are slightly different to those at commercial stations. 'They've got a slightly different group of pluggers, there's a lot of indies that visit triple j that don't visit commercial radio, like Remote Control and those kinds of labels—triple j is their bread and butter.' The pitch is also different. 'What you're pitching to triple j is a little bit different: they're looking for potential, they're looking for something that in a few years time is going to be bigger than Ben Hur—they want to champion something that's going to be big.'

In contrast, Green says, commercial radio is looking for sure bets. 'They're just looking for the fact that it's already popular, they're looking for stuff that's going to have a high familiarity rating with the listeners, something that's not too hard to break.'

When I asked Richard Kingsmill about this process, he told me that triple j pluggers meetings are conducted on tight timelines at the Ultimo offices. Stories of industry schmoozing, wining and dining are 'a myth'. 'We don't place faith in those research methods that the commercial stations use, we're looking at what people are requesting each night, but a lot of it is just gut instinct, we're basing it on the mood of this place,' Kingsmill said. 'We're employed to be music experts.'

Kingsmill's deputy in the programming department, Nick Findlay, explained how new songs are added to triple j's playlists. 'We add eight songs a week to rotation, which may not seem like much but is actually bursting at the seams in terms of adding new music.' In addition to the eight songs added to rotation, seven songs from the feature album are also rotated each week, and singles from previous weeks' feature albums are 'pushed up in the rotation'.

But it is also the case that Richard Kingsmill's musical tastes and sensibilities are only a marginal part of triple j's programming philosophy. The network is part of a demographic range that supports a diverse set of audiences. Triple j's own programming data show that the network's playlists sit somewhere between the commercial networks and community stations. Triple j's programming is shaped by the musical knowledge of its programmers and specialist announcers, as well as the demands of its listeners for popular songs by established artists. The result is a hybrid that accommodates a lot of diversity: big-name international artists jostle against indie bands and unknown hopefuls 'unearthed' from triple j's vast vault. Many more acts are played than on commercial radio and some acts are supported with a lot of enthusiasm.

According to Stephen Green, 'It's important that triple j doesn't stray too far left [of centre] because it's the vehicle for people's musical exploration.' Green explains it as a demographic shift whereby listeners' tastes develop as they age.

> You might start at *Video Hits* at age ten; by the time you get to your mid teens you've progressed onto Nova, they're playing more progressive stuff and it starts to open your mind a little. Once that's not enough for you, you jump to triple j: they're playing a couple of songs you've heard on Nova, but they're playing a lot of stuff you haven't. Triple j helps you get on that journey where you are listening to new stuff, that's the entry point to get you to listen to 4zzz and FBI. If you take triple j too left of centre, you are taking that link out of the chain of musical growth for people.

One way of understanding triple j's niche is to talk to those who sit on either side of it. Dean Buchanon is group program director at DMG's commercial FM network Nova. Nova out-rates triple j by a handy margin in triple j's key demographic of 18- to 24-year-olds, with a glossier and more commercial mix of music. Moreover, Nova's disciplined and focused advertising strategy of 'never more than two ads in a row' sees it deliver a less promotion-heavy radio format than triple j, whose various station IDs, tour support promotions, triple j-branded events and associated audio clutter have now progressed to the stage where you can hear a promotion for the Big Day Out or a Lily Allen tour on the ostensibly non-commercial national broadcaster.

Nova's national network of FM licences cost its corporate parent DMG Radio Australia hundreds of millions of dollars when it bought them in federal government auctions in the early 2000s. Critics thought DMG had overpaid, but Nova proceeded to steal market share from all its rivals, becoming the number-one radio station for under forties by 2003.

'We uncovered a massive audience that were interested in new music and music of all genres,' Buchanon explained. 'Once the Nova stations started to get critical mass, it started to change the landscape [in that] triple j was no longer the only domain for new music, the only brand that took risks on new music, and the Austereo stations were no longer the only ones that played hits.'

Buchanon believes triple j has moved closer to Nova's programming philosophy. 'Triple j appears to have become a lot closer to a commercial player like Nova in recent times,' he said. 'They'll play big commercial bands like Kings of Leon, where eighteen months ago they wouldn't have because they were commercially successful.'

At the other end of the spectrum in Australian radio lies the community sector. This large and diverse collection of more than 300 community radio stations includes niche, local and special interest radio outlets, ranging from small rural broadcasters to medium-sized FM music stations such as FBi in Sydney and 3RRR in Melbourne. Australia's capital cities have enjoyed a diverse and healthy alternative to commercial radio since the mid 1970s, with stations such as 3RRR and 4ZZZ becoming genuine landmarks in the cultural scene of their cities. Despite this, community radio in Australia remains underfunded, with most stations relying on volunteer labour and community fundraising to survive. It's a difficult environment, which has seen heavily indebted community station FBi in Sydney reach crisis point this year.

'We've always had a high debt that we've managed,' FBi's Dan Zilber told me on the phone from Sydney. 'What we've found over the last six months as the economy has declined is that our sponsors have had less money to spend with us and budgets have reduced.' FBi needs to raise $1 million to pay back these start-up loans. It's a challenging task in the current environment, but Zilber sees FBi as critical to Sydney's musical and cultural diversity. 'I guess I see FBi's job as reflecting Sydney back at itself, and perpetually reflecting the cultural fabric of the city back to the people.'

Stations such as FBi, 2SER, 3RRR, 3PBS, 4ZZZ and RTRfm generally support contemporary music of a quirkier, less commercial, more local and more independent nature than either triple j or the commercial networks. Although FBi maintains a relatively loose playlist, most community radio stations are completely unplaylisted, with announcers (often with deep and long-standing networks in their local music scenes) free to play whatever they want within station policies.

'Some people look at community radio as a feeder for triple j and commercial radio, but that's not true,' says FBi's Zilber. 'You can't deny a great pop song, but we're not going to play something just because it's going to be a real cross-over hit. We're a place of passion and enthusiasm—we're not just filling in a playlist.'

Kath Letch was station manager at Melbourne's 3RRR for fourteen years. 'I think the community radio sector is a really broad sector with both specialist and general services,' she said when I visited her at the station. 'You've got classical stations—the MBS stations—ethnic and multicultural licences, the general licences.' In contrast, 'triple j is set up in a particular way,' she continued. 'In comparison to community radio, it's a highly funded service, it's a staff-based operation, it has a more stereotypical structure and it's set up as a national broadcaster. I think that changes your content and how you produce content.'

Like nearly everyone I talked to while researching this essay, Letch acknowledges triple j's importance in regional Australia. 'Triple j has been a really interesting development in terms of regional communities and young people that I think had very little that reflected their perspective on the world. The extension of a specific youth-based service nationally has been a very good development for people's radio options.'

It's impossible to discuss triple j without debating the influence of music director Richard Kingsmill. The focus on Kingsmill is perhaps unfortunate, given all that triple j does, but it cannot be avoided. In our interviews, other triple j staff often deferred to him and waited for the music director to speak before giving their thoughts. There is a sense in which Kingsmill's musical tastes—in hip-hop, in indie rock and in pop—help define triple j's musical personality.

Whether you think this is a good or a bad thing will depend of what you think of the man himself. You could argue that the criticism that triple j is programmed by a small group of people led by Richard Kingsmill is not really a criticism at all. As one of the longest-standing radio announcers in the country, Kingsmill has shaped the voice and identity of triple j (and through it, Australian music in general) for more than two decades. In some ways, he can be considered a fascinating and important cultural figure in his own right. The wonderful thing about triple j's history, Kingsmill told me,

> is that we've had competitors and other media come along to rival our audience and rival what we do, but the station has always remained pretty fixed in its ideals. One is be a strong supporter of Australian music. We set a benchmark of 40 per cent Australian music, day in, day out, throughout the month. That figure last month was 42.99 per cent. So that commitment to Australian music is still there after thirty years, that hasn't changed. We've got a commitment to live music that hasn't changed in thirty years. We've got a commitment to discovering and fostering new Australian talent and bringing them up through the ranks, and it's also about trying to expose as much of the exciting overseas music as much as we can in amongst that as well.

Kingsmill is aware of the criticism triple j attracts, and doesn't hide the fact he finds much of it unfair. 'The mistruths are the ones that are most upsetting, that's when it hurts. I'm not saying we're perfect but we try really, really hard to get it right.'

After twenty years at triple j, and nearly thirty in radio, Kingsmill shows no signs of slowing down. In person he is quite intense, with a certain highly strung energy in his communication style; Kingsmill cares. 'We would never talk down to our audience. We engage them as much as we possibly can. The audience we've got now, it's a national audience, it's an excited audience, it's the same [size] audience as we had ten years ago, it's the same kind of people.'

Although music is triple j's focus, the network does a range of other things. Among the best of these is *Hack*, triple j's daily youth current affairs show. As producer James West pointed out to me, the show is unique in its ambit and scope. West, a 27-year-old with a degree in journalism from New York University, got his start as a junior reporter for triple j as a 20-year-old—another example of triple j's history of giving talented young presenters a chance.

West argues persuasively that *Hack* occupies some of the best radio real estate in the country: 5.30 to 6.00 p.m. on a national FM network. *Hack* has the resources to deliver high-quality radio journalism; indeed, the show can at times be every bit as good as that delivered by *Hack*'s more 'adult' colleagues on ABC Radio. West points to triple j's coverage of the *Pacific Adventurer* oil spill in Queensland's Moreton Bay, and Hack's exploration of the declining fortunes of Australian basketball:

We included an analysis of Firepower, the greatest corporate swindle this country has ever seen, and we were able to talk to young basket-ballers—promising athletes—and get out to courts in western Sydney and talk to people who had only ever been fans of American basketball . . . For me, *Hack* is one of the only venues that can really engage in a conversation with young people in what matters to them.

Ten days after I spoke to Richard Kingsmill, Nick Findlay and James West at triple j, the network held its One Night Stand in Sale. The event showed the network in its best light. In a town of barely 2000 people, triple j staged a sellout concert for 15,000 mainly young people that featured some of the most popular bands in the country, including Hilltop Hoods, Eskimo Joe and the Butterfly Effect, as well as indie rock up-and-comers Children Collide and Gippsland's Unearthed winners And Burn. Whatever triple j's quirks, its ongoing commitment to young music audiences in non-capital-city Australia continues to define the network at its most socially engaged.

Dr Kate Ames is an academic at Central Queensland University in Rock-hampton who studied triple j's impact on regional audiences for her doctorate. 'I moved to Rockhampton in the mid nineties, just after triple j had gone national. In Rocky at the time, there were only the two commercial AM sta-tions. What I really noticed when triple j came to town was that there was an almost automatic conversion of youth culture in Rockhampton. I was driving down the street and it was Jump for Js day, and all these people were getting out and jumping, and I thought, this must be something.'

Ames believes triple j is a crucial source of cultural capital for young people living in the regions. 'Triple j is a radio station that allows listeners to mentally leave the area they live in,' she told me. 'Triple j creates this sense of a virtual world that sits above where someone is located, it brings people together with a love of music, with a sense of being a little bit different.'

Kingsmill is proud of the Gippsland event. 'Initiatives like that are key to what we do, it's part of [our] philosophy . . . to broadcast to the whole of [the] Australian public.' For him, the One Night Stand in Sale is evidence that tri-ple j continues to deliver. 'Well, are we happy? Yeah. No-one around here goes "This place is broken" . . . there's nothing wrong with what we're doing, [although] there's always tweaks and improvements to make.'

Triple j emerges as a kind of rough diamond, a quirky but wonderful insti-tution that makes a unique contribution to the Australian cultural landscape. The network is sometimes mediocre, but often excellent. It does some things poorly, but does other things extraordinarily well. And it does some very important things, particularly in terms of its youth current-affairs program-ming and its outreach to independent bands and regional communities, that no other Australian cultural institution even tries. As cringe-worthy as triple j can sometimes be, the network is irreplaceable; it fills a unique niche in the Australian cultural landscape.

An MP3 recording of the author's interview with triple j's Richard Kingsmill and Nick Findlay is available on the Meanjin *website.*

REMEM-BERING BALIBO

SIAN PRIOR

Their eyes stare straight out at you from five grainy black-and-white photos on the wall. Such young faces, framed by luxuriant waves of hair in various stages of bouffant rebellion. The hair is unmistakably from the seventies, but those eyes could be staring at you from any decade. The men's facial expressions seem to cover the spectrum of human emotions. Malcolm Rennie is grinning, Brian Peters has a half-smile, and there's a faint wry twist to Gary Cunningham's lips. But Greg Shackleton is furrow-browed and there is something haunted in Tony Stewart's serious, wide-eyed gaze.

Resisting the tabloid temptation to interpret this as a look of foreboding, I remind myself that most of these photos were professional portraits, posed by media men whose working lives revolved around cameras. None of them expected to die for that privilege.

The photos hang on the wall of a small house in the village of Balibo, near the north-west coast of East Timor. The wall has had a fresh coat of powder-blue paint, courtesy of cash from the Victorian Government, and the house has been renamed the Balibo Community Learning Centre. Until recently, though, it was known as 'The House of the Flag'. The fresh paint has covered up the outline of an Australian flag hastily daubed on the wall by Channel Seven news reporter Greg Shackleton sometime on 11 October 1975, and shown in one of his last TV broadcasts from what was then called Portuguese Timor.

Now it is June 2005, and inside the dimly lit house there's a group of Timorese women doing a sewing workshop, and a handful of Australian travellers who've come to pay homage. The Timorese women nod and smile at the visitors but we Australians avoid each other's gaze. Tears seem self-indulgent here.

Back outside in the tropical afternoon, I consider climbing up to the jagged ruins of a Portuguese fort at the top of the hill to the left. But they look deserted so I turn right into the main square, where a clutch of children are milling around the foot of a monument. Erected by the Indonesians to celebrate East Timor's so-called 'integration' into the neighbouring republic in 1976, its plinth supports the triumphal figure of a Timorese man carrying a flag almost as big as he is.

I am reminded of images captured by television reporters in the previous century, pictures of giant statues of Stalin and Lenin being toppled by exultant crowds in post-communist Eastern Europe. Those images will be replayed over and over in decades to come, shorthand symbols of the human will to freedom and self-determination, and of the media's role in bearing witness to those moments in history.

Here in Balibo, the statue stands firm as the children kick a frayed soccer ball against the base and wait for their mothers to emerge from the community centre. The kids seem happy enough to have their photos taken by the latest Australian journalist to visit this town, and some of them hold their fingers up in a V sign. V for Viva Xanana Gusmão? V for peace? For victory?

Behind the statue, on the other side of the square, is a row of burnt-out buildings—roofless and daubed with fresh graffiti—the latest monuments to Indonesia's 24-year occupation of East Timor. They were torched by departing troops in 1999 after the East Timorese voted overwhelmingly in favour of independence. I move closer and take a photo of these charred shells of former homes, to remind myself of the criminal spite that accompanied that long-awaited separation.

Before continuing on my journey southwards, I return to the powder-blue wall to take a last look at those staring faces, and try to commit those five names to memory: Malcolm Rennie, Brian Peters, Gary Cunningham, Greg Shackleton and Tony Stewart.

In June 2009 I ask a class of Australian journalism students, aged between about twenty and fifty, if they have heard of the Balibo Five. When less than a quarter of them hesitantly raise their hands, I find myself wondering—when did this phrase disappear from our communal vocabulary? How has this Grimms tale of calculated murder and political subterfuge been allowed to disappear from the public sphere, and how should it be told now, to bring it back to life?

Once upon a time there was a tiny nation with large oil reserves and an aggressive neighbour to its west. When the aggressive neighbour decided to annex the tiny nation by force, another near neighbour to the south (with an appetite for oil) decided to turn a blind eye. But the southern neighbour had a long tradition of media freedom and so a bunch of intrepid news gatherers travelled north to the tiny nation to bear witness to these events.

The aggressive neighbour didn't want any foreign witnesses to the invasion, so when it found five of the intrepid newsmen filming its cross-border incursion into a small town called Balibo, it had them killed and their bodies burnt to cinders.

This was rather awkward for the leaders of southern neighbour, but nevertheless they continued to turn a blind eye to the murder and mayhem going on to their north, secretly hoping that the world would forget about the tiny nation.

But the colleagues, friends and relations of the murdered newsmen couldn't forget, and down through the decades the words 'the Balibo Five' became synonymous with a dirty little secret—a political cover-up—and a tiny nation of people who were still waiting and hoping for someone to bear witness to their story.

Queensland communications academic Alan McKee defines the public sphere as the virtual space 'where each of us finds out what's happening in our community, and what social, cultural and political issues are facing us . . . where we add our voices to the discussions . . . in the process of reaching a consensus or compromise about what should be done'.[1] The term 'public sphere' encompasses more than just the news stories being reported in the media—the trends and products of popular culture influence the so-called 'water-cooler' topics too—but the media have long had a central role in forming our collective memory and defining the stories we tell each other in this huge public conversation.

Gurus of contemporary broadcasting use a simple image to describe how radio presenters should conceive of their role in these discussions, advising them to imagine they are chatting with their listeners around the kitchen table.

Over the past three decades, the Balibo Five have drifted in and out of Australian kitchen-table conversations. Unless you were personally connected to any of the central players in this story, chances are you would only hear about them when one of the friends or relatives of the five men gained media coverage for their latest plea for a full investigation into the newsmen's deaths.

And there were understandable reasons why Australians of all political persuasions would be reluctant to spend too much time thinking and talking about the Balibo Five. Even if the exact details of the events of October 1975 remained unclear, enough information had been reported by interested journalists to indicate that, for reasons of political expedience and/or anticipated fiscal benefit, members of the Whitlam, Fraser, Hawke and Keating ministries had all been either active or complicit in covering up the murders of the five newsmen. Successive governments had tried to shape the official history—and thereby the dominant collective memory—of these events by framing the deaths as regrettable accidents amid distant and inevitable conflict. And we the Australian voters had let them get away with it.

Furthermore, any discussions about the Balibo Five led inevitably to consideration of the fate of the East Timorese people following their nation's forcible incorporation into Indonesia as its twenty-seventh province (a move whose legality was formally acknowledged only by Indonesia and Australia). Symbolically led by Timorese foreign-minister-in-exile José Ramos Horta traipsing the corridors of the United Nations in New York, small groups of Timorese ex-pats and international activists dedicated to the cause of their independence (including Greg Shackleton's widow Shirley Shackleton) persisted in reminding us of the violence being perpetrated against our Second World War allies by their Indonesian colonisers.

In short, this was a story that provoked feelings of shame, and nothing sends a conversationalist scuttling away from the kitchen table faster than a curdling sense of shame. But the story kept bubbling up, and as it was told and retold, new details were added and new and at times contested layers of meaning were attached to the lives and deaths of the Balibo Five.

Australian journalist Jill Jolliffe was in East Timor in 1975 at the same time as the five newsmen, and declined an offer to join them on their trip to Balibo. She remained behind in the capital, Dili, and was one of the two journalists (the other was the ABC's Tony Maniaty) who first reported the television newsmen missing.

Jolliffe's early involvement led to a three-decade-long personal pursuit of the truth about the circumstances of their deaths. She has since filed countless stories about East Timor and the Balibo Five for print and broadcast media, and in 2001 she documented her findings in forensic detail in her book *Cover-Up*.[2]

Jill Jolliffe's book also pays tribute to a sixth journalist from Australia whose story became inextricably—and fatally—linked to that of the five newsmen. By December 1975, AAP correspondent Roger East was the last remaining foreign journalist in East Timor and his final assignment was to try to find out exactly what had happened in Balibo. But Roger East was shot dead in Dili by Indonesian forces on 8 December, the day after their full-scale military invasion of the East Timorese capital began.

The author of *Cover-Up* is in no doubt about what she describes as the terrible cost for the Timorese of those six deaths: with 'the elimination of all independent observers to its actions . . . the invading force was no longer subject to restraint of any kind' (pp. 108–9). Furthermore, she asserts, 'the film (that the Balibo Five) had in their cameras could have changed the course of history' (p. 3). For Jill Jolliffe, the story of the Balibo Five is a tale of moral delinquency: 'Understanding what happened at Balibo is the key to understanding the complicity of successive Australian governments, Labor and Liberal, in the Indonesian military occupation of East Timor' (p. 6).

Tony Maniaty, the other Australian journalist who alerted his nation to the disappearance of the Balibo Five, agrees with Jolliffe that their story should be kept alive. These days Maniaty teaches journalism at the University of Technology, Sydney, but in October 1975 he was working in Portuguese Timor for the ABC and met the Channel Seven crew on the road as they were heading west to Dili. He was fleeing back to the capital after the invading militias had shot at him and his ABC crew in Balibo, and tried to warn the newcomers of the dangers they would face in the border town.

At the Melbourne launch of his new book *Shooting Balibo*, Tony Maniaty described how he thought the Indonesians would have responded to the Australian Government's inaction over the five deaths: 'They must have thought, how easy is this! Nobody's watching, nobody cares.'

But Maniaty's analysis of the impact of the five journalists' deaths differs significantly from that of Jill Jolliffe. 'People say that if they'd been able to get it to air, that film footage might have been able to stop the war against East Timor, but I don't think so,' he told his audience. And when I asked for his answer to the rhetorical question he poses in the book—'why the fate of a small group of journalists from a past generation matters in this one'—Maniaty's views again diverged from Jolliffe's: 'Speaking as a teacher of journalism, it's important that we go back to see what can be learnt from that tragedy. It's an opportunity to talk to a new generation of journalists about what went wrong and what *not* to do. Because no story is worth a life.'

And he's right, of course. No-one should have to die for the privilege of bearing witness to acts of injustice and inhumanity. And yet history is replete with examples of how these crazy-brave news reporters *have* had an impact—at times incremental, at times dramatic—on the course of events they have been covering.

There is now general consensus that without the startling Vietnam War footage gathered by cameramen such as Australian Neil Davis (whose work was celebrated in the 1980 film *Frontline* by another crazy-brave Australian, documentary-maker David Bradbury) and broadcast on the television sets of voting Australians and Americans, the war would have lasted longer than it did. And in East Timor, sixteen years after the events in Balibo, the actions of three courageous foreign news gatherers were to influence the course of the independence movement throughout the 1990s.

On 12 November 1991, two US journalists and a British cameraman were caught up in the massacre of around two hundred and fifty East Timorese mourners by Indonesian troops in the Santa Cruz cemetery in Dili. Americans Amy Goodman and Allan Nairn were beaten by Indonesian soldiers, and Yorkshire Television cameraman Max Stahl caught the violent events at the cemetery on film. Stahl's footage was later smuggled out of the country and, along with the eyewitness accounts of the two American journalists, broadcast around the world.

This irrefutable evidence of the Indonesian campaign of repression against the East Timorese not only galvanised pro-independence protests around the world, but it led to diplomatic reprisals against Indonesia by the Portuguese and US governments, and to increased debate in Indonesia about the ongoing annexation of East Timor. The widespread international media coverage of the joint 1996 Nobel Peace Prize awarded to José Ramos Horta and Bishop Carlos Ximenes Belo for their 'sustained efforts to hinder the oppression of a small people' reinforced the growing feeling in Indonesia that East Timor was a problem requiring a new solution. The debate culminated in the 1998 decision by then Indonesian President Habibie to hold a referendum in 1999 on 'special autonomy' for East Timor, and a quarter-century after the withdrawal of their Portuguese colonisers, the East Timorese were finally able to vote for independence.

We will never know whether the stories contained in the final film footage of the Balibo Five might have 'changed the course of history'. But like a classic Grimms fable without a happy ending, the story of their deaths has functioned as a morality tale in Australian public life. It has been a persistent reminder of how even the most apparently benign governments should never be trusted to tell 'the whole truth' about their motivations, actions and inactions when relations with other powerful nations are seen to be at stake—and of the vital role of a culture of investigative news-reporting in attempting to hold those governments to account.

As Jill Jolliffe documents so convincingly in *Cover-Up*, even after political pressure led two Australian foreign ministers (Gareth Evans in 1995 and Alexander Downer in 1998) to commission reports into the deaths of the Balibo Five,[3] key questions remained unanswered about exactly who was responsible for ordering the five deaths, and what role the Australian Government and its intelligence services played in the events in East Timor during and after October 1975.

More recently, following the 2007 coronial inquiry into the death of Brian Peters, the NSW Coroner concluded that the men died 'from wounds sustained when [they were] shot and/or stabbed deliberately, and not in the heat of battle, by members of the Indonesian Special Forces' and recommended that criminal proceedings be commenced against the alleged Indonesian perpetrators. As yet, however, no such proceedings have been instituted, and Jill Jolliffe is calling for a new criminal investigation into the matter.

For those journalists who have followed the story, either actively in the case of Jolliffe and Maniaty or (in my case) from a distance, the actions of the Balibo Five have been a kind of professional moral measuring stick. How far *would* you go to get the story, if you were convinced that it should be told? Would you go as far as those five men did—or as far as Roger East, who lost his life in pursuit of the story of *their* deaths?

In *Shooting Balibo*, Tony Maniaty uses the term 'survivor guilt' to explain why he has been consumed by the events of October 1975 for more than thirty years. He told the audience at his Melbourne book launch that 'no story is worth a life', and yet he also describes his own decision to leave East Timor before the full-scale Indonesian invasion as a 'strange failure'.[4]

Perhaps it is in part survivor guilt that has compelled journalists Jolliffe and Maniaty to keep asking questions about the fate of their dead colleagues over the past three decades. And the stories of these two journalists in particular have formed the basis of the new Australian feature film *Balibo*, released in August 2009.

Tony Maniaty claims to have first alerted filmmaker Robert Connolly to the cinematic potential of the events in Balibo when the two men met at the Australian Film Television and Radio School in 1993. Connolly produced and directed a short film written by Maniaty at AFTRS, and went on to write, direct and/or produce a number of award-winning Australian feature films, including *Romulus, My Father*, *The Boys*, *The Bank* and *Three Dollars*, before co-writing and directing *Balibo*. In 2008, at the invitation of Robert Connolly, Maniaty returned to East Timor for the first time since 1975 to relate his memories of those events to the Australian cast members during the film shoot.

Jill Jolliffe's book *Cover-Up* is listed in the film's credits as one of the key sources for the *Balibo* screenplay. Her reconstructions of the Balibo Five's deaths, based on the accounts of eyewitnesses whom she tracked down and interviewed over many years, are re-enacted in shocking detail in Connolly's film, as is the brutal killing of Roger East in Dili less than two months later.

Co-executive producer of *Balibo* Anthony LaPaglia, who also plays Roger East in the film, has said that it was the core group of Australian writers, activists and surviving relatives who kept the Balibo story alive: 'I asked them all the same question: Why would you devote your life to this? . . . There's an old saying: There's a special place in hell for those who witness atrocities and do nothing about it. And I don't think they want to go there.'[5]

Robert Connolly (interviewed in this issue of *Meanjin*) has carefully structured the film's narrative using the 'Russian doll' technique of a story-within-a-story-within-a-story. At the core is the re-enactment of what happened to the Balibo Five, as described to Roger East—whose own story is then related by a Timorese eyewitness to East's death. The Timorese woman's testimony opens and closes the story, and this plot device is a fitting acknowledgement of the fact that, while concerned Australians have played a part in seeking justice for this nation, and some have lost their loved ones—or their lives—in the process, it is the East Timorese people themselves who have suffered most for the goal of independence.

The filmmakers have incorporated in the movie some of the archival footage shot by the five newsmen, and restaged other filmed material, including the moment when Greg Shackleton daubs the Australian flag on the wall of the house in Balibo. They show the five adrenalin-charged young men doggedly pursuing that final footage which Jill Jolliffe believes could have changed the course of history—proof that Indonesian troops were pouring across the border into East Timor.

The film does not attempt to describe the subsequent political cover-up of what happened to the five newsmen, but by presenting their deaths as cold-blooded murders, it leaves viewers in no doubt about which version of history should be remembered when the Balibo Five are discussed around the kitchen tables of local film-goers. It remains to be seen whether the renewed interest in this story following the film's release could see the wheels of justice begin to turn again for the families and friends of the dead men.

But if you stay to watch the credits roll at the end of the film, you will find those same five grainy black-and-white faces staring out at you from the big screen, as images of the actors are replaced with photos of the real players in this memorable Australian story: Malcolm Rennie, Brian Peters, Gary Cunningham, Greg Shackleton and Tony Stewart.

NOTES

1   Alan McKee, *The Public Sphere: An Introduction*, Cambridge University Press, Cambridge, 2005, pp. 4, 5.

2   Jill Jolliffe, *Cover-Up: The Inside Story of the Balibo Five*, Scribe Publications, Melbourne, 2001; revised edition under the title *Balibo*, Scribe Publications, released in July 2009.

3   See, for example, Tom Sherman's *Second Report on the Deaths of Australian-Based Journalists in East Timor in 1975*, Department of Foreign Affairs and Trade, January 1999.

4   Tony Maniaty, *Shooting Balibo*, Penguin, Melbourne, 2009, p. 23.

5   Natasha Robertson, 'Balibo film gives voice to Timor victim', *Australian*, 15 July 2008.

FOOTY: THE SEASON OF LOVE, FAITH AND AGONY

MATTHEW KLUGMAN

My eldest son, Stephen, follows Fitzroy with the same dedication that Galahad showed for the Holy Grail. In this case for the Premier's crown.
—Oriel Gray[1]

and blessèd be the first sweet agony
I felt when I found myself bound to Love,
the bow and all the arrows that have pierced me
the wounds that reach the bottom of my heart.
—Petrarch, *Canzoniere* (trans. Musa)

1 Oriel Gray, 'Loss of a Homespun Legend', in Ross Fitzgerald and Ken Spillman (eds), *The Greatest Game*, William Heinemann Australia, Melbourne, 1988, p. 155.

SPRING. IT'S A WORD THAT conjures up images of a new beginning: blossoms unfurling, buds opening, sap quickening, rebirth. But in Australia the transition into spring never seems as clear and the trees hang on to their leaves all year. Wattles break out into cascades of yellow in the depths of winter. And spring heralds the end of a different type of season. A season that, like the weather, regulates the rhythms of life of so many Australians: the footy season. For September, the first month of spring, is finals time. And this brings a different kind of quickening, a crescendo that builds to the last Saturday in September: the grand final. This is a day that strikes people across Australia with 'a strange infirmity', as Manning Clark put it.[2] A day where football brings trauma and ecstasy in equal measure such that for a few hours, it seems like nothing else matters.

2 Manning Clark, 'An Entire Nation Stricken with a Strange Infirmity', in Fitzgerald and Spillman, p. 226.

If you think there's something strange about all this, you're right. There's something about Aussie Rules footy that is too much, that drives people to the edge of sanity. It produces suffering and joy, and an insatiable hunger for more. You can hear it in the roar of the crowd, in the thunders of triumph, the cries of distress, the howls of frustration and in the continual cycle of pleas, curses and cheers. It is there in the bodies that ride the game with the players: fists clenching, legs trembling, guts churning, eyes that long to look away but cannot.

Mad, fevered, obsessed, fanatical, addicted. These are just a few of the words routinely invoked to describe Aussie Rules barrackers by critics *and* fans. It's as if the strange passions of footy followers are pathological. And perhaps they are. For barracking is grounded in love. And love is the emotion most associated with excess—with extravagant devotion, extremes of trust and paranoia, and crimes of passion when it all goes wrong.

Yet footy followers are not driven mad by a single love. They are driven mad by a series of intertwined loves. First, there is the love that footy devotees freely name: the love of the club. This is an infatuation that binds fans to their club. It somehow leads barrackers to feel they are part of the club and that what happens to the club happens to them. This is a love of belonging: the club becomes a higher self, something that represents fans and connects them to the players (who are loved, and sometimes hated, in turn), so that every result is taken personally and fans are driven to comments such as 'we had a very good year', 'they absolutely destroyed us' and 'I hope we smash them'.

This imagined connection to the beloved club might seem bizarre enough, a naive union or a grand illusion. But there is a second type of love at play that lends a dynamic, intense and sometimes explosive character to the lives of footy followers. This is the love of the premiership. Not a unifying love, it is the lust for something that seems missing, the lack of which is all consuming. It's a love that inspires a quest. Like the lady wooed in the tales of courtly love, the premiership cup gleams with promise, tantalising fans with the possibility of an ultimate fulfilment at once familiar and forever out of reach. Obstacles are important, challenges essential, for the thrill lies as much in the chase of something that only the very best can win. But such pursuit comes at a cost, as the historian Denis de Rougemont explains:

> Happy love has no history . . . What stirs lyrical poets to their finest flights is neither the delight of the senses nor the fruitful contentment of the settled couple; not the satisfaction of love, but its *passion*. And passion means suffering. There we have a fundamental fact.[3]

3 Denis de Rougemont, *Passion and Society*, trans. Montgomery Belgion, Faber and Faber, London, 1956, p. 15.

The result is a seasonal cycle of anticipation and nerves, tension and release. All of which usually ends in a loss of some kind when the beloved club either crashes out of the finals after a defeat or, worse still, misses the finals altogether. Yet this recipe for suffering is also a recipe for excitement, dreams and fears. And the coming of the finals ramps this up a notch for those lucky enough to follow one of the clubs to have made it this far.

A third ingredient adds to this potent cocktail of footy mania: faith. For barrackers maintain the often absurd belief that their club will triumph in the end, that a time of glory has been foretold. We can see the power of this faith at the start of each season when fans come again to the strange hope that this will finally be the year that ends with joy rather than pain. This makes autumn, not spring, the time of rebirth for footy followers. A time of unfettered expectations centred on new recruits and emerging stars. We saw it this year with the wild excitement of Richmond over the second coming of Ben Cousins. But while the media circus that accompanied Cousins' every move was new, the millennial hopes that accompanied him were not. You only need to speak to Collingwood barrackers to hear of the great pleasure they took in the recruitment of Shane Woewodin from their old enemy Melbourne at the end of the 2002 season—a pleasure that echoed the earlier joy Melbourne barrackers felt after poaching Peter Moore from the Magpies in time for the 1983 season. In these cases the recruits were taken as portents of glory. It's as if footy fans are continuously willing a move from what Søren Kierkegaard described as the indifferent 'external and visible world' to the 'world of the spirit' where 'an eternal divine order prevails':

Here it does not rain on both the just and the unjust; here the sun does not shine on both good and evil. Here it holds true that only the one who works gets bread, that only the one who was in anxiety finds rest, that only the one who descends into the lower world rescues the beloved, that only the one who draws the knife gets Isaac.[4]

Barrackers continue to seek the signs that this promised world is at hand, that the great wrongs and humiliations inflicted on them and their beloved club will come to an end with a glory that makes all their suffering worthwhile. But by spring the hopes of many will have already been dashed. Indeed this year, the inflated hopes of Richmond followers collapsed in the first game. In such cases hope swings quickly to the bitter anger of those who've been betrayed, again. It will take the apportioning of blame—the scapegoating of a victim whose sacrifice somehow cleanses the sins of those who remain—signs of improvement (no matter how small) and new blood to bring fresh hope for the ensuing season.

But what about those whose club is one of the eight to make it into the finals? Even for these lucky ones, faith can pose a problem. At issue is the double-edged nature of the hope that faith inspires. For hope opens the door to the suffering that most football fans know only too well—the frustrations of failure, the anguish of lost dreams. Indeed at times it seems Friedrich Nietzsche was thinking of football fans when he pronounced hope to be the 'worst of all evils, for it protracts the torment of man'.[5]

As the grand final nears, the hopes of barrackers intensify, increasing the likelihood of further torment. Many fans respond by trying not to hope *too* much, trying to keep a lid on their expectations. But when the signs *seem* right, when everything appears to indicate that *this* will be the year, when a premiership victory looks fated, all restraint is lost. And in its place rises an unswerving belief that this time the flag will be won, the glorious pleasure of knowing that what has been promised will shortly come to pass.

Nadia remembers being taken by this spirit in late September 2003. Her team Collingwood was playing Brisbane on the last Saturday in September for the second year running. But while the Magpies had been firm underdogs in 2002, this year they were clear favourites. After their narrow loss to Brisbane the previous season, Collingwood had enjoyed a good season that culminated in a qualifying victory over Brisbane at the Melbourne Cricket Ground. This had entitled them to a week off, after which they comfortably defeated Port Adelaide to reach the grand final. While Brisbane had recovered to also reach the grand final, they were beset with injuries and had to overcome an underrated Sydney team to get there. The signs all seemed to point to a Collingwood victory. And all around her Nadia could see Collingwood followers glowing with anticipation, indulging in 'very strange and uncharacteristic' pre-match celebrations. A joyous Nadia joined in, recording the Collingwood club song for an Essendon supporter friend in Bangkok, and finding herself having these optimistic 'Collingwood conversations with shopkeepers of the sort that my father would have'.

A few years later, in 2007, Charlotte, a Geelong fan, experienced an even more marked transition. The Cats had been dominant since the early rounds of the season, but Charlotte and her fellow Geelong supporters, scarred by

4 Søren Kierkegaard [writing as Johannes de Silentio], *Fear and Trembling, and Repetition*, ed. Robert Perkins, Mercer University Press, Macon, Ga., 1993 (1843), p. 27.

5 Friedrich Nietzsche, *Human, all too Human: A Book for Free Spirits*, trans. Marion Faber, University of Nebraska Press, Lincoln, 1984.

earlier traumas, worked hard to minimise their excitement. Instead of raising their expectations, they waited for the 'bubble to burst'. But everything changed when Geelong smashed the Kangaroos in the qualifying final and then Collingwood, their opponents in the forthcoming preliminary final, had to play extra time and then fly back to Melbourne from Perth. Suddenly the attention of Charlotte, and of those Geelong followers she knew, switched to the grand final, as if victory against Collingwood was a given (a presumption that Charlotte would regret as soon as the game began, as we shall see).

This arresting, communal confidence can occur during finals games as well as before them. Some Western Bulldogs barrackers came to their 1997 preliminary final against Adelaide certain the Dogs were destined to win through to the grand final. Many others, however, were only cautiously hopeful. Yet after a slow start by their team, they quickly joined their fellow believers when the Bulldogs dominated the second quarter, kicking eight goals. Though Adelaide was still close enough to win, the irresistible play of the Dogs had convinced their fans that victory was assured. Their thoughts were already turning to the following week's grand final. By three-quarter time Daniel's mate already had a daughter queuing for grand final tickets, Walter had a tear in his eye, and the barracker with the 'nom de web' of Pembleton was over the moon:

> For the only time that i have been a dogs fan i had about 60 minutes where i believed we were going to the grand final. It wasn't a matter of 'isn't it great to be close to a grand final?', rather it was 'OMFG [Oh My Fucking God], we're finally going to a grand final'. For 60 minutes or so that day i experienced what it feels like to KNOW your team is going to a grand final, and i loved it.[6]

6 'Pembleton', 'Re: Only for the brave', <http://www. bigfooty.com/forum/ showthread>.

These three finals moments of absurd certainty point to the power the premiership holds for passionate footy fans and to the intoxication that comes when barrackers get so close they can feel it. But there are limits to this power. The heady rush of confidence requires signs that make it appear the premiership really *is* on the way. At issue is not the signs themselves, but the rapid conversion of hope into expectation that follows these signs. And fans are much more sober in the absence of such catalytic signs. Even if their club reaches the grand final, it might still seem, against this opponent, that they have little chance. At times like this, fans can find the strength to contain their hopes. In 2002, the year before Nadia's premature joy, many Collingwood fans were simply happy to have made it to the grand final against the all-conquering Lions. Fresh memories of deceptive expectations can even lead barrackers to extreme denials of hope. In 2007 some Geelong followers provided an absurd example of this after the team almost lost the preliminary final they had expected it to dominate. Though Geelong led Port Adelaide by more than 60 points in the third quarter of the ensuing grand final, some Cats fans still refused to believe that the long-awaited victory was finally theirs. But let us go back to the heights of intoxication that the apparent coming of the premiership can bring. For this intoxication frequently brings with it something else: agony.

How, you might be thinking, can a game of football produce suffering intense enough to warrant the term 'agony'? How can a bunch of boofheads kicking around a pigskin—to paraphrase one of the fans I interviewed—come to mean so much? Surely this is hyperbole. And maybe it is. But 'agony' is the word barrackers almost invariably choose when relating their experience of the grand final and sometimes even the preliminary final.

Part of what gives credence to their stories is the shock these experiences of agony bring. Helena, for one, could scarcely believe it. Nothing, she felt, had prepared her for the Sydney Swans' grand final match against the West Coast Eagles in 2005. The South Melbourne Swans had not made it that far in the twenty years or so that she had followed them before their move to Sydney in 1982. And Helena had stopped barracking for them in any serious sense for a time after their relocation. You 'really weren't supposed to like football' when involved in the women's liberation movement as Helena was, and though she held on during the 1970s, the move to Sydney was the last straw. She started reconnecting with the Swans through the early 1990s, and 1996 felt like 'a magic carpet ride' when the Swans unexpectedly made the grand final. But while Helena felt 'this would be the year', and the subsequent loss was incredibly disappointing, she was not yet sufficiently connected to the club for it to all mean *too* much.

In the early 2000s Helena and her mum rejoined as members, and attended as many of the Swans' Melbourne games as possible. By the time the Swans made the 2005 grand final Helena was right back into it. Inspired by the Swans players' ethos of teamwork, mateship and sacrifice, Helena became 'delirious' with hope as Brisbane and Port Adelaide—the dominant teams of the last four years—both fell away. 'I was like, could it be, could it be, oh my god it could be!'

Overseas because of her studies, Helena dragged her partner off to a pub in the early hours of a Paris morning so that she could watch the match. The match started at six, and the pub was cold, but soon Helena was drenched in sweat. Usually she concentrates fiercely, 'intellectually willing' the Swans on. That morning, however, Helena found herself 'channelling' *all* her energy into the game. In a tough, tight contest, the two teams were barely separated for the entire match. The effect on Helena was extraordinary. 'I'd never had such an intense football experience, I can't remember such an intense experience full-stop.' Her 'whole body was suffused with energy, anxiety, sweat' to the extent that she was 'aching, it was an incredible physical experience. And when it looked like they were going to run away with it, I was physically and emotionally in incredible pain . . . it was almost too much.' Tears were in her eyes throughout the last quarter, and Helena even found herself crying out to the heavens as the game moved towards its climax. 'I said, "oh please, we can't lose", I was sitting there with my head down saying "oh please, God, please, God", and I'm not fucking religious.'

Like Helena, Charlotte was shocked by the deep emotion a footy final could bring. So confident before the 2007 preliminary final between Geelong and Collingwood, Charlotte found the game 'one of the most excruciating' moments of her life. 'I was so nervous realising we could lose it. I couldn't conceive of what was going on at all, I couldn't understand it.' When she found out at half-time her cousin had just given birth, Charlotte was both excited by the news and relieved for the perspective it gave, but though she tried to hold on to this perspective when the game restarted, she was soon 'completely lost' in the footy again. As her anguish mounted, Charlotte developed an *'agonising* you-want-to-vomit feeling in your stomach'. She couldn't sit still, couldn't watch or completely look away, and kept asking, 'How long to go, how long to go?'

Other barrackers tell similar stories. For Margaret, the only thing you could compare the 1996 grand final to was the experience of going into hospital to have a major operation. 'You know you have to do it, but the process is *absolute agony*, like being strung out to an absolute level.' Every moment and contest in the game felt to Margaret like it was a matter of life and death. Stanley described his experience of the 1990 grand final in analogous terms. 'It was so stressful, every kick and mark counted and was magnified.' Alcohol tempered Stanley's anguish, but the intensity of every contest, of what was at stake, still made the game 'agonising'.

These are all tales of an anxiety beyond words that can infuse bodies with pain. We tend to associate such anxiety with the threat of loss and failure and the accounts of barrackers back this up. The possibility of loss caused Helena 'incredible pain', made Charlotte 'so nervous' and was likened by Margaret to death. Yet we do not find such extreme anxiety when defeat already seemed probable, when the signs of imminent victory were not found. The agony only comes when the premiership seems close enough to touch. Following the French psychoanalyst Jacques Lacan, we can therefore ask if this anxiety is at least in part about the consequences of winning the premiership. What intoxicates us also poisons us. And Lacan suggested that we fear getting those things we believe will fill us. For if we are finally made whole, what is there to long for? What is there to live for?[7]

7 See Jacques Lacan, *Seminar VII: The Ethics of Psychoanalysis, 1959–1960*, ed. Jacques-Alain Miller, trans. Dennis Porter, Norton, New York, 1992.

In 1995 Cats barracker John Harms was struck by a 'blasphemous thought' along these lines, which kept 'resurfacing' despite his attempts to suppress it:

> I have spent a lifetime waiting for Geelong to win the flag. I see the world this way; I know everything from this perspective. The only reality I know is one of hope. Would everything be irrevocably transformed if Geelong won the grand final? Would I be a different person? Would the World be a different place? I am a bit concerned.[8]

8 John Harms, *Loose Men Everywhere*, Text Publishing, Melbourne, 2002, p. 220.

Harms' concern moved him to compose a poem that ended with a warning of the hazard that awaited grand final victory, 'you can thrash the Tiges, / but Heaven help your whole existence / if you beat the Blues.' By the end of his composition Harms needed 'another Guinness' to calm himself down, but he was spared the threat to his existence by the fickle nature of footballing fate, as Carlton comfortably accounted for Geelong the following day.

Almost a decade later, Helena also discovered that the possibility of winning could provoke more anxiety than the certainty of losing. The occasion was the 2006 grand final, where the Sydney Swans again faced off against the West Coast Eagles. This time Helena was in the crowd and this time the Eagles dominated the first half. Dismayed and embarrassed by the performance of their team, Helena and her mother resigned themselves to defeat. But then the Swans started to claw their way back into the match. Instead of welcoming the comeback, Helena and her mum started saying 'no, no, not this *again*'. Helena felt she was 'being dragged back into hope'. She was happier for the Swans to get closer and turn a humiliating defeat into an honourable loss: to hope for a comeback victory was to risk greater disappointment when West Coast ran away with the game, as Helena was sure they would. The Swans kept on coming, though, and Helena did come unwillingly to 'a grim hope, mixed with threads of, oh my God, we could do this!' With the growing hope came an ever-increasing tension. Helena experienced 'a slow burning', an upward trajectory as though she was slowly being filled, but it was a gradual and difficult process, and just before Helena was full, the siren sounded. The Swans had lost by a point and Helena was suddenly deflated. She felt disbelief, but the previous year's victory meant she didn't feel shattered. Yet shortly after the game ended, Helena found herself reliving the pain of her reluctant hopes, asking 'if only, if only'.

The Swans' comeback, and Helena and her mum's protestations indicate that at least on one level they did not want to repeat the agony of the previous year, even though it had ended in victory. It is as if there were something overwhelming—traumatic even—about coming so close to the object of passionate longing, to the premiership that seemed to mean too much. Yet Helena's internal struggle against hope also suggests she was worried about the increased disappointment that elevated hopes might bring. And this hints at a second form of anxiety, one that acts as a warning of impending trauma.

Hope, as we have seen, often rushes beyond itself, investing in a future that comes to be expected. This expectation then sets the scene for disappointment that is traumatic because it was unanticipated. Barrackers whose clubs lose preliminary and grand finals they expected to win feel shocked into silence, tears or rage, unable to comprehend the awful nature of what has happened. Later they will even come to narrate these losses in tragic terms. They carefully detail the hubris, the lost chances and critical errors. They search endlessly for an understanding of what went wrong and what might be learnt, unearthing cause for renewed hope in a triumph that will redeem this great suffering, along with all those that preceded it.

Macabre as all this might sound, the suffering that so consumes footy fans appears to heighten the pleasure if and when the premiership is finally won. Outsiders cannot access the ecstasy that long-suffering barrackers feel when their club wins the flag. And even those who support the winning team do not feel the same extraordinary joy if they have not also been around for the pain. Leigh, a Collingwood fan, is a case in point. He only really got deeply into footy in 1990, when he and his 16-year-old mates started going to the matches together. Untouched by the Magpies' run of grand final defeats in the 1960s, 1970s and 1980s, Leigh was aghast at the great outpouring of emotion when Collingwood finally won the premiership. Grown men were crying with relief and joy, and Leigh 'thought they were just sooks . . . my uncle even said he cried just being there near the race where they came out'. Looking back, Leigh feels he 'didn't appreciate that victory enough'. He had taken the year for granted. 'I was born in the right year at the right time,' he explained, 'I was pretty lucky at that time.' But looked at another way, Leigh was unlucky. He was not yet initiated into the cycle of suffering and desire. Consequently he missed out on a pleasure so great it can be overwhelming.

Helena was on 'an incredible high' after Sydney defeated West Coast in the 2005 grand final. But even she was shocked when her mother told her on the phone that 'This has been the most amazing experience in my life', leading Helena to think: what about your marriage, what about giving birth to your first child? Helena's mother had endured the suffering of following the Swans longer than Helena had. But the indescribable nature of her ecstasy might also have led her to hyperbole. For victorious fans speak of the win often but seem unable to ever quite capture it. The best they can do is speak with wonder at the ineffable nature of their experience, as the North barracker Margaret did when she described the Kangaroos' 1996 victory as 'an extraordinary experience, like going somewhere you had never been before'. Even the voluble John Harms could hardly expand on the delight he felt when Geelong won in 2007. In his main account of the game, Harms notes tears of joy, his and others, and an 'overwhelming mood' of gratitude, but he can say little more than that: 'You must understand suffering to know the fullness of that joy . . . We feel blessed.'[9]

9 John Harms, 'The Grand Final', in John Harms and Paul Daffey (eds), *The Footy Almanac 2007: The AFL Season One Game at a Time*, Malarkey Publications, Melbourne, 2007, p. 509.

Whereas those stories of devastating finals losses attempt to comprehend the how and why of what happened, to explain the inexplicable, those who talk and write about wondrous grand final victories glide over the specificities of how it felt and focus instead on how people celebrated, on their deeds and actions. Both sets of narratives are wrestling with something they can never quite express. Those who have lost are confronted with the question 'why', initially in the silence of shock and bewilderment, and later in a painful questioning and storytelling. In contrast, the victorious barrackers are more likely to be active, to be doing something celebratory, something exuberant. It is as if they have a great bodily tension that demands expression. The losers feel drained of energy, of speech, sometimes of everything. The victors are full of joy, but perhaps a bit too full and in need of some release. The release comes from dancing, singing, shouting and, most typically, drinking to excess. It's as if many feel a need for further intoxication to blot something of themselves out, so as to better enjoy what they've got. But at the same time, most fans are trying to watch the game again, as if they've already lost a part of the moment—a part they enjoy trying to recapture over and over again.

Is there something dangerous in what the victorious barrackers have received? Death is certainly often mentioned by older fans, though it be in the form of jest. 'I can now die happy,' proclaimed Helena's mum, echoing the words of many an elderly fan in the moment of triumph. For some, though, victory is too much. Dan Quigley was a 'mad' Richmond barracker from the age of twelve when he arrived in Melbourne from Belfast in 1949.[10] But Quigley lost his passion after the fairytale year of 1967 when he not only saw the Tigers make the finals for the first time, but win the flag as well. The tremendous high that Quigley experienced after this victory was too much, rupturing his devotion to Richmond. For by 1969 the high had been replaced by a sense of disappointment that winning a flag would never feel so good again. The flag no longer gleamed with the fantastic promise it once had, and his interest in football waned.

10 Cyrus Wong, 'Me, I Like Football', in Kate Cummings (ed.), *Oral History: Brought to Book*, n.d., no publ., pp. 56–69.

Unlike Quigley, most fans find enough lacking in their premiership victory to want more: more glory, more ecstasy, and invariably more pain. Charlotte, however, found Geelong's 2007 grand final victory so lacking, she felt little ecstasy at all. The preliminary final win the week before against Collingwood had led to such 'complete elation' she felt happy enough to 'die'. The ensuing premiership win against Port Adelaide was too easy. Not enough of a challenge. She missed the almost unbearable agony the previous week had brought. Charlotte wanted more of that sickening, awful, somehow addictive tension.

And perhaps this agony is what footy fans strive to return to, a suffering that reaches its climax in spring with all the hope and excitement brought by the beloved club's quest for the gleaming premiership. It ends with a game on the last Saturday of the season, a day so often infused with excruciating pain and indescribable ecstasy, a day of collective obsession, which Manning Clark captured with his phrase 'a strange infirmity'. Clark too suffered from this infirmity. 'Anguish, ecstasy or despair', he proposed to pursue the premiership over and over again. Because, he confessed:

> I love it. I love it to the point of madness of repeating the words of the popular song: 'Just keep on doing what you're doing / Although you're leading me to ruin. Just keep on doing what you're doing. 'Cos I love what you're doing to me'. I love every minute of it.[11]

11 Clark, p. 229. For more on the seasonal passions of footy fans, see Matthew Klugman, *Passion Play: Love, Hope and Heartbreak at the Footy*, Hunter Publishers, Melbourne, 2009.

THE TATTOO

ELMO KEEP

So I had a great idea: I would get a giant tattoo on my back. And ow, my God, the pain! The pain, here it comes! Excruciating! Searing, searing, hot hot *hot*! Ow! It does not get any better! Ever! You do not 'get used to it'. At any time during the procedure (which, I have to remember, is voluntary). Help me, please. I'm dying. It burns with the heat of one thousand suns. Like the worst sunburn you ever had in your life, and that sunburn being stung by bees, many bees at once. It is almost, almost unbearable. Jesus, what? Why did I do this? It is exhilarating. Afterwards, I am invincible! But in the meantime, I think I will die before it is finished.

We have few chances in life to face our fears (bears, venomous snakes, tax returns)—in my case, needles and pain. For instance, when I have to give blood or, worse, when blood is taken from me and spirited away to a facility where it is analysed to be sure it does not contain traces of fatal diseases, say, I cry. Involuntary, embarrassing tears. Sometimes I wear a hat and pull it over my face so the nurse taking my blood won't see what a pathetic, quivering excuse for a girl I am. 'Just wait until you give birth!' This is often thrown at me and I just think: No, no! God, no! Just knock me out and wake me up and present me with my charmed and perfect infant! Instead I smile wanly through the tears and try to laugh about this horrible pain in my arm. And why are you taking my blood? I need that to live!

It's an hour before I have to be there. I feel as though I am preparing for some great battle. I eat a giant bowl of pasta. It has cheese on it, extra. I am ready? I am not ready. I am filled with both terror and impatience. Okay, shit. This is it. I am going. I am alone. Goodbye. I stop at the bar, conveniently right next door, just about, and swallow a shot of tequila. What? It's midday on a Monday, yes. Why are you looking at me like that? That reminds me, Get vodka, please. A lot, for afterwards. Thank you. Okay, see you later.

I was very specific with things about the fish. The fish are you and me. We are together, entwined, against the current, borne back ceaselessly and all that, only not so fatalistic. At all. This is triumph! The waterfall runs down (well, obviously) my back, cascades down my spine (this part is particularly bad, the pain, you will see), and the fish are swimming upstream. They are striving, you see, constantly. It was important that their facial expressions accurately reflect this inner state of their being, that they are you and me, respectively, though also, interchangeably. Depending.

So the faces of the fish, I had these instructions to give: their faces must appear determined. But not angry. Purposeful, but not aggressive. The look in their eye must signify forging, ever onward. They are happy to be doing this work, it is their choice. Do you see?

There is much mutual furrowing of brows between the tattoo artist and me.

'But you aren't really going to do any of that, are you?'

'No. Not really. I think I understand though.'

'Okay,' I say. When I go back a month later to look at the drawing it is perfect.

Why am I doing this? I wonder in knots of anxiety the sleepless night before. Do you not understand, it symbolises *X and Y* and all that? It will speak of the immutable us-ness of this moment. It will say certain things about me, on my behalf, that I am loath to articulate in case they come out wrong, but you will see them, *right there*. And it will say these things about me, and occasionally in the future to me, forever. This body is immaterial, some say. I agree, all is transient. It will wither and die, become (crossing fingers) old and give out, and then I will leave it behind. But until then it is mine and I will adorn it in the manner I see fit. So this is a permanence of some kind, such as we all crave for our lives, and when I put on my jacket no-one will see it. I will never see it except for when craning my neck in the mirror, if I am naked. But I will know it is there.

'You will regret this,' you say. I counter perhaps then, you don't know regret. I regret not seeing my father's body in the hospital. Not saying goodbye before then. I regret that we have so far not scattered his ashes, five years later, but instead I have carried them with me from house to house. 'It will hurt!' you say. Yes it will, it will hurt worse than anything I can imagine. It is molten hot, like lava on my spine: it will hurt. But it will not hurt as much as the time we said those things to each other, that time after which it was all broken and terrible. No, that was the worst pain, and still, I survived. I am here! Invincible after this pain.

I am looking at the tattoo stencil. It is very big. It will stretch from just below where my neck joins my body, and continue down, to just below my coccyx. It is buttressed on one side by the tender ridges of my spine, and on the other by the even more tender troughs of my ribs. It is very beautiful. I look at the fish and am pleased with their expressions of utter serenity/determination/intractable commitment that surely everyone will be able to see. I smile at them. They are swimming elegantly up the waterfall, down which float cherry blossoms over their smiling heads.

It occurs to me at this point, right then, that I will have to be naked from the waist up to get this tattoo, and this fills me with unbidden terror. This is it! I cannot be half naked, here, in public with all these people! That's crazy! This cannot go forward. Then I look and see the tattooers tattooing the tattooees, who are each as equally absorbed in their tasks of meting out and withstanding the scolding hot pain, and realise that no-one will look at me for even a second, and my escape plan is ruined. Don't punk out, I think. Don't be afraid. I'm extremely afraid.

I wish very hard for a moment that the tattoo might somehow magically attach itself to my body and be done, and finished and lovely. Or that someone will hit me in the head with a shovel and I'll wake up when it's perfectly over and done with.

No. *No*, no. I am lying face down, and gripping the legs of the table beneath me and listening already, to the five hours of meticulously selected music I will be listening to for the duration. It will help me zone out, zone it, go there, man, I'm on it, I'll find the centre, I am Zen, I am at one, my totem is—

SERIOUSLY! No! FUCK!

This is the worst! God, what are you doing? It is worse than you can ever, ever imagine. It is so bad. I am trying to imagine that I am anywhere else but here. I try very hard. I am at a rock 'n' roll concert, I am there, the music has taken me there, I'm down in front of the stage where the men are dressed like demonic, flying superheroes, with batwings, and the spitting of fire. There, that was a great show! I am right there, can smell again the engine fuel. And then I am yanked unceremoniously back to the immediate, awful present when the needle (which is puncturing like a sewing machine would, only without thread, and much, much faster, and you are the fabric passing beneath) hits my spine and something shoots along it, insanely quick, and ricochets into my skull, like a drilling I can feel through my body, rattling the table under me. But it was only for a second, then gone. And I am here again, in the room, on the table, looking very intently at the wall that I see I am hitting with a fist without realising. I can be nowhere but here in this moment, I am perfectly awake, I am wholly alive. It is terrible, terrible pain. It has been three minutes.

It was almost, almost over. A long time had passed, four hours and more.

Though I had a few breaks, for cigarettes and a chocolate bar, each of these ill-advised diversions was a false dawn, as the needle going back down was like ripping open a wound each time. Horrible. Still, I had done it. Without fainting—though I was nearly sick at about the 49-minute mark. Without whirring into an apoplexy of panic. Without leaving, halfway, never to return, never finishing, one of those idiots in that awful book of unfinished tattoos. Wimps. No. I did not cry, no matter what. Until I did.

I was thinking at that point, when I could just manage mentally to distract myself, really be somewhere else and away, that I was walking with you, in the park where you took me when I was little. Every weekend. And there was a very large clearing bordered by trees, and the sun I remember there, catching on leaves and other tree debris falling softly. And you piling me with leaves, until I was covered and hidden and then pretending to be greatly surprised when I emerged from them seconds later, as if from nowhere. Ah ha! I thought you were so scared of me. Of course you never were. We were friends.

Then we would walk around, very leisurely, and you would answer all my questions. Like why do planes leave white lines in the sky, like that one up there? And they were vapour trails, you'd say, from where the burning fuel meets the atmosphere. And I asked, how high is the atmosphere? And you said very high, you need to be in a plane to touch it, but you can't see it, even then. And I asked if we could catch a plane one day to see if maybe we could see it, and you said yes. I was very pleased with this news. And one day we did catch a plane, and I was too amazed by the curve of the Earth to remember to look for the atmosphere.

Then we would keep walking until we came to the house on the grounds, white and huge. A weird place, it had roped-off rooms where you could peer in and see, but you could never touch, you said. It wasn't allowed, because all the things inside the rooms were very old. And left like that, just how they were. Oh, I said. Okay. But I wanted to so badly. I wanted to jump all over the four-poster bed, and use the plates and bowls for a tea party for you and me.

So we walked through the house, from one end to the other, and we came to the outside again, where there was a pond. Slabs of sandstone ringed its edges and I would sit on them, and they were cold and smooth. And I would cross my legs and peer down into the murky water, very quietly, not breathing too loudly, until I saw it. The first one. It was shimmering, a deep, burnt orange, and huge, slowly moving the reeds to and fro out of its way. A koi. Then there would be one and then another. And I would count them all and tell you there were twelve this time! And then I would look back down at the water and see your reflection, smiling, looking over me. Not at the fish, but at me, at my delight at seeing the fish. They are very, very old, you'd say. Aren't they wonderful? And I would ask if we could take one—just one, or maybe two, so they could be friends—and take them home to live in the bath. And you would laugh and say No, they live here. But would you like some goldfish? And I would agree this was a good compromise, though the goldfish would never arrive.

And I was crying, hard and without making much sound, the hot tears slippery between my face and the leather of the bench. But not from the pain, I tried to explain, like I would to the nurse (I just hate needles, you see?). But it was from the pain, in a way I expect that you can see is obvious. Because I realised then, that five years was such a long time to have never done anything proper for you, but that it just wasn't possible, can you understand? Do you forgive me? I'm changing it now, from now on. This signifies the end, and the start. This was all inside, a (little, maybe not so little) hardness in me, emerging finally because I felt as though my whole back was burning, my flesh was *burning*. It was so hot.

So though I am sure I will die, I don't. This is obvious! I am alive! I am unstoppable. I am above humdrum, the petty disagreements and abysmal tiny failures of the day. The bills I keep forgetting to pay, the dishes in the sink, and whatever else! Did I make the wrong choice, once, sometime? A hundred times? I don't care now. I can withstand anything. I know why I did this. Now, I think. Yes.

NICK CAVE, MAN OR MYTH?

MARK MORDUE

MAN...

i am a crooked man and i've walked a crooked mile . . .
—Nick Cave, 'Your Funeral . . . My Trial'

THE FIRST TIME I EVER spoke to Nick Cave was in a phone interview to promote his second solo album, *The Firstborn is Dead* (1985), an ominous, blues-affected work that sanctified the birth of Elvis Presley and thereby rock 'n' roll itself in quasi-religious, apocalyptic terms. Our conversation around the recording was dry as spinifex, so slow and spacious it sometimes ceased to exist at all. As if Cave could not be less interested in what I was asking or saying and never would be. Given his notorious hatred of journalists this made for an uphill experience. I put the phone down with sweating palms and a sinking feeling in my heart. What a failure.

Dealing with Cave again, let alone meeting him, was not something I looked forward to. In 1987 I nonetheless lobbied to interview Nick Cave for Sydney's *On the Street*. Second time lucky, I must have been hoping. Face to face he had to be more approachable than that distant voice on an echoing telephone line. Besides, he was the pre-eminent Australian rock 'n' roll artist of his day. That made him hard to ignore.

Cave was in town to read from and preview a much anticipated literary work in progress, a book that would become known as *And the Ass Saw the Angel* (1989). He'd already gone so far as to declare himself 'more of a writer now'; disowning rock 'n' roll for its low-brow qualities and Pavlov's dog audience responses.

I was given a laneway address for a warehouse located directly behind Sydney's then alternative and bohemian gay strip, Oxford Street. Cave was apparently holed up there with a girlfriend or a dealer or criminal acquaintance: rumours varied, and as always with Cave rumours were all around him, as if his every movement across town were hot-wired into the gossip chambers of inner-city Sydney conversation. The only other wave-making machine of this kind that I would ever know of was Michael Hutchence.

When I knocked on the doors of what looked like an old garage, a key was hurled to the road with a vaguely familiar shout hovering invisibly on the Sunday afternoon air. I had let myself in before I heard footsteps on the wooden ceiling and the creak of a trapdoor above. At the top of the ladder-like stairs that rolled down to meet me with a thud there was now a hole in the ceiling where Cave himself stood, bathed in backlight. He beckoned me upwards like some awful figure in a B-grade horror film about a rock 'n' roll journalist come to interview a terrifying rock 'n' roll vampire. I gulped and set forth on my way to meet Nosferatu.

Once upstairs the atmosphere changed immediately. Cave was a solicitous host, while a young woman I took to be his partner bossed him about as if I had just entered a goth version of the British comedy *George and Mildred*. 'Get Mark something to eat, Nick,' she said briskly. A large serving of the very best fruits was then put before me—grapes, lychees, melon, apple—all prepared and presented in a grand manner.

As Cave was about to seat himself down and enjoy some of this banquet his partner said, 'Did you offer Mark some coffee, Nick?' Again he rose, mock lugubrious, stick-insect angular. Cave went over to an old metal funnel attached to a wooden workbench, poured in some coffee beans and began turning a handle slowly: 'Grind, grind, grind, it's the story of my life.'

With a variety of expensive biscuits now also arrayed before me, I was soon thanking the couple for their surprising hospitality. Cave asked me why it should be so unexpected. An evasive answer seemed tactically unwise. So I mentioned the Prince of Darkness thing around him, and his general reputation for treating journalists poorly. 'Who says that?' he asked a little surlily. 'Why the NME [*New Musical Express*] . . .' I began to say, in reference to the influential British music paper of the day. 'The NME!' he barked. Cave began to grind the coffee beans with much greater intensity. His partner looked at me and said, 'Don't get him started.' To Cave she called out in a calming voice, 'Now Nick . . .' Cave ground on, taking it out on the beans: 'The NME!'

Finally he came back over to us with a large silver coffee pot steaming with his efforts. A set of fine china cups were ready on a matching silver serving tray. Mid pour Cave lost focus, the coffee slowly streaming out of the spout and around—but not in—the cups in an ever-widening circle, till the serving tray was filled with black liquid as if it were a swimming pool—until Cave snapped back into consciousness and finally found the cups as well. Completing the task at last, Cave then asked me with all the decorum he could muster: 'Would you like milk or sugar with that?'

The next two and half hours felt rather like an interview taking place under similarly dark water. Each question seemed to demand huge reservoirs of concentration from Cave, not to mention frequent pauses and micro-sleeps. Cave's sometimes thin and creaky, sometimes sonorous and self-consciously refined speaking voice certainly had its hypnotic qualities. I felt suspended, unsure of what to do, or even how to leave. To be honest I'm not sure the interview *ever* quite ended so much as faded away. With everyone heavily relaxed, I departed once more through the floor.

It was yet another Cave interview in which I felt I had somehow failed, despite Cave's very best efforts to help me. This was largely because I didn't really understand how to write up what had happened. I also dreaded sitting down and transcribing the interview tapes, a process that would demand even greater leagues of passing time from me all over again.

Two nights later on stage at the Mandolin Cinema, Cave would recite from sections of his work in progress while an ambient soundtrack rose and fell with suitably ominous and dream-like affect around his reading voice. Looking every inch the 'Black Crow King' (one of many self-referential character songs that would add to his mythology despite the satirical swipes it took at his image and those who subscribed to it), Cave did not so much walk onto the stage as dangle, stoop and hang in the air as if from unseen strings. He would eventually fall off the stage at one point altogether. And yet the cinema was full to the brim with his fans, a sellout performance over two nights, and a success in terms of the mood created in reading from what appeared to be a credible, black-humoured, Faulknerian work of fiction well on the way to completion.

Almost a decade on from these readings and our warehouse encounter the boot would be on the other foot as I once again spoke to Cave over the phone in 1994. He was now living in São Paulo, Brazil, and by all accounts was clean as a whistle. For me it was an early-morning interview. Unfortunately I'd broken up with my girlfriend the previous night and not been home at all, to sleep or otherwise, barely brushing in the door to take Cave's call. Thank God for having prepared the previous day. When Cave asked me how I was I told him at great length: that I'd been out wandering all night, that I'd been here and there, felt this and thought that, a long wild emotional ramble that ended up with me saying I loved his new record *Let Love In* and finally asking if he had a favourite walk he liked to take in São Paulo.

Cave took this all in with a long pause and slight grunt—and we began to talk. It was a great interview and I liked him a lot. He seemed completely non-judgemental about my 'condition'; in fact I'd say he was both kind and curiously amused throughout. As for his answer to my opening question . . . 'Well, I make my favourite walk daily. Which is up to my local bar. Out the door, up the street, past the junkyard where the chickens and the old junkyard dog sits. And up a steep hill to my favourite bar, San Pedro's. There's this giant barman there who is the fattest guy I've ever seen. He is constantly described by locals as a huge woman, but he's a man with a moustache. He looks more like a giant baby to me. I sit there and read, drink, and contemplate the meaning of life. Then I walk back down.'

A few years on and I'd meet Cave again in 1997, at the offices of Festival Mushroom in Sydney, in a rather sterile fluorescent-lit room. Cave remembered me well enough, but his mood was odd and, I realise now, he was highly vulnerable as *The Boatman's Call*—a raw and revealing album that revolved around his break up with Brazilian partner Viviane Carneiro and a wounding affair with P.J. Harvey—was about to be released. None of that was public yet. I nonetheless asked him, almost randomly, if he thought the love of a good woman could redeem a man. It was a question that seemed to lead out of his lyrics and what they implied across the record. Cave looked at me as if I were a total fucking idiot and then away at the white wall as if he were a hopeless and God-forsaken case himself: 'How the hell would I know?' he said. And then he looked back at me and waited for the next question.

. . . OR MYTH?

I was just a boy when I sat down
To watch the news on TV
I saw some ordinary slaughter
I saw some routine atrocity
My father said, don't look away
You got to be strong, you got to be bold, now
He said, that in the end it is beauty
That is going to save the world, now
—Nick Cave, 'Nature Boy'

At its most extreme Nick Cave's life has been played out through a self-fulfill-ing philosophy of being damned—and now, it seems, redeemed at last. Cave has spiked this metaphor into his public persona with frequent allusions in song to the parable of the prodigal son (Luke 15:11–32)—especially notable as a regretful theme across his pivotal 1990 album of melancholy and melody, *The Good Son.*

The roots of this metaphor are archetypal and deeply personal: lying in the relationship between a rebellious teenager from 'Ned Kelly outlaw coun-try' in regional Victoria and a loving, if somewhat overbearing and artistically frustrated, schoolteacher father who imbued that son with a passion for Dos-toyevsky and Shakespeare.

Nicholas Edward Cave was already developing as a young musician with his glam-rock-cum-art-school band The Boys Next Door when he would hear of Colin Cave's death in a motor vehicle accident in 1976. As this news arrived, the then 21-year-old was in the process of being bailed out of a Melbourne police cell by his librarian mother Dawn after being held on charges of vandal-ism and being drunk and disorderly. It was not the first time the unruly third son had proved an embarrassment and a difficulty to this solidly Anglican, middle-class family of three boys and a younger girl.

That an element of shame was embedded with Cave's grief on the night is hardly the most penetrating analysis. That the death of his father would foster a sense of the inevitability of loss—and the perversity of fate—is again all too obvious.

And yet once these themes were branded into place Cave would explore them with a vengeance, pursuing a delinquent and self-destructive personal life that he celebrated and mocked in songs like 'Sonny's Burning', screaming out this invocation to his early audience: 'Hands up who wants to die?!' Yet as his first great love, Anita Lane, observed:

> Nick's got this incredible drive that's got him through everything. He's a workaholic. When we were younger I thought it was something he would grow out of and get over. He really wanted to impress his father and wanted him to think he was clever. His father would just laugh at him, he wouldn't take any notice. When his father died I wondered what was going to happen to Nick's drive, but it just got stronger.[1]

1 Anita Lane, quoted in Ian Johnstone, *Bad Seed—the Biography of Nick Cave*, Abacus, London, 1996, p. 57.

Mad, bad and dangerous to know (cf. Lord Byron), the young Nick Cave would make his mark as the heroin-addicted, rock 'n' roll wild man out front of his sensational group The Birthday Party: 'Sonny's Burning', 'She's Hit', 'Swampland', 'Mutiny in Heaven', 'Zoo Music Girl', 'Dead Joe', 'Deep in the Woods', 'Pleasureheads Must Burn', 'Six-inch Gold Blade', 'Big Jesus Trash Can', 'Wild World' . . . the song titles alone suggest something of their aesthetic.

The speed at which the band developed out of the gawky if promising origins of The Boys Next Door was manifest in a live show perpetually two steps ahead of the recorded material they were releasing, leaving audiences either thrilled or perplexed. Frustrated with an unresponsive and pub-rock obsessed Australian music scene, The Birthday Party set off for England in 1980 as young hopefuls on the expatriate trail. Cave in particular was developing as a showman and an expressionistically violent, erotic lyricist—much of that murderous energy focused on girlfriend Anita Lane, the muse to many of his songs for a decade.

> I didn't take it completely literally, that would be like believing in a soap opera in which a character has really died. It was like I was a character based in reality. I think Nick's writing is always one step removed from his true immediate feelings; it's [like] always having a literary eye on yourself.[2]

2 Lane, quoted in Johnstone, p. 99.

The Birthday Party's junkie primitivism was already well on display, a swaggering peacock quality guilded by sparks and slates of careening feedback from lead guitarist Rowland Howard, Cave's first great creative foil. This was complemented by Cave's deep-voiced singing and primal grunts and howls—while his lyrics increasingly showed the influence of writers such as Flannery O'Connor and Samuel Beckett (a writer he devoured with zeal in the grim squats of London), not to mention a sarcastic fascination for 1950s-style hoodlum images of glamorised violence and rebellion.

It was a sound that drew on the confrontational hedonism of The Stooges and the B-grade rockabilly theatrics of The Cramps, as well the intellectual rage of The Pop Group (minus their overt politics) and the dislocated melodic sensibilities of Pere Ubu, along with a taste for free jazz and its brash improvisatory attitudes. The unlikely net result of these varied influences was an act—in both music and appearance—that moulded together an original, hillbilly Australian Gothic.

In tapping into this spirit of colonial darkness as well as an exaggerated white trash, criminal aura, The Birthday Party would ironically connect with English audiences and their latent stereotypes about those from the land Down Under. All the while the band's lyrical concerns and experimental approach to playing rock 'n' roll revealed an obvious intelligence at odds with their stagey inclinations towards thuggishness and chaos. Champions such as the BBC's renowned DJ John Peel and an eventually adoring New Musical Express magazine were bowled over by the force of the group's sound and their artistic ambition, a demonic grandness that did not seem to stop when the show was over. As Robert Vickers of The Go-Betweens explained:

The Birthday Party were the leaders among the group of Australian bands who moved to London in the early 1980s . . . the Go-Betweens, The Triffids, The Moodists and a host of others. They were the most charismatic and the most self destructive; the most successful but the worst organised. They never had places to live and moved around like a travelling circus with a wild collection of fascinating girlfriends who had come over from Australia with them.[3]

3 Robert Vickers on The Go-Betweens, quoted in Amy Hanson, *Kicking against the Pricks: An Armchair Guide to Nick Cave*, Helter Skelter Publishing, London, 2005, p. 45.

If The Birthday Party's sense of humour was underestimated, as Cave and his cohorts always claimed, it was because it became another aspect to their more obvious malice. Cave would satisfy himself with that blend when he persuaded the American artist Ed 'Big Daddy' Roth to provide the demented and slobbering hot rod/bubblegum cover art for The Birthday Party's 1982 release *Junk Yard*. In the meanwhile their biggest 'hit', 'Release the Bats' (1981), had been conceived to mock the goths who were embracing them in England. Much to the band's horror, very few people got the joke.

Cave felt as if he were becoming a performing monkey for audience expectations that had built up around the group: whether he did another back-flip on stage, or simply kicked someone in the head who was annoying him, spitting on him or even attacking him in the punk rock spirit of the times. In an aside that reflects on this ugly streak to the band's performing history, Rowland Howard would nickname one of their last sojourns across the UK and Europe in *Rolling Stone*: 'The Oops I've Got Blood on the Tips of My Boots Tour'. Cave would later comment:

We wanted to go out and really abuse people and assault them and hurt them. And I think our integrity shines through in that as soon as we got to a point where everyone was coming along to have all this happen to 'em, we folded up the group and went on to other things.

After blowing a hole through the UK post-punk music scene at the start of the 1980s and establishing themselves as the most exciting live act of the era (they rated only The Fall and Joy Division as opposition), The Birthday Party began to devour themselves. The first to go was their much bullied drummer and old school friend, Phill Calvert. Bassist Tracy Pew was then jailed for eight months on a drink-driving charge in Melbourne. The creative friction between Rowland Howard (who had written their early hit, 'Shivers') and the dominant axis of Nick Cave and multi-instrumentalist Mick Harvey was growing. Remarkably it led to their finest recordings. The band sounded as if it were dying like some ferocious animal across the final two EPs, *The Bad Seed* (1983) and *Mutiny!* (1984). Call those last recordings a brilliant spasm of overtly violent creativity, if you wish: swastika cover artwork with syringed blood red finishing off the artistic quest to repulse as much as attract. Not for the first time would Cave associate himself with Jesus in a brilliant image of twinned lovers that also marked out his own druggy mythology—'post crucifixion baby and a little undone', to quote from the latter-day Birthday Party classic 'Wild World'. Howard had simply stopped turning up at the studio. Harvey, sick of the disorder, quit. The band was now finished. Fucked.

It was therefore a surprise to see Cave somehow reform the Birthday Party in everything but name that same year (with Hugo Race filling in for Howard on guitar) for a lucrative solo tour of Australia called 'Nick Cave: Man or Myth?': another joke, this one inspired by an old book entitled *Ned Kelly, Man or Myth?*, a bushranger biography precious to the singer because Cave's father had written the introduction for it.

'Nick Cave: Man or Myth?' was not the last attempt the singer would make to laugh off or push away his larger-than-life reputation—or to be free of the absurd level of cultivated aggression that had given him such a dangerous name. A blur was well established now between the theatre of his songs and his aggressive, dissolute performances, and the tendency for that to become an all consuming reality around him. It would plague Cave for a long time to come. How much he fed it, and how much it consumed him, is of course one of the dilemmas he would have to face.

By the end of 1983 the singer had nonetheless settled in what was then West Berlin, revelling in that divided city's decadent historical ambience and bohemianism—lurking in the illegal all-night bars and associated backroom poker-and-drug dens that encouraged a freewheeling lifestyle. There Cave began establishing a solo career with what would become his new backing band, The Bad Seeds, to be led once more by Mick Harvey. The former school friend and Boys Next Door/Birthday Party associate had already been through a lot with Cave—but Harvey would confirm himself as the singer's crucial right-hand man and musical arranger for the next two decades. How someone as controlled and organised as Harvey could work with a figure as turbulent as Cave remains one of the more mysterious questions in modern music—it's a partnership yet to be analysed, and for that matter even fully appreciated for its significance.

In Berlin it became obvious Cave measured himself beside his heroes—Bob Dylan, Leonard Cohen, Neil Young and Johnny Cash (who would later cover 'The Mercy Seat' and invite Cave to sing with him on one of his last records)—and that he was doing his best to catch up with them. Between 1983 and 1987 Cave produced the albums *From Her to Eternity*, *The Firstborn is Dead*, *Kicking against the Pricks*, *Your Funeral . . . My Trial* and *Tender Prey* in rapid succession, and completed—with some difficulty—what would become his debut novel *And the Ass Saw the Angel*. He also took time out to help develop a script for, write the soundtrack for and act in the hardcore Australian prison film, John Hillcoat's *Ghosts . . . of the Civil Dead*.

Under Harvey's guiding hand, and with German 'anti-guitarist' Blixa Bargeld adding his uniquely deconstructive, textural style of playing—variously described by Cave as 'destroyed' and 'mournful'—The Bad Seeds brought a more blues-affected, melodically organised and cinematic sense of drama to Cave's songwriting. This culminated in *Your Funeral . . . My Trial* (1986, an overt reference to his father), without doubt Cave's first masterpiece as a solo artist. It was a flawless statement of his broadening narrative concerns, his growing preference for mood and atmosphere over rapturous aural assaults, and a capacity for surprising beauty in songs like 'Sad Waters'. The sorrowful Kurt Weill fairground creep of an extended narrative such as 'The Carny' caught the interest of film director Wim Wenders, who invited Cave to perform in and contribute music to what became *Wings of Desire* (1989). Cave had effectively become an icon of Berlin, affirming its place as one of the world's contemporary arts and music capitals.

By 1988 Cave would nonetheless flee Berlin: profoundly addicted to both speed and heroin, in debt to his dealers and acolytes, and all but socially disgraced if not notorious. Cave has described *Tender Prey* (1988), the last recording of his that could truly be associated with his life in that city, as 'one long cry for help'. In spite of this it yielded one of his greatest songs, 'The Mercy Seat' (a vision from the electric chair) and his first 'pop' hit, 'Deanna' (a love song concerned with lust and abortion). It was a do-or-die effort Cave could not afford to sustain:

> I've always worked really hard, I've always worked at a desk, and I've always put in long hours, despite the circumstances of my life . . . I wrote a novel, and you don't do that on a lark. You have to fuckin' sit down at the typewriter day after day just to get it done, just to get the words down. That I did nothing but lie around and take drugs is just a misconception. It's a misconception by people who don't really understand the nature of drug-taking. I think there's a general idea that if you take drugs, your life must be out of control, and you're kind of going nowhere. I don't see this as being true at all.[4]

4 Nick Cave, interviewed by Keith Phipps at the AV Club, 24 November 2004.

To this day many argue that only Keith Richards has had a larger role in glamorising heroin use to a rock 'n' roll audience, an allegation that offends Cave and ignores the role of media obsessed with the taboos and romantic allure of his outlaw image. Ironically enough, one of Cave's adolescent heroes at art school was the heroin-addicted Australian painter Brett Whitely. Cave's ambitions and constitution have played their part in his survival, allowing him to endure where others have fallen by the wayside: notably brilliant but troubled fellow musicians such as one-time Bad Seeds bassist Barry Adamson and The Birthday Party guitarist Rowland Howard, both of whom would struggle with addiction and its psychological impact on their more fragile personalities.

In 1986 these personal losses would become even more serious when bassist Tracy Pew, Cave's boyhood friend and closest personal associate in The Birthday Party, died after an extreme epileptic fit possibly worsened by a history of binge drinking and drug taking. The death of Pew, the spiralling downwards of the Berlin years in 1986–88, a drug bust for Cave in the UK, and numerous other close calls in seedy circumstances combined to push the singer into making his first serious if reluctant steps towards rehabilitation. His friend and song-writing partner Mick Harvey saw the obvious downsides to it all:

> One tendency Nick has is to rewrite history from his current perspective. He tends to describe what his motivations were then through the perspective of what his motivations are now. In 1987, during *Tender Prey*, he was getting so fucked up but now he sees it as being confused about what he wanted to do in finishing the record, recording in four different countries and half a dozen studios. At the time, in 1988, it

was affecting his work, that's when it had to stop because up till then it hadn't. If that wasn't the case he'd still be using now. I think it also had a lot to do with why the book [*And the Ass Saw the Angel*] wouldn't take form, why it dragged on. Nick, you see, would argue that a lot of the creative aspects of it were inspired by it, which is valid, but it affected ordering what he had created. That was the problem. He couldn't decide whether what he was doing was good or bad and he couldn't look at it again, or on occasion even be able to find it. It had all just turned to mayhem. A lot of people just let it take over but Nick would never let that happen.[5]

5 Mick Harvey, quoted in Johnstone, pp. 241-2.

After coming out of rehab in the UK, Cave yearned once more to escape the shadow of his public image—and the less than healthy opportunities provided by eager fans offering him the usual amalgam of sex and drugs for their rock 'n' roll kicks. London and Berlin felt used up; his hometown, Melbourne, was a backward step. Where to next? It was on a 1988 tour of Brazil inspired by his interest in the South American child prostitution film *Pixote* that Cave found his answer: it came in the form of a fashion stylist called Viviane Carneiro, a brunette who caught his eye from the stage and to whom he gave his entire performance.

Cave would move base to São Paulo to be with Carneiro in 1989. There he found inspiration in the extremes of the city, in its mix of cosmopolitanism and the contrasting poverty and crime of the surrounding *favelas*. He was also inspired by the deeply musical and religious nature of the culture, symbolised by the famous statue of Christ the Redeemer that overlooks the city. Cave would say it changed its countenance from benevolent to sinister depending on the time of day, as if orchestrating the darker and lighter moods of the city. Cave was still wrestling with demons of his own, trying to stay off heroin while continuing to compensate by drinking. He would later admit he was terrified his muse would desert him when he went 'straight' after depending for inspiration on drugs and disorder for so long.

Instead, his next record, *The Good Son* (1990), marked another revolution in Cave's career: stately, regretful and sweeping. Known in some quarters as his 'post-rehab' album, it reflected Cave's relatively stable life with Carneiro and the birth of their son, Luke (another son, Jethro, to whom Cave is now reconciled, was born in Australia a mere ten days before Luke in São Paulo). After being dogged by his notoriety in the UK and Europe, it was a pleasing contrast for Cave to land favourably on the front pages of the local newspapers for choosing to live and record in Brazil. He moved freely about São Paulo as a much admired 'gringo' who had fallen in love with the city, almost something of a local hero.

The Good Son developed naturally as a calling into account of Cave's life thus far, even as an extended prayer for forgiveness. Cave expressed it this way:

> We all experience within us what the Portuguese call *saudade*, which translates as an inexplicable longing, an unnamed and enigmatic yearning of the soul, and it is this feeling that lives in the realms of the imagination and inspiration and is the breeding ground for the sad

6 Nick Cave, *The Secret Life of the Love Song / The Flesh Made Word* (spoken word recording), King Mob, 1999.

song, for the Love Song. The Love Song is the light of God, deep down, blasting up through our wounds.[6]

Unfortunately, Cave's romance with Carneiro began to wither. Language difficulties further isolated him as he grew disenchanted with São Paulo and an outsider status he could never really shake. In the end he was still, and always would be, a 'gringo'. The couple moved briefly to New York, then to London in 1996—to no avail. Cave had thrown himself back into work, perhaps his greatest addiction. Carneiro and their son Luke would return to São Paolo, from where a long-distance relationship wrought its inevitable strains, memorably evoked in Cave's song 'Into My Arms':

I don't believe in an interventionist God
But I know, darling, that you do
But if I did I would kneel down and ask Him
Not to intervene when it came to you.

If *The Good Son* had been a stately creation, Cave began moving quickly through a series of albums that reflected his restless energy and emotional turbulence: the somewhat frustrating *Henry's Dream* that showed him looking for new directions; the rock 'n' roll return of *Let Love In* that finally unleashed those restless marital energies to spectacular effect (pairing him once again with long-time cohort and production genius Tony Cohen); and *Murder Ballads*, which would become his most successful album ever thanks to 'Where the Wild Roses Grow', a duet with Kylie Minogue.

By the time Cave was recording what would become *The Boatman's Call* in 1997 he and Carneiro had split irrevocably. He had meanwhile become involved in a devastating affair with fellow singer P.J. Harvey, a romance that had sparked before the cameras during the filming of a video for the song 'Henry Lee' off the earlier *Murder Ballads* album. *The Boatman's Call* reeked of the aftermath of these relationships, and worked as a raw-to-the-bone confessional, as naked and close as Cave would ever be.

It's a record Cave admits to being embarrassed about, even a little ashamed of. In his view the music and lyrics were simply too direct, certain lines too bitter or obvious. The presence of The Bad Seeds on the record is restrained to the point of almost being non-existent; the musicianship extremely spare. Perhaps most significantly, the record also marks the first involvement in The Bad Seeds of Dirty Three violinist Warren Ellis, the man who would become Cave's next great musical partner.

Cave would take some time to recover from his personal troubles. It had become clear since *The Good Son* that he was on a reflective trajectory and unlikely to return to the furies of The Birthday Party years, or even the drug-fuelled, mercurial extremes of *Tender Prey*. A break-out rock 'n' roll masterpiece like *Let Love In* looked increasingly like an anomaly as Cave turned more and more to the piano as a basis for his songwriting. He was also articulating his deepening religious interests in songs such as 'Brompton Oratory', where the connections between music and solace were obvious. It was a song tainted by a suggestive slippage back into addiction, and a tone of resignation, as if he was not just letting go of a relationship but climbing out of a greater weakness as well.

> I was reading the Bible a lot through my 20s, mostly the Old Testament, just because I was knocked out by the language and the stories. I felt that the God being talked about there, who was this insane, vindictive patriarch—it was kind of thrilling, and titillated something in me at the time. It seemed to me that the world deserves a God like that. Then I started reading the New Testament, and it spoke in a totally different way to me. It was much more mysterious, incredibly beautiful, and I think it turned my way of thinking around in some way. It struck a much more personal note.[7]

7 Nick Cave, interviewed by Keith Phipps.

The collapse of his relationship with Carneiro and the more intense affair with P.J. Harvey would spark another shift in direction for Cave. It was during this emotional hiatus that Michael Hutchence befriended the singer in London. Cave would eventually become the godfather to the daughter of Hutchence and Paula Yates, Heavenly Hiraani Tiger Lily. The thought of these two somewhat dissolute rock 'n' roll dads sharing play-dates and morning conversations in London has an air of exhausted sweetness about it. These were definitely quiet times for Cave, and outwardly the beginnings of his least productive period ever after an almost manic performing and recording career lasting some twenty years.

Ironically, 'Into My Arms', the song Cave had written for Carneiro when their relationship was foundering, would become the song Cave found himself playing for Hutchence at his funeral in 1997. Hutchence had died in ambiguous and tragic circumstances from what was at first a suspected suicide, and later declared 'death by misadventure' due to an overdose of drugs and auto-erotic strangulation.

> Michael was a good friend of mine. We liked each other very much, but we came from different places musically, obviously, and I think we both understood that, and we didn't go into each other's music all that much. He was a very beautiful guy with a generous spirit, and he was very honest about things to me, and I appreciated that.[8]

8 Nick Cave, quoted in Hanson, pp. 114-15.

In 1998 Cave was invited by Canongate Books in the UK to write a foreword to a special edition of *The Gospel According to Mark*. Cave's lecture 'The Secret Life of the Love Song' (Vienna, 1999)—made available as a spoken-word CD and broadcast on radio internationally—developed this religious theme by linking his ideal for love songs with a desire for divine communication and healing.

His friend the author Will Self would later sum this up more aesthetically in an introduction for *Nick Cave: The Complete Lyrics* (2007) by declaring Cave was a songwriter who had 'the aching heart of Smokey [Robinson], implanted in the tortured breast of [Robert] Zimmerman [alias Bob Dylan].'

Cave's public resurgence began with *No More Shall We Part* (2001), then the remarkably strong, almost bragging scope of his next two-CD set *Abattoir*

Blues / The Lyre of Orpheus (2004), followed by *Nocturama* (2006). He would also be invited to sing with Johnny Cash, to work with Marianne Faithfull and to perform across the world on the Leonard Cohen tribute concert. The associations with these iconic contemporary figures pointed out what was now obvious: Cave was an international artist with a remarkable body of work, and an icon in his own right.

Sail away to where your troubles can't follow.
Sail away, save your tears for tomorrow.
—Nick Cave, 'Sail Away' (2008)

It's as if Cave had been writing, and even anticipating, his life story all along, and marking that path with his songs. Certainly Cave always had a theatrical vision of himself, and he has presented this vision to the public, albeit with a tang of resentment and a goodly dose of irony: from the contrary dark prince, 'Hamlet (Pow! Pow! Pow!)' of the post-punk music scene in Melbourne and London; to the junkie blues nightmare retaliating from Berlin against all his goth admirers in 'Black Crow King'; to a decadent, then washed-up and eventually dead rock star of biblical proportions in the title track to his latest LP, 'Dig, Lazarus, Dig!!!'

It's this mix of menace and camp, grief and cabaret, poetry and pulp crudity that has kept Cave and his audience on their toes for three decades. And beyond all that a genuinely deep trace of autobiographical feeling that has never allowed the theatrics to slide into empty gestures.

His latest renewal can easily be connected to meeting and marrying the former model Susie Bick in 1999 and becoming the father of their twin sons Arthur and Earl, now aged eight. Indeed *No More Shall We Part* is sometimes referred to as 'the wedding album'. Cave openly discussed his new regimen at the time: a highly disciplined nine-to-five working day in his studio 'office' surrounded by depictions of cats painted by the nineteenth-century schizophrenic artist Louis Wain. As Wim Wenders had astutely remarked years earlier: 'His [Cave's] songs deal with a desire for pure love or this longing for peace in spite of all the turmoil and unrest happening inside him.'[9]

9 Wim Wenders, *The South Bank Show*, ITV, UK, 10 August 2003.

Secluded in the seaside tourist town of Brighton & Hove, Cave is now the very picture of domesticity, a domesticity that does not seem to have tamed him. Cave has said in interviews he is 'obsessing over sex more than ever'. It's a theme relished in recent work where he deals with growing old disgracefully in everything from side-project Grinderman's 'No Pussy Blues' and 'Go Tell the Women (that we're leaving)' to The Bad Seeds, 'Dig, Lazarus, Dig!!!'. As if to cement this 'ironic' perspective on himself he told *Rolling Stone* in 2004: 'I consider myself to be first and foremost a comic writer.'

Note: Apart from the above references I must also mention a larger debt to Ian Johnstone's biography *Bad Seed* as well as Robert Brokenmouth's *Nick Cave—The Birthday Party & Other Epic Adventures*, Omnibus Press, London, 1996. And to Robert L. Miller, who initiated me into this 'wild world'.

With his band Grinderman unexpectedly recalling the raucously inventive savagery of The Birthday Party with a more overt dose of ribald wit and pop-rock buoyancy, Cave appears capable of being as energetic and unpredictable as he ever was. His last recording with The Bad Seeds, *Dig, Lazarus, Dig!!!*, has meanwhile been heralded as one of the group's best albums ever, seeding itself from the upbeat, guitar-oriented energies of the Grinderman project and lashing out accordingly.

Cave and fellow Bad Seed member Warren Ellis continue to work on highly regarded soundtracks for theatre productions and major films such as *The Proposition* (which Cave co-scripted with friend and neighbour John Hillcoat), *The Assassination of Jesse James by the Coward Robert Ford* and *The Road*. Looking like Rasputin reincarnated on stage, Ellis's energising effect on Cave has nonetheless spelt the end of the long-time partnership with Mick Harvey, who left The Bad Seeds in January 2009. Ed Kuepper, the iconic guitarist for the Saints and The Laughing Clowns, was announced as Harvey's replacement. Something that makes The Bad Seeds a veritable rock 'n' roll supergroup.

So it goes. Nick Cave, aged fifty-one, still evolving, still coming at you with everything he has—shedding expectations like so much dead skin while his body of work grows in substance and reputation across the world. From being invited to present the 2008 Turner Art Prize in the UK to curating the All Tomorrow's Parties events at the 2009 Sydney Festival and in Mt Buller, from being inducted into the Australian Record Industry Association's Rock 'n' Roll Hall of Fame in 2007 to the release of his second novel, *The Death of Bunny Munro*. A sardonic thriller about a horny travelling salesman, the novel recalls the pulp kicks of Jim Thompson at his most evilly amused, as well as Martin Amis and Will Self's flair for moral vertigo and pornographic rushes of energy. What comes next, one has to ask? A Booker Prize? An Academy Award for Best Soundtrack? An even sleazier moustache?

There's certainly no doubt Nicholas Edward Cave is the epitome of the sophisticated and successful international artist; and that he is enjoying a renaissance in every aspect of his career. These days he does not take drugs, or drink, or even smoke. When not performing, writing and recording at a furious pace, he simply busies himself with his young family and keeps in touch with his two older boys Jethro and Luke. Who could have guessed that marriage and fatherhood would be so kind to him?

HAVE RELATIONSHIPS LIKE ROCK STARS: A TWITTER EXPOSÉ

MEERA ATKINSON

Sometime last year my ex-husband discovered Twitter and his 'tweets'—mini-blog messages limited to 140 characters—started showing up on his Facebook page, dutifully proffering answers to the quintessential Twitter question: what are you doing? Frankly, I couldn't see the point.

But then all of a sudden it seemed like the world was abuzz about Twitter. My curiosity got the better of me and I signed up to see what all the fuss was about. By this time my ex had lost interest and no longer twittered, and I expected to follow suit. In fact, as one who is not fond of inane conversation, the prospect of a flood of sound bytes from strangers left me quite cold. Even worse was the thought that you could not only twitter on the web; you could 'tweet' and be tweeted at via mobile phone. There's even an 'adult' Twitter. Had humanity given up on the notion of peace of mind all together?

Twitter cuts a broad swathe across communities around the world, from soccer mums to celebrities, including Hugh Jackman and Ashton Kutcher, who beat CNN in a race to reach 1 million followers. Even Barack Obama twitters.

Sycophant that I am, I follow lots of famous people, including DAVID_LYNCH and stephenfry. Although there are fake celeb twits, the real deal often grant their followers a refreshing sense of their humanity—they eat, they breathe, they tweet, just like the rest of us. They admit to nerves before events, talk about their daily chores, their kids and their projects.

JohnCleese posts tweets like 'Weighing up minty plenitude against tongue-cavorting freshness'; yokoono is delightfully Yokoish with updates such as 'Remember, we are all water in the same ocean'; and ben_stiller tweets about his obsession with sea monkeys and his 'mini man crush' on the latest *Star Trek* Captain Kirk, Chris Pine. Never before has there been such a direct route of communication between the famous and the un-famous and such an instant avenue for contact between widely diverse people. It unsurprisingly stands to reason that the famous are not as sure to follow us as we are to follow them but I am being followed by the writer JohnBirmingham and KevinRuddPM (or whichever intern is busy maintaining his Twitter form).

Some celebs on Twitter are confirmed, others not so much. I decided to follow isla_fisher, whose credibility has been debated among twits, when I caught a tweet teasing that her pal Nicole Kidman had just joined up under an alias. Some 'Isla' tweets sounded convincing enough but when she began sending me direct messages, tweeting in sloppy English and sounding plain obsessed with Our Nicole, I took side with the sceptics. On this count I feel for the famous. Not only are they hounded and photographed and gossiped about in magazines but now their very identities are being hijacked. It's hard to imagine how it would feel to have someone spouting all manner of nonsense not just about you but *as* you.

I am also being followed by an array of spambots including VAGINAPOWER and myteethwhiten. Those with a professional agenda range from individual artists, bands and journals (*Meanjin* tweets) to aggressive sales people peddling their many wares. The beauty of Twitter though is that I don't have to follow them back. Marketers can knock themselves out but I have the option of not listening. I can even block selected entities from following me.

There are times when Twitter's superficial and opportunistic qualities are outweighed by its powers of good and its importance as an instant and uncensored form of communication. When violence broke out in Iran following the defeat of presidential candidate Mir-Hossein Mousavi and the re-election of President Mahmoud Ahmadinejad in what many claimed was a rigged count, Iranians turned to Twitter. AAP reported that after the Iranian government shut down media and banned foreign journalists from covering protests, Twitter was one of the only ways those inside Iran could relate events to the worldwide community. The US government even took the incredible step of asking Twitter to hold off on site maintenance to ensure the twitstream remained open to Iranians.

When I first started I knew personally only one dedicated twit: my old friend 'First Dog On the Moon', a cartoonist for *Crikey*. Having joined up a year ago,

Firstdogonmoon has become a popular twit, partly because of his adoring fan base and partly because when News Limited tipped him as one of Australia's most interesting twits several months ago his followers jumped from around 600 to more than 1300 in a week.

Firstdogonmoon's cartoons are available daily to subscribers of *Crikey* and once a week they're offered free. This gives Firstdogonmoon an opportunity to throw his loyal Twitter admirers and new followers alike a proverbial bone by linking to the free 'toon. This is the kind of subtle promotion strategy artists, media and organisations are routinely employing on Twitter, and there's no denying Twitter and other online forums can boost public profile. 'I didn't go on specifically to promote the cartoons but I assumed I'd be able to do that,' says Firstdogonmoon. 'Some people just think I'm a nice guy but the majority know me as the cartoonist.'

But for all the stars and snake-oil salesmen, the heart and soul of the Twitter experience is 140-character interaction with mere mortals who, just like me, ponder the issues of the day and exercise brainpower before an audience of etherised others.

For Twitter virgins let me explain. To get started you select a username, which is what shows up when you tweet, along with a thumbnail image. You log other optional information, such as a real name, location and bio, and this shows up on your profile along with your list of followers, followees, number of updates (tweets) and your history of updates. Tweets, once twittered, can't be edited but can be deleted. If someone follows you and you follow them you have the option of sending a direct message (DM) to each other. If you want to direct a tweet to someone in the twitstream rather than send a DM, you tweet in the usual fashion but with what's called an @reply ahead of the message. This means the tweet shows up with an @ followed by the username of the person you're addressing. And thus do tweets become more like snappy conversations than simple reportage on activity. The tweets of a user and their followees are relayed in a continual live stream. This is referred to as the 'timeline'.

Tweets aren't limited to simple text—an entire culture is now evolving. You can post links, reference Twitter groups (trends and groupings of special interest twits and tweets indicated by a 'hashtag' that shows up as the # symbol followed by the name of the group), and you can blip songs. This involves becoming a Blip.fm DJ, which enables your track selections to post on Twitter as a song others can listen to. You can give 'props' to blips you particularly like or even re-blip them (done by posting RB @ reply original blipper) before the blip. There is a 'Follow Friday' custom, which involves recommending who others should follow, as well as a convention of acknowledging good tweets by retweeting them, which is done by typing RT @reply the original tweeter, followed by their tweet.

But enough Twitter 101. So it was that @firstdogonmoon was the first twit I followed. He promptly received email notification that I was following him, under the handle of Gertrudesteinjr, and though I'd withheld my real name on my profile I had posted a photo of myself in the thumbnail so he quickly followed in return. I DMd asking how to get going on the following front and next thing I knew Firstdog had posted this tweet to his 2500-plus followers: 'Follow @Gertrudesteinjr because it is my birthday. Also, she is a special big brained rabbit.'

In no time I had a flurry of followers whom I immediately followed back. Thus my Twitter life was born. I confessed to my new friends despite my Twitter name that I was not a frumpy dead Jewish-American lesbian genius and I watched baffled as jargoned messages sailed by with acronyms and emoticons I didn't understand, such as tyvm (thank you very much), :P (tongue poke) and :D (grin), and the in-jokes of established conversations.

I looked down the list of welcoming tweets and caught sight of an attractive guy in thumbnail called sswayze. My thinking went to the obvious.

'Do people flirt on twitter and even fall in love?' I tweeted, followed by: 'Hey sswayze, want to have my babies?'

'Lol,' he replied [laugh out loud]. 'Usually the flirting comes before the babies.'

And so, with a slightly compulsive back and forth of DMs and tweets, my twittership with sswayze flourished complete with lashings of witty repartee, intellectual camaraderie and a shared love of music. We impressed each other with unpredictable blips. He gave me props for The B-52's 'Give Me Back My Man', 'I Want You to Want Me' (Cheap Trick) and the Frente cover of New Order's 'Bizarre Love Triangle'. I gave him props for the *Tommy* highlight 'See Me, Feel Me' (The Who), Peter Frampton's moment of greatness 'Do You Feel Like We Do' and Gil Scott-Heron's 'The Revolution Will Not Be Televised'. Though we remained keenly aware of the enormous geographical distance and the impossibility of a friendship of the normal variety, it was, for all its limitations, a downright fun exchange.

The man behind sswayze is Sean Swayze, a Canadian computer scientist, certified genius, hard-core twit and avid blipper. Beginning with comic flirtation, our preliminary banter morphed into a curious twittership, one of several that brought to light the inherent and deep-seated need for connection and validation common to all humanity and very evident in the Twitter revolution.

Sean, who has been tweeting regularly since the end of last year, had started a Twitter account a few years back when it first began. 'It was very slow and there was almost nobody on it, no followers. The whole idea was immature and people hadn't latched onto it or built a community,' he says.

When Sean and I progressed from DM to email and live Skype chats I asked him outright if he was a geek Lothario, a Twitter Don Juan. He was offended and protested that no, he most certainly was not. He had just emerged, battle-scarred, from a 15-year relationship that produced a now nine-year-old child and in which he had been staunchly monogamous. He preferred the company of women, he said, and perhaps engaged in harmless flirtation but nothing more nefarious. And harmlessly flirt he did, most notably with Blackittyblack, an attractive 27-year-old single mother and artist from Okalahoma City. I had no interest in viewing sswayze, charming though he was, as a prospective partner so I was embarrassed to register illogical and ridiculous twinges of jealousy over his attentions towards kitty. How was it possible to experience even a hint of such feelings in relation to someone you've known less than two weeks, whom you've never met in person, and on whom you have no designs?

Herein lies the magic of the internet. One cannot know or love another online in the usual way and there is an unavoidable unreality and spectre of absence in all online relationships that denies closeness in the normal sense. At the same time, as if we are masked at carnival, the internet loosens inhibitions and tempts us to reveal ourselves more quickly and in ways we might not day to day. People do cyber-porn in place of real-life sex for two reasons: it both suggests eroticism and refuses it. It offers the form without the content. The content is frightening: exposing yourself to another, and not just physically, requires outrageous courage and maturity. When that courage and maturity (or the opportunity to develop them) are lacking but the desire remains, the form can become fetishised and accessed 24/7 on the internet. In short, online connection provides a facsimile of what's possible, an illusion of relationship without the usual risk or challenge.

So it is that online relationships, with their suggestion of what's possible, however remote, can trigger strange reactions. Internet friendships can be a genuine meeting of minds, and heartfelt connections made online, via Twitter or other forums, often result in real-life relationships (there are Twitter meet-ups taking place all over, including in Sydney, Melbourne and Brisbane) but so long as they are limited to an online existence these relationships, like cyber-sex, offer a concentrated form of connection without its full-bodied, complex and unlimited potential, which creates a condition of confusion. When you hit it off with someone, like I did with Sean, without the solidity of bodies and the boundaries they establish, free-floating vulnerabilities can come into play that are more to do with a facsimile of possibilities than reality or intention.

Might Twitter then, like internet porn, be seen as addictive, a substitute for concrete engagement, a sign of ailing spiritual health? When I first joined up and tweeted that I probably wouldn't stay long I was met by a knowing and good-humoured reassurance that I too would end up hooked. I asked Sean, who seemed to be constantly tweeting, for his thoughts. 'I'd like to think it's not addictive but I have spent a fair amount of time there,' he admitted, before adding, 'Anything that feels good and doesn't hurt anybody—I don't know if that's a problem.'

The thought 'classic denial' came to mind. I do think Twitter's addictive but then I'm of the view that almost anything and everything can be and that rather than being the exception in this culture addiction is the norm. As I told Sean, in my experience addiction is located in the person rather than in the substance or process itself (though some substances are also, of themselves, physically addictive). And so when I noticed a somewhat compulsive quality to my tweeting in those first couple of weeks I recognised it as an old tendency to seek connection to avoid feelings of loneliness and seek validation to avoid feelings of inadequacy.

After a couple of weeks of regular contact sswayze seemed to disappear. Not entirely—he still tweeted at times, though much less frequently and he was absent from the timeline and Skype for long stretches. I fretted that maybe I'd said something that bothered him. I recalled a previous discussion, about Aboriginal art, and a comment I'd made about taking him to see some if he ever made it to Australia and I cringed at the thought that my friendly, throwaway offer might have been misconstrued as romantic hope. Finally, after some days I emailed and asked why he hadn't been around. He replied sweetly about being busy with offline work, spending quality time with his daughter and being consumed with RL (real life) 'nonsense'. And so, after its heady beginning, and in the face of respective RL demands and the time difference, our twittership slowed to a more evenly paced dialogue maintained by blips, spots of jousting in the timeline and occasional Skype conversations.

My twitterverse is largely inhabited by American and Australian twits due to the fact that the majority of Twitter users are American and Firstdogonmoon's introduction of me ensured a substantial Australian base. Though Twitter is, by nature, global, individualistic and non-nationalistic, there are notable differences between the styles of American and Australian twits. Americans are prone to earnestness and the circulating of profound quotes and pearls of wisdom, while Australians tend to be dry, ironic, cynical and above all irreverent.

For example, in response to the #followfriday trend, in which Americans tweet a string of recommendations of who to follow, fulltimecasual, a Melbourne-based, self-described 'New Media Fucktard', posted the following tweet: '@people @who @do @a lot @of @these @tweets @are @really @fucking @annoying #followfriday.' Once, after I had tweeted that I had things to do I didn't care for, followed by the statement 'fuck the chores', OkayStill excitedly suggested we start a group called #fuckthechores.

One of the lovable smart-arses, sicsicsic, started a 'twibe' called #cuntards, of which I am a member along with Glebe2037, SylviaDiscount and several others. The group is supposedly about being mindless lemmings, dental floss and genetic mutation but mostly it's to do with being silly and taking the piss.

It's easy to see why a novice would be unimpressed. In May Nielsen Online released a report stating that though people were signing up 'in droves', more than 60 per cent stop using Twitter after a month. This research cast into doubt the hoopla about Twitter taking over the world, particularly when it made the point that Facebook and MySpace had double Twitter's retention rates when they were starting out.

Needless to say this news was tweeted and TheMonkeyBoy summed up the attitude of the core community: 'Good riddance. The best ones keep going ;-) People that give up stick to their status updates on Facebook.'

Firstdogonmoon has a different take on those who fail to get the Twitter point. 'To people who don't understand Twitter I say to them, "Do you sit in front of a computer all day?" And if they don't—tiddly pom. For someone who does you run it as another application in the background and why wouldn't you?'

Like Firstdogonmoon I spend most of my Twitter time with those who share my date and time zone and who sit in front of a computer for much of their waking life as we do. There's Brisbane-based sweetheart kissability, photographer and all around good guy Glebe2037 and resident wise guys yonderboy and ninjamoeba. OkayStill is a smart and funny earthmother who tweets from Townsville and TagAlongTess is, like me, currently manless and catless; we exchange blips and quips about singledom. Then there's SylviaDiscount and middleclassgirl, the adult embodiment of the cool kids at school. They tweet warmly to each other and to certain other twits but not so much to me.

I want to be Sylvia's friend and appreciate her droll one-liners such as 'Covered in cats' and 'Listening irritably to young people talking'. She also relays announcements about her 'fella'. Once she tweeted, miffed, that he'd returned from having spent the day with his ex, another time he was giving her grief for accidentally melting his hat in the dryer. Indeed Sylvia, more than any other twit I know, makes a kind of art form of her tweets, which I sometimes think of as one-sentence novels. I am surprised by the evocative poignancy of tweets like 'Once a girl that worked in a shoe shop told me she hated people's feet' and 'Train. Financial planner explaining in detail to his companion how his pay rises are structured over 3 years.'

It's hard to know to what degree you're being deliberately shunned or rejected on Twitter because the twitstream moves fast at times. People are often multitasking and regularly moving away from their desks, so tweets inevitably get missed. Sylvia and I do tweet occasionally but middleclassgirl and I rarely engage.

For those of us who like to think of ourselves as too evolved and highbrow to be seeking the approval of faceless, sometimes nameless 'entities', it can be confronting to experience moments of self-doubt in a medium that is at once meeting that human need for connection while also frustrating it. As well as being enjoyable and compulsive, Twitter can be boring and hurtful, though I'm yet to witness any serious spats or bad behaviour, perhaps because I tend to follow a more mature and literary crowd. Firstdog, who also blogs at *Crikey*, has written about Twitter, specifically the business of following and being followed and the insecurities that surface when favourite twits don't follow you in return. This is no small point: the crux of Twitter is whom you follow and who follows you. This is what will define your Twitter experience. 'You find your community,' says Firstdogonmoon. 'Mine is a geeky, cartoonist, weirdo, lefty community and we reinforce each other's fabulousness.'

For some Twitter becomes a popularity contest that promises vital affirmation. These twits are driven by a need to get as many followers as possible and seem to dedicate their online life to recruiting and campaigning to that end. There are those who might rather die than have fewer followers than followees. Some seem obsessed with being useful. Java4Two, a young mother and educator from Minnesota, posts such a dizzying number of helpful links I get tired just watching her. I imagine her furiously negotiating countless open windows, searching, cutting, pasting, updating. Twits like Java4Two often list 'social networking' or 'social media' as their raison d'être in their bio.

There are even tragi-comic Twitter guides and videos available that offer tips on successful twittering. One guide promises to show people how to 'have relationships like rock stars'. I posted the following tweet in response: 'Twitter guide says, "Have relationships like rock stars"—what, you mean do coke and fuck 15-year-old virgins?'

What is it then that we get from a community like Twitter? Why tweet?

'I like the immediacy of it. I like that I can drop in and out of conversations. I like that I laugh at it all the time because people are funny,' says Firstdog. 'People say it's micro-blogging but I say it's mini-showing off. You go on there and say, "I thought this. Aren't I clever?" '

'This is the first time we've ever been given the opportunity to communicate freely and easily with each other. Before the development of the internet communication was slow and controlled,' says Sean. 'There's a global consciousness awakening and people are becoming more aware we're in a fishbowl and the differences between us are mostly trivial. I think it's a positive force in the world and that's why it has such a huge uptake. It's building a beautiful communication network where like-minded people get together and solve problems in a way that's quite egalitarian. Everybody has a voice.'

It's not hard to imagine some serious-minded philosophy student working up a poststructuralist or post-poststructuralist reading of Twitter. If I were such a student where might I begin?

One could go old school and employ Jacques Lacan's 'mirror stage' notion of the lifelong structure of subjectivity, the ego-ideal 'I', and the sense of self established through the identification with the images of others (or narcissistically with a reflection in the mirror, which becomes a kind of other), with which to posit that desire (born of lack) for the Twitter timeline is the desire for the Other as a locus in which speech is formed.

One might reinforce that with a spot of deconstructionist theory by way of Derrida's analysis of *différance*, which, like Lacan, views the 'I' (along with all signifiers) as generating its 'self' relationally. One could take a different route and try on some Deleuze and Guattari for size, dressing Twitter up as a 'body without organs', the 'virtual' dimension of the body that houses potentials not manifest in the actual body and which may be actualised through union with other bodies by way of 'becomings'. Or one could ponder Twitter keeping in mind Nietzsche's statement 'Talking about oneself can also be a means to conceal oneself' but that might make for a very short thesis.

It's hard to imagine the young philosophy student going past Jean Baudrillard, whom Nicholas Carr refers to as 'technology's prophet' in his March Encyclopaedia Britannica blog entry <http://www.britannica.com/blogs/2009/03/technologys-prophet-its-jean-baudrillard-not-marshall-mcluhan>. Baudrillard, suggests Carr, is the obvious guru of the ether age, beginning with the premise that 'Those that know the technology cannot see beyond it, and those that don't know the technology cannot see into it. Both end up trafficking in absurdity.' Baudrillard, asserts Carr, described 'the twitterification phenomenon ten years before it became a phenomenon', before concluding that 'Mass media reaches its natural end-state when we broadcast our lives rather than live them.'

Twitter is a contemporary community like no other in the history of humanity and yet sometimes I find myself staring at the scrolling timeline, weary of wordplay and small talk, unmoved to join in. There are moments when I feel empty and lonely in the face of it, when I long to say or hear something more than potted platitude, textual posturing and nano-confession, when I pine for not just connection but intimacy. This is when I know it's time to go offline for an experience not available on Twitter or anywhere on the internet—that of going deep within and far beyond the performative self.

Some say Twitter jumped the shark when Oprah joined in April, that its hipster movers and shakers are poised to bail as its moment of glory is consumed by the baser aspects of mainstream culture, but Paul Boutin, writing for the *New York Times*, insists 'that's like saying the Beatles were over after they appeared on "The Ed Sullivan Show" ' and that 'Twittermania has only begun.' Only time will tell.

CLASS ACT: GOOGIE WITHERS AND JOHN MCCALLUM

BRIAN MCFARLANE

As I talked to the McCallums in May this year, I had to keep reminding myself that they are both in their nineties and that they've been in the business of entertaining us for over seventy years. Anyone who saw them in any of the films or plays in which they co-starred will know how well they played together professionally. As you watch them together now, complementing (and complimenting) each other, you can't help wondering how much of their professional success was a spin-off from a stimulating partnership off-screen or off-stage. It seems timely to pay tribute to them for what they achieved in the performing arts in Australia and elsewhere.

GOOGIE

Googie Withers came to prominence in British films in the 1940s, when British cinema was enjoying its finest hours and when there was a flurry of memorable women stars. If they are not well known today, they certainly were then: Sally Gray with the eloquent voice and slightly melancholy mien; patrician Valerie Hobson; Ann Todd of the ambiguous, chiselled blonde features; Phyllis Calvert, so much smarter than the goody-goody image that was foisted on her; Margaret Lockwood, flaring her nostrils and baring her cleavage in a refined version of passion; sexy bad-girl Jean Kent getting into a lot of entertaining trouble; and Anna Neagle being so ladylike that you wanted her to slip on a banana skin. But Googie Withers was something else. She was bold, beautiful and sensual. She routinely gave men a run for their money, and they were better men for it, in films such as *The Loves of Joanna Godden* (1947), as a lady farmer who succumbs to a neighbouring chap but is still wearing a tie at the end, so that he needn't think she's going to go all frilly and feminine.

Withers had been around for more than a decade before this, having made twenty-five films in the 1930s. Many of these were 'quota quickies' (films made to satisfy legislation about how many British films exhibitors had to screen), but there are two things to note. Several of these swiftly and cheaply made program-fillers she appeared in were directed by maverick master Michael Powell, who would be important to her later career, and one that was distinctly *not* a quickie was *The Lady Vanishes* (1938), directed by Alfred Hitchcock. She is in the opening sequences, in her underwear at first, then in a no-nonsense plaid cloak. 'And *there* was another unpleasant man,' she recalled of Hitchcock, having just summoned up some of Powell's cruelties to actors and others. They didn't, however, intimidate Withers. When we discussed this she recalled how she'd told Hitchcock off for some nastiness, and she said, 'I was as assured then as I am today.' John McCallum, who happened to be passing at this time chipped in with, 'And that's very assured.' No wonder, then, that in the forties she commanded the screen with such éclat. 'I never wanted to play the Phyllis Calvert parts,' she said (neither did Phyllis Calvert, but that's another story).

Having made a start, in the thirties, on Hitchcock and Powell, not to speak of gormless Lancashire comedian George Formby (in 1939's *Trouble Brewing*, she ended up in a vat of beer with him), Withers imposed herself on the forties with apparently effortless authority. She was involved in two 'Resistance' war films, *The Silver Fleet* (1943), with Ralph Richardson, and Powell's *One of Our Aircraft Is Missing* (1942), in which she spirits a British bomber crew out of occupied Holland, and you actually believed she *could* do it. Sliding up and down the social scale as few British actresses could, she sashayed through the immaculate high comedy of *On Approval* (1944), undaunted by her distinguished and much older co-stars, Beatrice Lillie and Clive Brook; murdered her way through *Pink String and Sealing Wax* (1945), prior to throwing herself over a Brighton cliff; ran a sheep farm in *Joanna Godden*; helped a convict ex-lover to escape in *It Always Rains on Sunday* (1947); dealt with a mermaid threat to her marriage in *Miranda* (1948); and wielded a stethoscope with conviction in *White Corridors*, the 1951 release that crowned a decade of memorable achievement in film. And just to keep herself busy, she was also starring on stage, in plays as varied as J.B. Priestley's Utopian allegory *They Came to a City* (1944) and Noël Coward's brittle but dazzling comedy *Private Lives* (1945) as the maddening, mercurial Amanda.

The accommodating arms into which Withers surrendered herself in *Joanna Godden* belonged to John McCallum. He was born in Queensland, where his father was a well-known producer and entrepreneur and ran the Cremorne Theatre, but was largely educated in England, including drama training at London's prestigious RADA (Royal Academy of Dramatic Art). Withers was in Hollywood when she was told that her leading man for *Joanna Godden* was to be John McCallum. 'Never heard of him,' she said, and she returned to England, to the Romney Marsh, where it was to be filmed. As she came down the stairs of the hotel they were using on location, a small elderly man at the foot of the stairs introduced himself as John McCallum and watched with great amusement as her face dropped. Well, he *was* John McCallum, but father of the handsome leading man whose proposals she resists through the film, accepting them on a partnership basis at the end. Among the ranks of leading men at the time, he struck a convincingly virile, intelligent but sturdily uncomplicated note: less dangerous than James Mason, less leery than Stewart Granger, much taller than Dirk Bogarde or John Mills, and refreshingly free from limiting class associations.

He'd had theatrical experience before the war, both in Brisbane and in the United Kingdom, with the Old Vic Company no less, but after war service he was back in Australia, co-starring with musical-comedy diva Gladys Moncrieff in *The Maid of the Mountains* and *Rio Rita* in 1945. He directed his first play there, *The Wind and the Rain*, and this is worth noting in view of his later multi-faceted career, when he was as likely to be directing as acting. As to film, he greyed his temples to play Muriel Steinbeck's second husband and step-father to Ron Randell in Eric Porter's family melodrama *A Son Is Born*, but if you wanted a film career in 1946, Australia was hardly the place to be, so he took himself off to England on the *Aquitania* with a lot of homeward-bound ex-servicemen. In his first film there, *The Root of All Evil* (1947), he showed Phyllis Calvert that a woman's true vocation was marriage rather than business, and got away with this in a way that would be unthinkable today—or to Withers even then, as his next film, *Joanna Godden*, would show.

His leading-man image didn't act to straitjacket him in films. He was equally convincing as the patient farmer suitor in *Joanna Godden*, Withers' unshaven convict ex-lover on the run in *It Always Rains on Sunday*, the cyclist hero of *A Boy, a Girl and a Bike* (1949), the Australian pineapple-grower who rescues the beauty queen from who knows what corruptions in *Lady Godiva Rides Again* (1951), and best of all as the police officer in *The Long Memory* (1952), tormented by his wife's involvement in the case he is investigating. *The Long Memory* was directed by the great Robert Hamer, who had sent Withers over that Brighton cliff in *Pink String*, put her in danger from McCallum on the run in *It Always Rains on Sunday* and did some uncredited work on *Joanna Godden*.

He will do as the nexus that links the subjects of this piece, especially since they both admired him more than any other of their directors. And by this time they had become, in Withers' words, 'what would today be called an "item" '.

GOOGIE AND JOHN

Individually impressive as their work was, and on film at least the evidence is still there, the *partnership* has been extraordinary. There have been other distinguished theatrical/

cinematic duos: for a decade Laurence Olivier and Vivien Leigh dazzled us and bestrode the entertainment world, almost inventing the notion of 'celebrity'; Sybil Thorndike and Lewis Casson were married for sixty years and often performed together, in Australia and elsewhere. However, it is arguable that no other combo has exhibited quite the same *equality* of achievement. Thorndike's larger-than-life personality on and off stage tended to overshadow Casson's more muted persona, and the Oliviers' glamour foundered on personal difficulties and her nagging sense of not being up to the acting standards he set. In the McCallums' case, Withers has an immense filmography and theatrical role-call, whereas he has the more diversified involvement. She is an actress par excellence; he is a director, producer and theatre company CEO as well.

It used to be said (perhaps sometimes by disaffected local actors) that Australian commercial theatre wasted money on bringing from overseas acting names who were well past their prime—if they had ever had one. There was some truth in this, I suppose, when one thinks of the likes of Jessie Matthews or Evelyn Laye, who had shared fame (and a husband, though not at the same time) in 1930s England, but were no longer in a commanding position when they reached Australia in the early fifties. But this unkind perception was not to be levelled against the Oliviers in the late forties or the Cassons or Ralph Richardson in the mid fifties, and it was certainly not the case with the Withers–McCallum partnership when they arrived in 1955. In fact, the mid fifties was a very bullish period for commercial theatre in Melbourne. The Cassons and the Richardsons (with wife Meriel Forbes; Withers remembers their fractious relationship) were doing two plays by Terence Rattigan, *Separate Tables* and *The Sleeping Prince* at the Princess, while round the corner in Exhibition Street the McCallum partnership made its Australian debut with Alan Melville's comedy *Simon and Laura* and yet another Rattigan, *The Deep Blue Sea*.

These latter two plays drew very fruitfully on the McCallum–Withers co-starring team. In *Simon and Laura* they played a pair of married television celebrities whose off-screen sparring is at odds with the ideal they present on the box. It was a smart, witty satire at the expense of television procedures and images, perhaps a case of one medium feeding off (or slinging off at) another, and the supporting cast drew on Australian stalwarts such as Bud Tingwell, Lettie Craydon and Bettina Welch. McCallum and Withers had made a couple of amusing lightweight comedies for the Rank Organisation in the late forties—*Miranda* and *Traveller's Joy* (1949), both from West End successes—and they brought a snappy stylishness to the eponymous pair in *Simon and Laura*. The other play they did in that year (they toured the two round Australia and New Zealand in 1955–56), *The Deep Blue Sea*, offered a contrasting dramatic challenge. McCallum played the RAF-ish and raffish lover of Withers's suicidal Hester. Jean Kent, who'd also played this role in England, as had Dames Peggy Ashcroft and Celia Johnson, had no hesitation in saying to me in interview (1989) that she thought Withers was the best in the role. Indeed, in contrast to the sophisticated comedy playing of *Simon and Laura*, she was here heartbreaking in her delineation of a passionate woman trying to hold on to Freddie, her unreliable lover. John McCallum told me that he didn't feel he was right for Freddie, the role played by Kenneth More on London stage and on film, but somehow the greater inherent firmness of McCallum's persona worked very effectively, and perhaps more subtly, in suggesting and highlighting Freddie's defining shallowness.

As McCallum pointed out, these plays ran for six months in Melbourne then, whereas now, perhaps a result of the dominance of television, they'd be lucky to last four weeks. His views on the changing patterns of the entertainment arts in Australia, where they settled in 1958, are worth noting as he has been influential at various times in theatre, film and television. When he wasn't acting, and for more than a decade in the sixties and seventies he wasn't, he was otherwise engaged. He'd accepted Frank Tait's offer to co-manage J.C. Williamson Theatres Ltd in Australia in 1958, and in this role he was responsible for administering the company's eight theatres, which meant keeping them full with shows the public might be expected to patronise. This position meant that he also directed a number of these, as varied as Ray Lawler's *Summer of the Seventeenth Doll* follow-up play *The Piccadilly Bushman* (1959), the second company of *My Fair Lady* (1960), which had been such a huge hit in Melbourne that Sydney was getting restless for its own production, and in 1970 he directed it again at Her Majesty's Theatre, Melbourne. He was also responsible for JCW's production of the musical *Camelot* (1964), which is much remembered for the evocative settings designed by Melbourne's John Truscott, who went on to win an Oscar for designing the film version.

He also took Williamson into film production with *They're a Weird Mob* (1966), negotiating an agreement between the firm and British director Michael Powell (Withers' 1930s and 1940s director) to make the film for $600,000. It was a great hit in Australia, though the rest of the world was largely immune to its affectionately drawn stereotypes. But the decade for cinema in Australia was the seventies and by that time McCallum was deeply involved with the burgeoning local television scene. The children's adventure series *Skippy* (1968–70) spawned a film spin-off, *The Intruders* (1969), starring Ed Devereaux and the titular kangaroo of the series (there was a rumour that a number of kangaroos had shared the title role but that is surely a matter of interest only to other kangaroos). He was looking for subjects that would be peculiar to Australia and the next two series he produced qualified indeed: they were *Barrier Reef* (1971–72) and, drawing on Arthur Upfield's popular crime-solving Aborigine, *Bony* (1972–73), in which New Zealand–born James Laurenson played Detective Inspector Bonaparte. McCallum had difficulty in selling *Boney* in the United States, where potential buyers felt there should be guns on obvious display and in frequent use. Withers guest-starred in several episodes and I'd particularly like to see the episode called 'Boney Hunts a Murderess'. Surely her murderess-training in *Pink String*, at Ealing in 1945, would have stood her in good stead for this, in which McCallum also played a role.

He directed and designed Neil Simon's *Plaza Suite* (1969–70), in which Withers starred, a play that gave scope for her gifts for provocative comedy. (She'd done chirpy, mischievous blonde comedy leads in the thirties, more elegant high-comedy types in the forties, and thereafter her comedy style blended sophistication and human warmth.) They were happy to act together, and did so many more times both here and in London, in *Cocktail Hour* and *The Kingfisher* in Melbourne, and, as late as 1998, a revival of Wilde's *An Ideal Husband*. They were fondly regarded by critics and audiences as a team, but, as they point out, they were prepared to work separately when it seemed appropriate and it was never made a condition of employing one of them that the other should also be involved. And while McCallum was occupied elsewhere, Withers would appear as a slatternly wife who nearly loses her husband in *Woman in a Dressing Gown*, at Melbourne's once-lovely Comedy Theatre, or Madame Ranevskaya in *The Cherry Orchard* and the conniving adventuress, Mrs Cheveley, in *An Ideal Husband* for the Melbourne Theatre Company (both 1972). Or as the smartly dressed prison governor in the long-running TV series *Within These Walls* (forty-two episodes, 1974–75), which was bought for Australia but suppressed after five episodes so as not to compete with the Grundy Organisation's *Prisoner*. In England it was hugely popular and Withers remembered being greeted everywhere as 'Governor' or 'Gov', and a street delinquent coming up to her and saying, 'I wish you were my mum.'

Withers starred under McCallum's direction in *Nickel Queen* (1971), the mining-boom comedy set in Western Australia. It is a good-natured film in which she plays a pub proprietress with her ear to the ground for a nickel strike, and she does it with style and good humour. The film was a big hit in Western Australia but didn't enjoy this success elsewhere. She subsequently played in two more Australian films, both with European connections: *Country Life* (1994), the outback reworking of Chekhov's *Uncle Vanya*, in which she wasn't pleased to be made to look frumpy but is a warm, human presence in the film; and *Shine* (1996), the David Helfgott biopic in which she incarnated Katharine Susannah Prichard, despite the latter's son telling her she was wrong for the role. When I taxed her for not making more films here, she said there were no others she could have done because she never felt she'd mastered an appropriate Australian accent.

McCallum, meanwhile, was producing more television series (*Bailey's Bird*, *The Highest Honor*) and got entangled as executive producer in the fraught filming of *Attack Force Z*, with its stars-of-tomorrow cast led by Mel Gibson, Sam Neill and John Waters. Their last appearance on the Melbourne stage was in 1998 in a handsome production of *An Ideal Husband*, which they'd done at the Old Vic two years earlier—Withers this time as Lady Markby deploring the upward social mobility of curates, and McCallum with an amazing range of 'harrumphs' expostulating his way through Lord Caversham, disapproving father of the play's dandy hero. And there was a final brush with Wilde on the London stage in 2002 with Vanessa Redgrave in *Lady Windermere's Fan*, a mere forty-eight years since the McCallums first appeared together there in Ronald Millar's *Waiting for Gillian* (1954), presented by Laurence Olivier at the about-to-be demolished St James's Theatre. Withers recalled a semi-drunken rebuke from Michael Redgrave's mother, Margaret Scudamore, to American Sam Wanamaker correcting him when he called it *Saint* James, instead of St James's. Withers co-starred with him there in *Winter Journey* (1952), in the role of the put-upon wife she so movingly repeated in Australia in 1960.

    McCallum and Withers had once been prepared to do all the necessary publicity to promote plays and films; like real troupers they never underestimated the importance of keeping in the public eye. Talking to them now, there is something inspirational about them. To films they brought the kind of character-training the stage had required; to the stage they brought the kind of easy naturalism that film had demanded. Yet it's not just a matter of what they've achieved, separately and in tandem, but also of the rich sense of an amused, tolerant humanity they now exude.

LOCAL LUNAR LANDINGS

MICHAEL WINKLER

When I am away from home I find it comforting to look up at the night sky and know that my family and I are all under the same celestial blanket. This was why I stood on a road in Ernabella looking at the blazon of night stars as the desert temperature neared zero. I was with a local teacher and we talked about indigenous and European astronomy. I had read about the astronomy of the Boorong people, but this was quite different. It seemed that perhaps we are not all beneath the same sky after all.

In the space of one week, by serendipity rather than design, I visited both ends of the Australian continuum. My week began under stars in a remote Aboriginal community in the Anangu Pitjantjatjara Yankunytjatjara Lands. It concluded in a high-rise apartment on Gold Coast Highway, Surfers Paradise, where the flamboyant wattage renders stars invisible.

While the two destinations fit into easy dichotomies—desert/coastal, spiritual/hedonistic, poverty/rampant commerce—my experiences of them had unexpected similarities. Continuums are curved. The extreme at one end bends to touch the extreme at the other.

The desert terrain was mesmeric, transfixing. It was an ecology based on the almost total absence of water, with landforms that might be found on the moon. I have visited Aboriginal communities on a few occasions. This Anangu community on the Pitjantjatjara Yankunytjatjara Lands was superficially familiar to my middle-class eyes—the omnipresent dogs, the cars and trucks left lying where they conked out. But it was also different to the other communities, in the way that Aboriginal peoples across the nation are different.

Anangu culture is strong. Being with the residents while they spoke together was a profound reminder of my European status. I talked to whitefellas who have lived and worked in the community for years, who speak the language but accept that they can never truly understand the culture. Being an outsider hoping to know Aboriginal culture is like looking at the night sky: you might learn every star on display, but can never know how they are linked together, never grasp those connections every bit as mysterious as the constellations that lie beyond, present but out of sight.

I still had red dust on my boots when I arrived in Surfers Paradise. That was a second lunar landing of sorts, and the culture shock was no less profound than it had been in the desert. In the Anangu community, I could not get over the suspicion that I was on a different globe. In Surfers, among my fellow tourists, I could not shake the feeling that I was overseas.

A friend once suggested to me that if the *Big Brother* household provided the entire gene pool and made everything crude and loud all the time then you would have something like Surfers Paradise. Commerce is triumphant. Flesh, 'fun' and the free market are rampant. Tomorrow's temperature matters; global warming does not. You eat ice-cream, look through shops full of foreign-made Australiana souvenirs, marvel at the tans and enhancements of the golden-haired locals.

In the Central Australian community you can buy art and have it shipped to any address, anywhere. You just won't understand it. In Surfers, I tried and failed to find a post office. Perhaps Australia Post seems too akin to a public sector entity—an affront to the one true path of capitalism. Dozens of shops will sell you a postcard, but only a sleuth can find a stamp or a post box. After the initial sale, the transaction is over. Maybe no-one ever writes on the things. Maybe visitors are rendered pre-literate by the primitive attractions of the sun temple.

After landing at Coolangatta we drove inland to visit relatives, then approached Surfers Paradise from the north. My first view of the city made me laugh aloud—the skyscrapers scraping the sky, a cartoonish rendition of Gotham in pastel and grey. And the glass! It conjured other cityscapes, at other times, glimpsed firsthand or with an artist's eye, but the applicability to Surfers was tangential rather than direct.

When I initially encountered 'On First Looking into Chapman's Homer', I thought Keats was describing a completely new discovery, the great vivid wash of Chapman's text splashing across a tabula rasa. Later I learned that he had already read Homer in translations by Pope and Dryden and perhaps others; when he sat up all night with his pal reading the Chapman text, the wild surmising and planetary swimming was due to the (pleasing) variations from the versions he already knew. Keats was not quite twenty-one, but already had enough background information to analyse his reading through the frame of already acquired knowledge.

So it is today—only more so, with the easy accessibility of information. The surprise for me, given that I live in the suburbs of a city, was that I was more disconcerted in a metropolitan setting (Surfers) than in the desert community. Like many Australians of my generation I have read plenty about the central desert, but little on Surfers. For a place firmly lodged in our national consciousness—'a trip to the Gold Coast' might be the second-greatest Australian dream—it is decidedly underrepresented in our culture.

There are exceptions: Helen Garner, whose eye never fails her, wrote in *Postcards from Surfers* that '. . . blurred in the milky air, I see a dream city: its cream, its silver, its turquoise towers thrust in a cluster from a distant spot'. Later she records that: 'In the morning the rising sun hits the front windows and floods the place with a light so intense that the white curtains can hardly net it. Everything is pink and golden.'

Google helps me establish that both John Tranter and Liam Ferney have written poems called 'Surfers Paradise'. Gig Ryan namechecks it in 'Loose Red'. John Millett released *The People Singers: The Surfers Paradise Poems* in 2005. I hadn't previously come across any of these poems. When songwriter Kev Carmody's Elly leaves the Diamantina River country and enters prostitution, 'She gazed up at the tall glass and concrete walls / At Main Street Surfers Paradise.' Carmody, a long-time outback stockman, nails Surfers not just as the Janus face of the bush but also a site of sin.

I cannot find any other cultural items minted in honour of—or in response to—the great Australian holiday destination. Where are the visual artists intersecting with the glass sarcophagi of Surfers? Where are the songs, the comics? Where are the novels that pull apart the entire Surfers phenomenon and explicate something central to the national consciousness? It seems an odd lack, and something that could be profitably redressed; this is a place of personal resonance for generations of holiday-makers, somewhere as worthy of explication and exploration as, say, Central Australia.

By contrast, the vast red interior is not only part of our national race memory, but also part of our cultural iconography. As has often been noted, it is extraordinary that a nation with such extreme demographic distribution—clinging to the coastal rim like frosting on a glass—should maintain a cultural obsession with the desert. I remember schoolrooms with faded prints of paintings by Albert Namatjira and Tom Roberts and spooky Russell Drysdale. School library books offered bush yarns and impenetrable, unpleasingly elliptical dreamtime stories. As an adolescent I read a dozen or more of Arthur Upfield's ponderous Bony novels, absorbing knowledge about 'half-castes' and the dingo fence and bores identified by number rather than name. I didn't know about Burleigh or Broadbeach or boardriding.

Films from *Jedda* (1955) onwards have gloried in the interior, and several movies from recent years are indispensable for anyone wanting to know about Australia beyond the concerns of coast dwellers. Certainly they inform my response whenever I venture outside my sphere of comfort (roughly bounded by the limits of the Melbourne tram network).

Desert Australia's modern story is examined in the underrated *Dead Heart* (1996), which depicts some of the hopelessness experienced by those who try to work on either side of the racial divide. It is hard as flint, tough on all characters regardless of pigmentation. Equally valuable is Ivan Sen's *Beneath Clouds* (2002), in which sweeping visuals match the rookie actors' performances in breadth and impact. The other crucial modern outback film is *Welcome to Woop Woop* (1997). It is horribly flawed and was derided by critics on release ('as flat as a kangaroo spread across a highway', wrote Luke Buckmaster for *In Film Australia*; and 'desperately unfunny' according to Stephen Holden in the *New York Times*), but the guts of this film—the surreal Woop Woop and its shambolic grotesques—is important and potent. Creator Stephan Elliott's representation of remoteness is as resonant and valuable as Arthur Boyd's urban insights in his Brueghel-influenced 1940s phase or his outback meditations in the 1950s. Elliott's dystopia and its denizens add a layer of valuable discordance to our apprehension of non-coastal Australia.

Woop Woop is a screeching contrast to the ballyhooed Tourism Australia cinema advertisement by Baz Luhrmann. The latter provides a Manichean vision of an Australia where desert sand functions like stardust, where toilers in Manhattan's dark satanic mills have greed-grime washed away by Kimberley waters, and a whole continent bends to the urgent task of a Stateside sales manager's self-renewal. It uses an Aboriginal child not as a decorative bauble but as an otherworldly talisman. It pretends Australia is a nation without Surfers Paradise. Apart from any marketing success it might have had, it was culturally worthless because it had no grounding in truth.

These books and films provide foreknowledge that shapes my vision whenever I step into red dust regions—not powerful enough to obviate the urgency of direct experience, but providing a prism that prevents me completely apprehending new things as 'new'. In a recent *Text*, Moya Costello wrote that Murray Bail's *The Pages* is 'set in the same anonymous west of the Blue Mountains [as] *Eucalyptus*. I barely remember my pre-Bail perception of the bush, so dominated is it now by Bail's representations . . .' For me, travelling to Aboriginal communities in Central Australia involves the (involuntary) recognition of dotted lines between current experience, past memories and cultural antecedents—in this case, most prominently, the films mentioned above plus Peter Goldsworthy's *Three Dog Night* and that novel's odd, lingering character Felix.

It seems to me that the centre of this country is inherently strange. This is its attraction, or part of it. Perhaps if I lived there permanently it would become less strange. Perhaps you have to be born there, part of a people born there for multiple generations, to avoid dislocation, however partial. If you are not part of the land, you are not part of it. You are just a visitor with a head full of cultural way-paving.

And yet it has a place in me. So many attempts to explicate it, from stumble-footed 1970s television documentaries to the contemporary online magic of 'Us Mob' (www.usmob.com.au), have guided my response to this geographic, social and emotional frontier country.

But in Surfers Paradise there is no cultural frame. There is no Gold Coast equivalent of *Woop Woop* unless you count the unintentionally askew *Coolangatta Gold* (1984) or the little-seen *Crooked Business* (2008). Counter to intuition, I have less cultural guidance in this oppidan agglomeration than I had in the desert. The gaudy verticals are as difficult to explicate as the centre's insistent horizontal. There are echoes of Jeffrey Smart's urbanscapes, but an equally apt visual reference point might be the drawings of Escher. In a bad mood, you might consider staging a Kafka adaptation in any of the high-rises—but I was in a good mood. I was somewhere new.

So we trawled slowly along the shopping strips, looking for the middle of the city. Wrong: there is no middle. Real estate commerce dictates that property value is calibrated in linear distance to the beach, not radial distance to a civic hub. Searching for a centre means you are asking the wrong question; being anywhere in Surfers means you are already in the middle of where you want to be. This confidence can easily transmute into arrogance. The proliferation of skyscrapers is architecture as hubris. The notion of constructing teetering towers above sand dunes, oblivious to potential rises in sea level or falls in tourist favour, is breathtaking. Allowing buildings of such design that they obscure the sun for beachgoers during the best portion of the day may seem like vandalism to some, but it is also a feat of derring-do. Conventional laws do not apply. Similarly, the ongoing presence of 'meter maids' (shabbily clad and depressing, the two I saw, their thick layer of fake tan insufficient to keep out the cold) is a refusal to accede to the modern world's understanding of common-sense feminism. Surfers builds its own meaning and as long as tourists arrive, it can keep doing so. This pigheadedness is worthy of wonder, if not of admiration.

You can't see the stars from Surfers at night. You can't see the sun from the beach in the afternoon. You can't see a post office anywhere. There is excellent surf, but most people swim in small hotel pools. A pleasant middle-aged woman stopped us on a street corner and offered $10,000 if we went to the top floor of a nearby building and heard about the apartments they had for sale. She was not the least perturbed when we declined. During the day, tourists are sucked into the suburban hinterland to visit 'the worlds'—Wet'n'Wild Water World, Dreamworld and so forth. Movie World is the big daddy. We spent a ponderous day there celebrating our heritage through leaden tributes to *Lethal Weapon, Shrek* and *Scooby-Doo*. Along with thousands of our fellow revellers we then funnelled back into the heart of Surfers Paradise for food and accommodation, because everywhere in Surfers—as we know—is the heart.

I do not dislike the place. On the contrary, I found its oddness captivating. I just struggled to fit it into a frame, handicapped by the paucity of cultural interpretations that may have assisted me with understanding a place as alien as anywhere on this continent.

With eagle eyes I stared at the Pacific. Silent, upon a peak in Cavill Avenue Mall.

GRIEF AND DESIRE

MAGGIE MACKELLAR

There is a storyline in the popular medical drama *Grey's Anatomy* where one of the main characters, Izzie Stevens, continues to have a sexual relationship with her dead lover, Denny. This man, a patient with a chronic heart condition, dies shortly after the two discover their love for each other. He dies despite Izzie's heroic and morally dubious efforts to save him. Izzie is suitably tormented and grief stricken. Eventually after cooking batches of muffins, uncontrollable bouts of crying, not leaving the house for weeks, Izzie hauls herself from the edge and rejoins society, albeit in a terribly fragile state. Then, just as things seem to start going well for her (we know this because she has returned to work; she is washing her hair; she is having sex with a gorgeous new boyfriend), Denny reappears as a ghost. Izzie can see him, speak to him, feel him, taste him and have much enviable sex with him. Poor Denny seems as trapped as Izzie. He is unable to leave Izzie or convince her to leave her new boyfriend. And Izzie won't let Denny go either, she hangs on to his presence despite her increasingly fluid grip on her own sanity. Eventually, after much soul searching and hand wringing, Izzie tells Denny he can't visit her any more and he walks away from her one last time.

Apart from the amount of sex she was having, I found myself identifying with Izzie Stevens. Desire and grief are odd bedfellows and yet the writers of *Grey's Anatomy* have brought to life the very real disconnections between the grieving body and mind.

Of course they can't help but spoil this when they later reveal Izzie has aggressive cancer, which is the cause of these vivid hallucinations. But still, for a moment they articulated desire in grief.

Anne Carson, in the introduction to her recent translation of four Euripides plays, *Grief Lessons*, asks why tragedy is so vital an art form. Her understanding speaks to our modern obsession with soap operas: for Carson the tragedy becomes a frame that can be put around our grief. Inside the safety of that frame the violent expression of grief and rage can be played out without 'you or your kin having to die'. Watching unbearable stories about other people lost in grief and rage may 'cleanse you of your darkness'. Nobody, writes Carson, wants to 'go down into the pit of yourself all alone'. This idea, of having actors go into the pit for you, is exactly the sacrifice Izzie makes for us, the viewer. Her longing for sexual intimacy with her dead lover articulates loss at a primal level. The writers, by making Denny real to Izzie, show her grief running from anger, denial, sadness, tears through to an alarming depression. Then finally they allow her desire. For all its taboos it seems a legitimate question to ask: what happens to desire when you are living in the thick mist of grief? Desire, that swirling presence in the night.

My husband—closest companion of eleven years, father of my five-year-old daughter and an unborn son—died with intent. He was in hospital, in a supposed safe ward for people who cannot leave alone the thought of harming themselves. He was in a session with a doctor and his parents; he walked out of this session, scaled a three-metre wall, ran to a cliff and placed himself in an impossible position from which to be saved. In the end, despite the efforts of rescue workers, he fell to his death. This was not a new thing; this was something he had tried repeatedly to accomplish over the preceding few months. And yet this was such a new thing that I, his wife of more than a decade, still cannot quite accept this was my husband at the centre of an inevitable drama played out upon a cliff top in the wind and rain of a squally July afternoon.

How do I tell you about us? About him and me, I mean. How do I stitch for you a pattern where you might peek at what I had and what I lost. You see, I'm being seduced in my dreams. My anger is being unpicked even as I hug it closer.

You think you know someone. You are so sure of someone. Then, one morning there is this new Thing. This new Thing that is a very old Thing. A Thing that has been buried so deeply that the skeleton, when it appears, is prehistoric. It is something you do not recognise as being of the world that exists between the two of you, you and the person you thought you knew. It is a dinosaur. It is a monster. You feel like it eats you alive.

One day he says, 'This has happened before.'

'What has happened before?'

'Losing my mind,' he says.

'Oh, really? What do you mean?' I'm scrabbling, for air, for the ground, for something to hang on to.

He says, 'You don't know everything about me. There's something I've never told you.'

'Oh.'

Then there appears a terrible pit. Knowledge is a strange and powerful weapon. Before it I'm destroyed. Our life together, the last ten years, is sliced up.

'What do you mean you had a breakdown?'

'I spent six months in and out of hospital when I was eighteen . . . I spent my nineteenth birthday in the psychiatric ward . . . They wouldn't let me out . . . I actually don't remember how long I was there—sometimes it feels like it was my home— sometimes I forget I was ever there . . . They diagnosed me . . . They never diagnosed me . . . I walked out and never suffered from such a moment again . . . Until we met I suffered from these episodes but never told anyone.'

The contradictions darken the sun.

I have been loved, cherished, celebrated and I have been deceived, manipulated, treated as less than nothing—all by the same person. When I stand in the daylight I can see no track back to my golden husband. It's only in the dark, in the stillness of the night that he appears before me. He comes softly; he comes to me from a deep cave. I retreat, run from all we had and still his body presses and I feel it against mine. It quakes, and the memory of the movement is steeped in my blood, branded on my skin. I've withdrawn, laid my weapons down, turned my back but still he pursues me.

Some context—a little chronology—a touch of clarification perhaps, so this trajectory is laid out. I am pregnant. My husband gets sick, very sick, very quickly. He dies. Ten weeks later I have my second child. A beautiful boy. I have a job as a lecturer in the history department at a university. I publish my first book. My mother helps me bring up the two children. Life starts to look possible. She enables me to work by taking over much of the child care. My son turns two. My mother is diagnosed with cancer. Ten weeks later she too is dead. I struggle on working full-time. Without my mother I can't keep going. I take some time off from teaching and return to the farm where my mother grew up and where I spent much of my childhood. At the end of my leave I don't return to my job. I realise I've come home to stay. I have escaped the city and the pressure and I've rescued my children. But I haven't left the grief behind.

I'm being seduced. The dreams come long after he's gone. Coming back to the farm has allowed him access to me. While I was working the stress of getting through the day suppressed him constantly. I could go to sleep and know he wouldn't break the water again. In this time my anger had shifted and solidified, so it no longer surfaces, hissing. But just as I begin to believe sleep to be a safe place he returns. When he first comes my anger is so fierce it breaks though the crust of time and I run, hurling abuse for him to stay away. I wake sobbing, my eyes as dry as ice. The next night and the next night and the night after that he comes back. I greet him cautiously. I find myself questioning the certainty of my anger. Could I really be so angry? Could my body really be so heavy? Could our future be so destroyed?

He coaxes me out. Dares to touch me. He may be back in my dreams but as he pursues me I wake to remind him that he is no longer in my life. How could he think that my trust would tremble and re-form before his touch?

But my dream body and his dream body deceive me. They know each other so well. Soon, though it's a long time since he died, he's back in my bed. He visits with increasing frequency but I resist. Desire rises. Curled in bed on a night where cold presses down like death, I half wake and his shudder runs the length of me. I reach out to hold him and my body, released from the discipline of the day, roams free. But these are places I don't want to revisit. There can be no happy ending here. Say I forgive him. Let him stay. Where does that get me? Does it get me to peace? I think not. It leads to a place where I'm naked under the sky, where the world around is edged with mountains and the earth underneath is scoured by fierce cold, and heat and wind.

The weak light pushes in against the cold, it plays with the presence of the night, but it's relentless and soon the dark is gone. When I wake the world is white, frost has reached the top of the trees and the murmurs of early spring are silenced. I reach over to the place warmed by his body. The sheets are cold. I stay in bed, buried beneath the blankets, unwilling to face another day. A song rises in my head: 'heavy blankets, heavy blankets, cover lonely girls'. I wonder again how I got to be here.

Who knew that his absence would change the shape of me physically? I keep expecting people to comment. It's so obvious to me that my body shouts his departure to the world. I move differently, I stand on the earth with less certainty. Those close to me must put my changed appearance down to my struggle to cope, or the grief I'm living through, or perhaps they just don't want to look too closely. But it's more primal than these explanations; quite simply, my body is different without him. Its boundaries have shifted, I no longer know where I start and finish. I used to be so physically confident. I used to feel powerful. But I've changed and there are times when I feel so disconnected from who I used to be that I wonder whether I'll ever reclaim myself. This body is as foreign to me as the life I'm living without him.

In Sydney for a visit, I go to the Korean Baths. In this hidden female place I squat and scrub beneath the shower, and something of my reserve is sloughed off. I've booked myself in for a massage; a Korean woman strides into the room and calls my number. I follow her and she motions to me to climb onto the massage table. My identity has been stripped along with my clothes and almost blissfully I embrace the anonymity of being naked. The room is full of slabs of female flesh. I'm doused in warm water, wrapped in warm towels, pummelled, pushed and most divinely touched. Why do I think the hands that run over my back can feel his absence? Does this sound so strange that neutral hands, indifferent hands trace the shape of my desire? My body misses him in a craven way. It's not tormented by deceit, by hope turned sour, it simply wants. In this desire I am trapped. I feel duplicitous. Duped by my own body into wanting him back.

There is so much hurt, so much that can't be said, so many unfinished conversations. Yet still I desire. It's easier now I can acknowledge this. One of the harder things has been to shield others from the anger he lit in me. People expect grief in the form of tears, they expect softness and vulnerability, and I can't seem to show that I know I am not performing my grief *properly*. I know people want me to fall to pieces so they can comfort me. And it's not as if I don't want rescuing, I do, but I can't seem to give in to the expressions of missing him that people seem to feel they need to see. Instead they see me working, looking after my children, *coping well*. If only they could see him stalking me through my sleep, perhaps then they would understand.

Living out here I'm being reconnected to the land. Its mood seems to reflect my own sense of entrapment. For my inertia is made worse by the sudden return of the drought. We've waited for autumn rain. It hasn't come, the ground is hard and the nights are now too long and cold for the grass to grow. Tension curls around my waiting, flexes its muscle.

Last night it did rain. It fell as I bathed children, lit the fire and cooked dinner. Our house was a cocoon of warmth and light. Rain lashed the roof and windows and fled into tanks. There is nothing more intoxicating than the tattoo of rain on a tin roof. I slept inside its rhythm.

But there is not enough rain. It's violent and heavy and washes away some of the dust and fills the tanks for a moment but all it leaves in its trail is enough moisture to encourage a carpet of catheads—those vicious burrs sometimes called three-cornered jacks—that cripple the dogs and cause the new lambs to stagger and fall. The catheads have some strange component to them, because the sheep become addicted to them and won't eat anything else. The toxin in the catheads causes the sheep to swell in the sun, their heads become misshapen, their ears blister and fall off. Those most severely affected must be locked up in the dark of the shed and fed hay until the poison slowly leaches from their system.

I held myself so tight at his funeral, I felt absurd, but the tears wouldn't come. Instead I was swollen with our child, my tummy rounded and awkward, my breasts full and heavy. Fluid gathered in my body. Perhaps that was where all the tears were hiding, in my ankles and under my skin, supporting my swollen legs, my heavy head.

Who wants to be that dramatic trope of the pregnant wife farewelling a husband who will never meet the child so obviously present in her body? I smiled and groped my way through the day. I kept bumping into things, hitting myself on objects that loomed out of the dark. My body carried me through. I seemed to float some way above the crush of people. Only a young person's funeral attracts such a turnout. Everywhere around me tears flowed, but for me there was no release, the tears stayed trapped beneath my skin, a poison, which changed my shape.

The day of his funeral is a dream I find hard to wake from. I walk outside into the night and the smell of the sheep camped behind the house under the trees hits me like a shot to the head. I have to wake from that day, I have to find myself again, claim back my body and leave the spell of him behind.

I had this other dream, about another man. Can you believe it, me and another man!? I'm still so ensnared by my husband that I find it hard to believe my dreams are introducing me to someone new. Don't worry, it hasn't happened—yet. But in this dream I met a new man and straight away we fell in love. He was dark, possibly Italian with curly hair. He was wildly rich and thought I was beautiful. At last I had a new body and I felt long and slender in it. He seemed to have other girlfriends, but this didn't worry me unduly. We were in the city. Then we went to America where he mostly lived. We went to his university and while there I felt as if we wandered among his many girlfriends. Suddenly, as happens in dreams, there was an exam. I didn't have to do it but I did it anyway, and it seemed important to do well even though I had never taken the subject. I wrote and wrote; the essay was partly concerned with Australia, I can't recall what I wrote, only that the ideas came to me fully formed and fast and that all the other women wrote very little and seemed perplexed. I was connected again—my body firm, my mind strong.

It was such a strange dream, to be loved by someone other than my husband. Though as I think of it now, I can't recall feeling any love in return. There's a blankness, as if all the love I have to give has been poured out and whatever it is this new man and I share, it's not what I had before. But this absence of love seemed of little significance. It was comforting to imagine myself attracted to someone without sacrificing everything. I did feel clever in comparison to the other women in his life, I was different to anyone he'd been with before. For this new man had many women and he didn't care to hide them. I craved to see his past and what I needed to show him was that I was not naive, not young, not deceived by his wealth or good looks.

But despite this dream, I can't let go. I go back over the day of the funeral and I see I didn't really participate. Others farewelled my husband, made their peace, tried to understand, but I was a bystander. The crowd streamed past me. They took him with them, all their different versions of him. But I was left standing there on the side because now he was dead I didn't know him any more. I had no idea to whom it was I needed to say goodbye.

What I want is some precise definition, something scientific, that can be measured telling me who my husband had become and where the man I married went. Is this perhaps why I persist in seeing my grief as something that must be mapped? I want to see its outline, because perhaps in its shadow I will be able to see him again.

I use words to find my way back into him. His illness stole everything I thought I knew about him. Four years later, after a birth, after my mother's death, after saying goodbye to him under the light—it's only now as summer comes on, as the drought tightens, as the words spill out that I finally give in to tears and then find it impossible to staunch them. I'm no longer easily comforted. I'm no longer caught in the whirl of imagining juggling his illness and a newborn baby. Instead I'm thrown back into the memories of our ten years together. I hear his laughter as we paddle on the ocean. I see him tossing our daughter high in the air above the waves and I look at our children and count, once again, what he and I have lost. I want to take a sharpened flint stone and cut myself from breast to breast. I want everyone to see the scars and know that however they imagine loss to be, it's bigger, harder, higher and deeper.

I'm left now without even dreams to sustain me. I don't know why they've stopped, or where they've gone, but now I have to conjure him from memory, he doesn't come when I'm unaware. While I was dreaming, my love and anger were both fuelled. Without them, without him, I'm empty, somehow made passive by his absence. Death defies me.

The calendar on the kitchen wall marks the marching days and I watch, detached, as anniversaries pass; birthdays, death days, ordinary days all seem unlived. One of my most valued ways of coping was to have that calendar full, especially on the days when I didn't want to look at the date. But despite my careful planning, C disarms me by requesting his father put in an appearance on his birthday. He's actually not fussy about which father—the whole concept for him is rather vague—fathers are definitely something everyone else has, but his puzzled expression pulls me up and I wonder if I've been right in not actively seeking a replacement for these kids.

C's confusion is not so hard to understand, because parts of me refuse to acknowledge the movement of time. How can four years have passed while I still struggle daily with his absence? Mostly he put out the garbage and now it mounts with frightening frequency and still I turn away, hesitant with the expectation that the job is not mine to perform. At least in Sydney all I had to do was drag the bins up the stairs and out to the street. Out here there is no garbage service and I wonder how I could have been resentful at the short walk from the side of the house, the huff and puff up the stairs and the miracle of empty bins in the morning. Now I let bottles and papers spill in the corners of the garage, the bins stink as I stamp another bag of rubbish into the top of them. I make an effort for a while, washing milk bottles, shrinking them up, rinsing tins and squashing them down, but inevitably life takes over and before I know it I'm surfing the tide of rubbish out the garage door. Eventually a trip to the tip cannot be avoided. On Sundays a procession of utes and trailers pass my front gate on the way to the tip. I square my shoulders, load the car and join the blokes in the line-up.

I fight every definition his death throws at me. I fight till I can fight no more and lie exhausted in the dust. He is the invisible adversary I shadow-box through the day. Every gathering I go to, every kids' birthday party, swimming carnival, trip to the beach, every ordinary moment, I have to push him away so I can see what I need to say, what I need to do. I wonder as I walk away from a group of people if they can see us jostling together on the edges. I wait for his response, his opinion, his insight. Do others see the pauses in my conversation? Do they hear the gaps he should fill?

I finally ring a man who calls himself the 'PacMan', he's in the local yellow pages under 'rubbish'. For twenty-eight dollars a month he will take my garbage to the tip. It's a bargain.

Last night I woke because there was a snake in my bed. I had turned over in my sleep and as I turned I sensed a presence and opened my eyes. There was the snake, not curled beside me, not poised to attack but working its way across my pillow. I leapt for the end of the bed and then stopped, terrified it would see my flight as an attack. I was unsure how to get out of the bed without being bitten. I was frozen but my heart pumped against its cage and I was soaked in sweat. I inched my way from the bed, then panic took over and I scrambled for the floor. It was not until I was out of bed that my mind began to convince every other part of me that it was distinctly unlikely there really was a snake in my bed. Only then could I sneak my hand towards the light, my senses prickled, not believing it was safe. So you see I had a very different dream last night.

I head to the web for interpretations. I have a thing for snakes. I'm not alone in this and I'm never sure whether it's just low-level paranoia or if it's something else. But I sense the snake before I see it and often I'm convinced of its presence even if I don't see it. There is a spot as I walk down the lane to get the horses where I've seen a huge king brown and sometimes when I walk past I know it's beside the track watching me. I've had snakes in the chook shed and in the garden and we get some big ones up at the sheds and stables. These aren't harmless snakes. They are deadly browns, aggressive and quick to strike. My uncle is adept at killing them, though he'll leave them be if they are out in the paddocks. I'm not adept at killing them, though I'm determined to become so. But a snake in my bed! The dream-interpretation sites talk of transformation, shedding old lives, of learning to live in new skins. Perhaps . . .

THEIR HOOKS FIND HOLD DEEP IN OUR FLESH: PART SIX

AUTHOR Kate Fielding, ARTISTS Ben Fox and Mandy Ord

The extracts presented in this and the previous five issues of *Meanjin* are taken from a longer work created by author Kate Fielding and artists Mandy Ord, Clint Curé, Elizabeth McDowell and Ben Fox. It was originally presented as an honours thesis in the History Department of the University of Melbourne, and has been subsequently reworked with support from the Australia Council for the Arts.

Hummocks at Armstrong's Bay, between
  Warrnambool and Port Fairy Tocwool
Large Swamp between Merrang and Minjal
  Stations Yan-yeen. (Query—Yan Yan
  reservoir, water supply of Melbourne.)
        NAMES OF THINGS AND WORDS.
Fire Ween.
Lightning Yarone.
Thunder Mordan, meaning noise.
Rain My'ang.
Wind—Oorndoonk.
Sea—Meirtick.
Sky Moorneong.
Sun Tirng.
Moon Koorntarreng.
Stars—Kacki-tirng sisters of the sun.
The ground Merring.
Sea sand Kolak.
Stones—Mart.
Wood—Ween.
Leg—Yoorak.
Water—Pareetch.
Waterhole—Kilink. Sound produced by
  stone plunged into waterhole Kalink.
House Bard-ba-moorndook, meaning habi-
  tation erected by blows.
Knife—Marnhoot, marnhoot mattai, oat eat
  meat.
Dray—Barrangoart.
Axe or tomahawk Bartbartkoort.
Opossum rug Baloongo.
Blanket Kn'eolarr.
Opossum-skin ornaments worn round the
  loins at corroboriee Barrinteh.
Kangaroo-teeth necklace Maramar.
Boot Walle-walkeep dinang.
Hat Kn'ooparbirn.
Hair net Koorair Beem (net for head)
Ornament of emeu feathers worn round the
  loins while dancing Teerbarrum.
Basket—Bunaar.
Eel basket Narrabau.
Bucket—Popair.
Bone—Backie.
Stump—Tootoooort.
Fence—Nalloobun.
Yes—Ka.
No—K'ne k'ne.

In 1870 the *Australasian* featured an article written by Isabella Dawson that discussed Indigenous languages with which she was familiar.

The young girl who had played with the local kids...

...was now a woman taking notes.

In placing the following before your readers, the writer begs them to understand that, although the orthography is questionable, it is the nearest to convey sounds of many native words almost inexpressible.

Note.—When the letter k forms the commencement of a word with a consonant following, the k is not sounded, as in knee.

HUMAN BEINGS AND MEMBERS OF THE BODY.
White man—K'nauma'teitch.
White woman—K'nauma'teitchar.
Aboriginal man—Marr.
Head—Beem, a general name for all heads.
Hair—Arrat.
Forehead—Mittinch.
Ear—Wirng.
Eye—Mirng.
Eyelash—Knarrat-mirng.
Nose—Kapoong.
Lip—Woorong.
Teeth—Tung-ang.
Tongue—Talling.
Mouth—Oolang.
Throat—Yan (which means to pass or go, a person leaving; yannan, gone; yaunakie, must go).
Neck—Allum.
Shoulder—Kok.
Chest—Mart.
Waist—Aloork.
Navel—Pe-koorn.
Stomach—Tookooie.
Spine or Back—Aw-oorn.
Leg—Pirn.
Knee—Parring.
Foot—Toomang.
Hand—Wookartang, the giver t...
RELATIONS.
Grandfather—Kna'poorn.
Grandmother—Koorooky'e.
Father—Peepye.
Mother—Kneerang.
Brother—Wardii.
Sister—Kakii.
Cousin—Tow...il.
Uncle—M...min.

Cockatoo—I'youk.
Yang Yang parrot—Merrān.
Black cockatoo—Willān.
Rose-bill parrokeet—Kootch-kootch.
Blue Mountain parrokeet—Kallang'high.
Small green parrokeet—Yoo'kootch.
Lorry (common) parrokeet—Yoo'rakootch.
Pigeon—Koorāy.
Crow—Wāugh (cry).
Laughing-jackass—Koonett.
Swallow—Wee-which (cry).
LIZARDS.
Guana—Wirrakoot.
Lizard (common)—Moonie.
SNAKES.
General name—Koo'rang.
Black snake—Moo'rang.
Whip snake—Kir'tonsh.
FISHES.
Whale—Counter'bool.
Shark—Toorong.
Sting-ray—Mardān. When an object is hit by spear or weapon ... blacks exclaim "Mardān," in ... blow inflicted by the ... the tail of the sting ...
Blackfish (in fr... ...ar.
Trout—Yoo'ni...
Eel—Koo-yang.
Small fishes re... ...and only eaten by wom... ...oort-coort.

Common small b... ...ae-chook.
Bull-dog ant—Koo'n...
Jumping black ant... jump jump,
Sugar ant (large)—...
Flies—Menning.
Blow fly—Wooro...
March fly—Mor...

Crawfish—Ya...
Cuttle-fish—...
...rimp—Y... ...fingers.
...ou...

The Dawsons had returned to the Portland Bay District in the early 1870s, renting the farm 'Wurrong' near Camperdown.

Here in 1876 James Dawson was appointed the Local Guardian of the Aborigines — a government position designed to account for the generally older Indigenous people who refused to move from their land to mission stations. As well as 'overseeing' five Kooris who resided in the area, Dawson was an important point of contact for Indigenous people who had been removed to Framlingham. During this time, until his death, he was a frequent contributor to newspapers, local and otherwise, on issues surrounding the treatment of Aboriginal people. He was adamant that the violent dispossession of Indigenous people not be forgotten. When in 1884 Henty Jubilee Festival organisers debated whether to allow Aboriginal people to perform a 'Korroboree,' Dawson publicly expressed his disgust that 'the original owners of the land' would be excluded from 'participation in the festivities so deeply concerned with their fate'. When consulted by the 1877 Royal Commission on the Aborigines for his opinions of the missions, James asserted it was a 'mistake to imagine that they [Indigenous people] are not fully aware to the position the occupation of their country by the white man has placed them in, and of their strong claims on him for proper maintenance and protection'. He also contended that Indigenous people should be allowed to practise culture and to move freely on and off the missions, an opinion shared by few of his contemporaries.

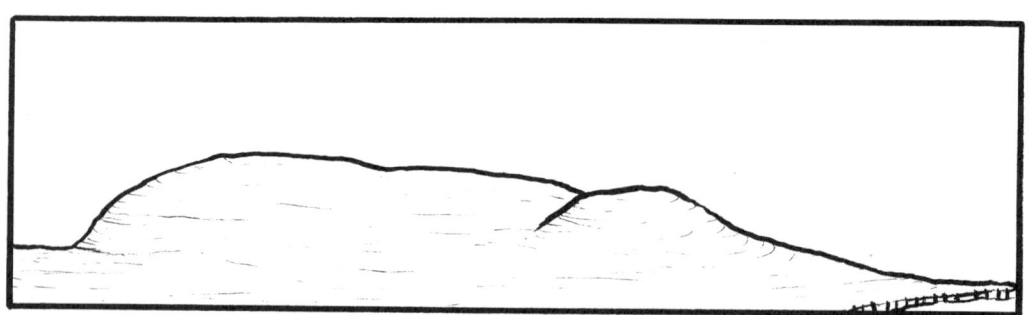

... his interest in Indigenous people also had more morbid scientific overtones. Dawson had provided the 1873–76 Challenger scientific expedition with a skull and other skeletal material from a local Indigenous person.[3]

As well as supporting the collecting interests of others, Dawson amassed his own extensive collection of 'ethnographic' objects from local Kooris, which he displayed in a local museum along with his collection of taxidermied animals.

These actions were driven by the popular scientific notion that Indigenous Australians were a race doomed to die, a belief both Isabella and James publicly declared. The tragedy of the Dawsons is that, like von Guerard's painting of Tower Hill, they were simultaneously representing and creating the 'dying race'.

In 1881, driven by an urge to present the language and culture of 'an ill-used and interesting people, fast passing away' James published an amateur ethnographic study of Western District Indigenous culture, *Australian Aborigines*.[4]

While James claimed authorship, Isabella's central role in the project is indicated in Dawson's introduction, in the similarities between the letter she wrote to the *Australasian* and the book, and by surviving photos of her 'taking notes' from groups of Indigenous people. James is eager to state that his text was based directly on the words of the Indigenous people whom he described, and it seems Isabella's linguistic dexterity was thus crucial to the project.

Despite his anxiety to highlight his superior sources, James tells us little about the identity of those 'sable friends'.

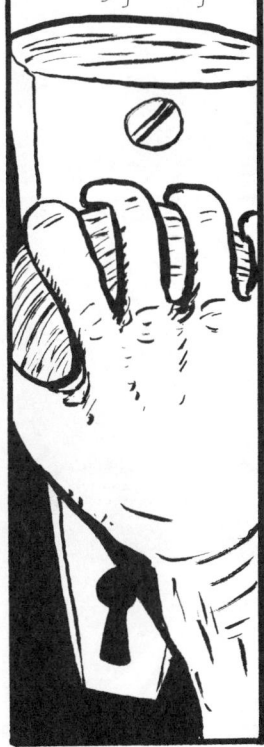

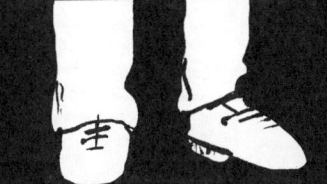

It is instead through the work of a later historian that we know something of their lives.

YARRUUN PARPUR TARNEEN 'VICTORIOUS'
Daughter of chief of Morpor tribe
'The very Intelligent Chiefess'
M. Wombeet Tuulawarn
Resided Framlingham Mission
d. 1882

WOMBEET TUULAWARAN
M. Yarruun Parpur Tarneen
Resided Framlingham Mission
b. 1832
d. 1882
'Rotten Spear'

WEERATT KUYUUT
'a Professor of languages, astronomy and geography'
b. c. 1801

Adult during 1840s Interracial Conflict

JOHNNY DAWSON
b. 1842 Instigated that Kangatong Reserve be designated for Aboriginal Use

HENRY DAWSON
b. Kangatong
Protested removal of 'half-castes' and closure of Aboriginal Missions

In his conviction that Indigenous Australians were a dying race,

James Dawson metaphorically buried his friends even as he collected their words, memories and culture. Pitched as a study of a valuable but vanishing culture, *Australian Aborigines* missed out on the scoop. It is a valuable, if patchy, reconstruction of pre-contact Indigenous culture. But because they maintained a limiting fascination with rarified 'traditional' or 'pure' culture, Isabella and James lost the chance to record the contact zone history and culture of which they had been a part.

James undertook a literal burial of this 'dying race'. In 1884, at significant financial and emotional cost, he exhumed the body of his friend Wombeetch Puyuun ('Camperdown George') with his own hands,

and reburied him under an obelisk.

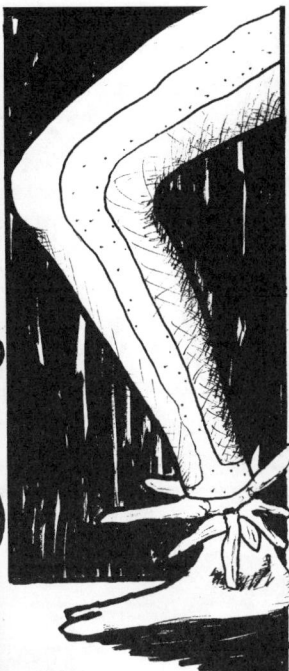

And yet the Dawsons surrounded themselves with living Kooris. In May 1884, upon James' return from holiday in Scotland, Isabella organised a corroboree to celebrate.

James' hidden authors, Isabella included, represent a diverse range of experiences of the contact zone.

The Kooris told her how the first white man spied by Kooris at Port Fairy was considered to be made of fire, due to his smoking pipe...

... the first ship considered to be either a huge bird or a tree growing from the ocean ... and the first bullock, with a sheet of tin tied across his face, a Muurmup.[5]

They told these stories with 'great glee' at their ancestors' mistakes.[6] The Kooris were able to laugh at their misconceptions, but the Dawsons were barely aware of theirs. Imagine if the Dawsons and their 'sable friends' had conspired to tell the tale of the Europeans' arrival and settlement in the south-west with a particular eye to the misconceptions of *both* sides.

Imagine if instead of an anthropological study, the Dawsons had undertaken to publish an account of European settlement in the Western District, incorporating the perspectives of a variety of Indigenous and European people who had lived through that time.

Imagine if, instead of being told stories of girls dragged from the sea,

I had been given a book collaboratively written by Yarruun Parpur Tarneen, Wombeet Tuulawarn, Weeratt Kuyuut, Isabella Dawson, Johnny Dawson, Henry Dawson and James Dawson.

NOTES

1   James Dawson, response to letter requesting opinion of present state of Aborigines dated 28 February 1877. Royal Commission on the Aborigines, 'Report of the Commissioners appointed to inquire into the present condition of the Aborigines of this colony: and to advise as to the best means of caring for, and dealing with them, in the future, together with minutes of evidence and appendices', John Ferres, Government Printer, Melbourne, 1877, Appendix C: Certain correspondence, Letter no. 5, p. 100.

2   L. Bayer to A.G. Stephens, 6 June 1903, Ab 120 Bayer L., catalogued under Dawson, Mitchell Library. Extract in Jan Critchett, *Untold Stories: Memories and Lives of Victorian Kooris*, Melbourne University Press, Melbourne, 1998, p. 232.

3   Critchett, *Untold Stories*, p. 233. This not the only example of apparently contradictory concern for welfare and science—though honorary superintendent of the Society for Prevention of Cruelty to Animals, he was also a passionate hunter and taxidermist: from obituary for James Dawson, *Camperdown Chronicle*, 21 April 1900.

4   James Dawson, *Australian Aborigines—The Languages and Customs of Several Tribes of Aborigines in the Western District of Victoria, Australia*, facsimile edition, Australian Institute of Aboriginal Studies, Canberra, 1981 (1881), quote from Dawson's preface, p. v.

5   Dawson, *Australian Aborigines*, p. v.

6   Critchett draws this quote from an inscription on the back of Weeratt Kuyuut's portrait: Critchett, *Untold Stories*, p. 142.

WAXWORK

RACHAEL WEAVER

HE FIRST PRINCIPLE OF A wax model is not just verisimilitude, but to be lifelike, though wax reproduction is a form obsessed by death. The affiliations between wax and mortality seem intuitive and easy to trace. Everyone has observed, or at least heard about, the waxy complexion of a corpse. Morticians and embalmers have much in common with waxwork artists; they all strive, in various ways, to display death to its best advantage. The associations come to us automatically. When startled by some commonplace ghoul—a stranger lurking unexpectedly, perhaps, in the back room of a poorly lit junk shop—it's his waxy skin we remember later. Lifeless, glassy eyes are nearly always set off with a deathly waxen pallor. Cadaverous traits are often expressed in terms of the strangely neutral medium of wax, which carries nothing of the stink of the grave, of decomposition, of leaking fluids or parasitic infestation, though it does have a kinship with grave wax, or adipocere, the crumbly white substance that sometimes forms from the fatty tissues of a rotting corpse. The process is known as saponification and can protect the flesh indefinitely from further deterioration, preserving body parts and facial features and sometimes even organs in a naturally occurring cast.

Wax's pliability and luminosity as well as its surprising durability have made it the ideal material for replicating and exhibiting the dead, in death masks and waxwork effigies, most popularly, of crime victims and their murderers. The early works of legendary waxworks proprietor Madame Tussaud accomplished this almost at the moment death occurred. Under the careful tutelage of her uncle Curtius during the French Revolution, she drew inspiration as well as many of her subjects directly from the guillotine. After the severed heads were cast the victim's real hair was sometimes added as a finishing touch, along with vivid splashes of artificial blood. Tussaud continued her work long after her uncle's death from suspected poisoning, carrying on his legacy at the Cabinet du Cire with her husband until their separation in 1800, and a short time later she left France for England, never to return.

As well as transporting many models and historical relics from the original collection to her new quarters in the Strand, Tussaud took with her the guillotine used during the Terror, to be employed as a symbol of authenticity in future wax displays. In the first decades of the nineteenth century she toured the English countryside, exhibiting waxworks in provincial theatres and town halls. Following complaints about propriety by an Oxford scholar in the 1830s, the criminals were separated from royalty and the Chamber of Horrors—known initially as the Dead Room—was born. As the century progressed, the trade in murderers' relics greatly enhanced the gallery of villains and victims with the weapons and personal artefacts of notorious killers such as Maria and Frederick Manning, James Greenacre, and the poisoner William Palmer included in the exhibits. William Calcraft, one of London's longest-serving executioners, would often use his privileges to supply Tussaud's museum with a murderer's final set of clothes.

Famous murder trials always led to press and public speculation over the prices paid for particular items, such as Hampstead murderer Mary Pearcey's ominous black perambulator or the kitchen where Frederick Deeming killed his wife and children at Rainhill. The museum also received a cast of Deeming's head as a gift from Australia, taken after his execution at Melbourne Gaol in 1892. Murderers' relics and death masks share similar powers: they derive their potency from intimate contact with the dead. As Marina Warner writes, 'the crucial character of a death mask depends on its status as a relic, as the nearest remnant that can be preserved of a body before its disintegration'.[1] In celebrated cases, though, time was also pressing, so that living subjects were sometimes modelled and revealed to the public for exhibition moments after death, a kind of instant reincarnation in wax.

1 Marina Warner, *Phantasmagoria: Spirit Visions, Metaphors, and Media into the Twenty-First Century*, Oxford University Press, Oxford, 2006, p. 24.

Convicted felons often took pleasure in their future as wax celebrities and approached the drop courageously to perform their final words. Colonial waxwork entrepreneurs were as quick to claim the corpses of hanged felons as the wax artists of the great metropolises, lining up to wait with the anatomists while capital sentences were carried out. At a triple execution in Melbourne in August 1864, one of the condemned, Christopher Harrison, used his dying speech to offer his corpse to a local medic, Professor Halford, while another, William Carver, sought a place in the waxworks, with a request that 'his history should be published throughout the world'.

The cosmopolitan glamour of prurience and sensation offered by the waxworks was evident to aspiring subjects and audiences alike. In 1879 a man named Hilton threatened to knock his wife's brains out to secure a place in the Melbourne waxworks, while local theatre critic and coroner Dr James Edward Neild noted with wonder and pleasure 'how such things find their way out here to this new city where in general our home friends look upon us as dwelling in tents, and feeding on mutton, tea and damper'.[2] In a similar spirit of metropolitan sophistication, 'Mrs Jarley' conducted waxwork installations that toured Queensland and Western Australia, a homage to the seedy waxworks proprietor from Dickens' *Old Curiosity Shop*. Such associations appealed to a fascination with the macabre inherited from Britain and Europe, but in the early 1890s one colonial speculator established a floating waxworks to offer the old world something in return.

2 Quoted in Mimi Colligan, 'Waxwork Shows and Some of Their Proprietors in Australia 1850s–1910s', *Australasian Drama Studies*, vol. 34 (1999), p. 86. I have also drawn on some details from Colligan's account of Melbourne's waxworks for this essay.

Marketed to audiences as a convict ship, the *Success* was originally a passenger barque, built in the East Indies in 1790, and used for trade by the British. After a helmsman was killed at the wheel, a small wooden coffin was inlaid in its deck, marking the *Success* forever as a ship of death. On arrival in Melbourne in 1853, the crew abandoned sailing for the goldfields, and the ship was recommissioned as one of five new prison hulks moored in Port Phillip Bay, with seventy-two cage-like cells installed to contain 120 of the growing numbers of criminals—many of them ex-convicts—attracted to Victoria by the discovery of gold. After a prison gang murdered John Price, inspector general of penal establishments, in 1857, the hulks were abolished and the ship became a prison for seamen, a women's prison and a boys' reformatory.

In 1890 the *Success* was resurrected as a show ship and filled with wax figures of convicts from different eras. Models of bushrangers such as Henry Power, Captain Moonlight and the Kelly Gang were locked up alongside Price's killers, author–criminals Owen Suffolk and Henry Garrett and many others. Instruments of punishment and torture such as the 'necklet' and the 'coffin bath' were also shown, with lecture tours telling 'gruesome stories of atrocious horrors committed long ago'. Protests against airing such sordid colonial histories led to the vessel's deliberate sinking at Sydney's Port Jackson, but after six months on the ocean floor it was rehabilitated and the barnacles removed. Denied clearance by customs, the prison hulk finally left Australia for London surreptitiously in 1895, embarking with its cargo of wax criminals on a voyage of transportation in reverse. It remained on exhibition in the Thames for several years, a kind of floating monument to the return of the repressed.

The longest-surviving waxworks museum in Australia was in Melbourne's Bourke Street. Opening as 'Madame Lee's' in 1857, it was taken over and expanded by wax artist Ellen Williams the following year, who added several topical new displays, including effigies of the notorious murderers Chong-Sigh and Hing Tzan, who had recently killed a woman named Sophia Lewis, slashing her throat with a razor and almost cutting off her head. Williams also amalgamated the collection with the phrenological museum of her partner (soon to be husband) Professor Philemon Sohier and they began utilising the overlaps in their professions. Their 'Australian Waxworks Exhibition' soon became one of the city's most popular amusements, offering a comprehensive catalogue of local and international murderers and other criminals, as well as a range of more tasteful subjects, such as a tableau of the explorers Burke and Wills. A growing cast of live performers and freaks came to enhance the plastic displays, replacing an earlier series of subtler 'drawing room entertainments'.

By the late 1860s the family had become wealthy enough to sell off all their Australian interests except the Sydney branch of the waxworks, for which they were unable to find a buyer. They retired to France for several years before setting out on the return journey to Australia in August 1870, accompanied by 100 wax models, a dwarf, a giantess, two or three albinos and 'other nameless horrors' to replenish the Sydney show. But in sympathy with the kinds of tragedy and darkness that come so naturally to waxworks, the Sohiers never made it. Their ship, the *City of Sydney*, went missing in the southern Indian Ocean, somewhere around the Crozet Islands, and was thought to have struck ice, the corpses of its drowned passengers and crew floating in the bitter waters surrounded by all those waxen bodies, which probably outlived (or at least outlasted) them.

In 1873 when signs of life were detected on nearby Amsterdam Island, Sohier's brother in Nantes raised hopes that some of those aboard the *City of Sydney* may have survived. The British Admiralty was called on to investigate, and crew members of HMS *Pearl* soon discovered a neat cabbage garden and a well-made hut stocked with a range of domestic utensils on the island, but no castaway population. The remote place had been carefully cultivated, tidied and mysteriously abandoned.

The Melbourne waxworks continued operations under Sohier's partner Maximilian Kreitmayer, a German medical modeller who had bought into the company in 1863 and become sole proprietor in 1869. He went on to merge the waxworks with his Bourke Street anatomical museum, adding lurid (essentially pornographic) specimens and models of diseased body parts to the galleries of royalty, politicians, criminals and victims, and increasing the Vaudeville-style entertainments.

But the 'Chamber of Horrors' remained the waxworks' centrepiece, working—like Madame Tussaud's or Paris's Musée Grévin—as a kind of three-dimensional newspaper, in which contemporary and historical atrocities were re-created. The published catalogue shows the way child killers Francis Knorr and Sarah Makin were lined up near 'homicidal maniacs' such as William Colston and Deeming, while the usual cast of colonial Australian bushrangers kept company with urban murderers such as Thomas Dooley, Robert Landells and George Dean. Adding to the general feeling of violence was a model of the gallows from the Melbourne Gaol in nearby Russell Street, as well as a set of torture devices such as the 'pitch boot' and the 'iron broom'.

The popular desire for proximity to wax murderers has sometimes extended to criminals and their friends: the Melbourne *Herald* reported in October 1866 that Bourke the Bushranger visited the waxworks as his only outing when living as a fugitive at a pension in Lonsdale Street (he thought the waxworks should be blown to pieces). In 1880 while Ned Kelly was being held at Melbourne Gaol, the Kelly women supposedly visited the waxworks after calling by the prison, to critique models of their relatives as they were being created.

Wax effigies themselves have also been known to invite violent or criminal acts. At a Liverpool waxworks in August 1883 three men destroyed the wax figures in a display representing the Phoenix Park murders in Ireland a year earlier, in which Lord Frederick Cavendish and Thomas Henry Burke were assassinated. In Melbourne in May 1892 a woman attacked a likeness of Frederick Deeming with her walking stick, while as late as February 1954 a man smashed models of lords and politicians including Winston Churchill and the British home secretary with a hammer in Madame Tussaud's grand hall.

The kind of visceral power sometimes created by such attractions is hard to name. In a way, the uncanny impact of a waxwork killer—as an arch criminal's creepy double—is only an exaggeration of the sinister potential already possessed by such a being. Perpetrators of incomprehensible violence such as motiveless murder may display all of the outward characteristics of an ordinary human, but the moral blankness and brutality suggested by their crimes renders them unfamiliar, literally inhuman. Perhaps this is where the thrill of the waxwork lies: in the liminal zone between human and not human, real and artificial, living and dead. There always seems to be pleasure taken in blurring these distinctions, as shown in the 'Chamber of Horrors rumour' described by John Theodore Tussaud (Madame's grandson). The rumour, which persisted well into the twentieth century, consists of a 'popular delusion that Madame Tussaud's will pay a large sum of money to any person who spends a night alone with the criminals assembled'.[3] The story goes that nobody was ever crazy enough to try it for fear the wax villains would suddenly come to life, stumble forward like zombies and strike them dead.

3 John Theodore Tussaud, *The Romance of Madame Tussaud's*, Oldhams, London, 1920, p. 261.

INTERVIEW

IMMERSING THE AUDIENCE

SOPHIE CUNNINGHAM TALKS TO ROBERT CONNOLLY

Robert Connolly is the writer and director of the feature films *The Bank* (2001), *Three Dollars* (2005) and, most recently the film that is the subject of this conversation, the extraordinary *Balibo* (2009). He is the producer, together with his business partner John Maynard, of *The Boys* (1998) and *Romulus, My Father* (2007) (which won four AFI Awards including Best Film). Robert received a Centenary Medal for services to the Australian Film Industry in 2001 and was recently appointed to the new board of Screen Australia. We met to discuss the writing and making of *Balibo* just a few days after Connolly returned from East Timor and the film's first public screening in that country—and the day after I'd attended an early screening. The film had a profound effect on me.

Sophie Cunningham: Balibo is the most explicitly political of all your films, isn't it?

> *Robert Connolly: Yes, it's a piece of history, it needs to be looked at with great rigour, and it's uncomfortable for a lot of people. Think of the 1980s, of John Pilger's documentary of Gareth Evans and the foreign minister of Indonesia in the Lear jet flying over the East Timor oil and gas fields, drinking French champagne and signing the deal to share it, and celebrating sharing it when we know below a third of the population was dying and a massive famine was happening on our doorstep. I think there's every reason for that shame to be part of our own national story.*

The Boys was loosely based on a real story but it was much more fictionalised, wasn't it?

It was.

This was the first time you've worked so directly with a historical event.

Absolutely, yes. We used to talk about Peter Shaffer's play *Equus* where he'd read in the paper 'A young boy gouged the eyes out of eight horses', that's all he read, and he went away and thought: my God, why would a boy do that? and wrote a play about it, but never researched the specifics of that. *The Boys* was the writer responding to the Anita Cobby murder—'How is it that three brothers could do a crime together?'—but not researching the Cobby murder. *Balibo* is a piece of history, though it falls into the camp of speculating about what may have happened between characters and people.

Was it hard to keep on top of the creative process when you felt so much responsibility?

Yes. I met all of the families, those of the Balibo Five and Roger [East], and I met a whole range of Timorese activists and historians; I also met the President of East Timor—who is a character in the film. I was up there, and I think I mentioned in my speech at the screening, I was in Dili screening it for José Ramos Horta, I was sick in the stomach . . .

How did they respond?

They loved it. For example, in the massacre that we depict on the wharf, there's a woman who hands a child over. It's just a little moment. She was based on the wife of Nicolau Lobato, the president of East Timor at the time. For Australians it's just a moment in the scene, but for Timorese it's an iconic moment in their history. They killed Isabel Lobato. She handed over her child who is now in his forties and in the Timorese Government.

It was incredible to be in the cinema with them because it's their story. It was one of the great experiences in my life, actually.

Have the families seen it?

All the families have seen it.

I don't know how they sat through the murder scene.

Shirley Shackleton got up after it and went into the bathroom, she said she threw up, and then she came back and watched it again.

Each family watched the film separately at their own screening, and they were all quite incredible experiences to be part of. In casting those actors, I wanted to find actors who took on that responsibility too. They almost felt like they had to get permission to play those men.

There's something about the seventies re-creation footage of the Balibo Five ... I had a very emotional response to the film partly because of remembering news footage shot in the way you shot those scenes.

With cinema, it's a case of how do you take the viewer into that state? How do you create a sense of immersing the audience in something? As a director you've got someone sitting in a dark room for 100 minutes, captured. They can't get out—or they don't try to generally! How do you create an emotional space that they inhabit for that time rather than necessarily just a narrative ...

So in what conscious ways did you do that?

For the Balibo Five sequences you just mentioned we used the old lenses from the seventies, the Angenieux lenses. We did do some colour grading in post-production with this amazing colour grader, a South African guy, Brett Manson (he graded a South African film called Tsotsi, did you ever see that?). So he's incredible and he had a great eye for the colour. But because we shot on these beautiful Angenieux lenses ... there's so much you can do digitally now but I think imperceptibly those lenses really helped us.

Is it a blue light?

The colour palette is different and they're a little bit softer.

And you used those for the scenes of the five but not of Roger East.

The other stuff was really sharp: modern lenses to get more of a typical political thriller look.

It's such a complex story. How do we even know what happened to the Balibo Five? Because Roger East died, did the circumstances under which the Balibo Five were murdered have to be re-created?

East got some of the story out there. Horta did find three witnesses for him in real life, and those witnesses were the basis on which East got out the gist of what happened—that they were killed and that they had been murdered. Then there is Jill Jolliffe's book [Cover-Up: The Inside Story of the Balibo Five, Scribe, 2001] and her re-creations and witnesses.

I think the scrutiny that's been applied more recently though, the rigour with which the coroner, Dorelle Pinch, considered the events—she brought out lots of Timorese witnesses—has finally given us a definitive version of what happened. I'd been working on the script for five years so obviously it had been developed a lot before the coroner's findings, which were released in December 2007. That created a challenge.

I had wondered if there would be DNA evidence left, even today?

I know that there's a big issue about the remains. There's a box of bones that was buried in Jakarta. It's an amazing bit of history. On 16 October the Balibo Five get killed, 7 December is the invasion, which Australia clearly knows is about to happen, so in the interim period a rushed funeral is held in Jakarta for a box of bones, which is the Balibo Five.

And the Australian Government said they were killed in the crossfire?

They said that a bomb had blown up the house or something and there was talk of crossfire. But why at that point in history the Australian Government didn't take a deep breath and say 'We need to scrutinise this, five Australian-based men have been killed'... The Australian Government just accepted Indonesia's official line, and so quickly buried the bodies, which was all part of laying the clear foundation for this invasion that was about to happen that Australia had signed off on, as had America...

Is the current Australian Government nervous about this film?

I think on a practical level the Australian Government is deliberating about whether to honour the findings of the coroner of eighteen months ago, which were that two Indonesians who are significant figures in the Indonesian Government should be charged with murdering the Balibo Five. The coroner's findings went to the attorney-general, who then gave it to the federal police. They have to respond in some way at some point. This film will, on a very practical level, bring to public awareness this story in a way that will put pressure on the Australian Government to come to a decision about what it's going to do. I know that's the families' hope. There's part of me that can't quite believe that we're still so afraid of events of thirty years ago. If you think about the Vietnam War and how cinema has scrutinised that war ... it started only a few years after the war with films like The Deer Hunter.

The Australian Government doesn't know how to deal with the Indonesian Government, I suspect...

That's right, yes. And that anxiety is ill-founded because, as we know, history reveals all truths anyway. We know that the history of this time, whether it happens now or it happens in another ten years, will be explored.

Was it a decision not to mention specific Australian politicians? There was no mention of the specifics of the Australian Government's machinations. Was that because it was hard to do that in a naturalistic way?

There are two moments in the film where Whitlam is referred to. What I had to decide was, do I overtly make this like a documentary analysis of what was happening or do I use little moments and hope that they reverberate through the film? It's such a fine line because in feature films you need to allow the characters to not become a mouthpiece for the filmmaker's political views, but by the same token I knew the film would lack courage if it didn't refer to Whitlam and Suharto and the time. So it was a fine balance during the process of editing the film how much or how little to have of that.

Can you tell me when you made decisions to fictionalise and when you made a decision to stick with the 'facts'—and how that process worked?

I think we approached it with a very strong view that the murder of the Balibo Five and the murder of Roger East and the massacre on the pier were two significant moments in East Timor's history and in our own history. And that, as they were being contested and as over so many years they'd been concealed, we didn't want to further complicate people's view of what the truth of those events was.

It took so long to uncover the truth that to then add or change details would be problematic?

Yes. The coroner's findings were very helpful in that regard. We know that Brian Peters went outside. It's assumed that Tony Stewart was killed out the back...

The detail about the asthma attack, how did that...?

That came from a great interview with Shirley [Shackleton's wife] where she talked about Greg's asthma and about how scared he was about having an asthma attack up there. So that was part of a hypothesis about how the individuals were responding to the situation. But the essential thing is these men declared they were journalists and they were murdered because they were journalists, and they were murdered in cold blood. It was easier to depict the murder of Roger East, because the Indonesians killed him in broad daylight. I've always asked the question, if the Australian Government had shown more spine and stood up to the Indonesians about the murder of the Balibo Five, would Roger East have been executed so blatantly in public seven weeks later?

Why is his story less known?

I think when you're adapting any piece of history you begin with what you know from the public sphere, but when you dig deeper there are things that surprise you. For me, I approached the story about the Balibo Five, and then you discover the story of Roger East, and Roger East being a journalist in his early fifties. He's less glamorous, he was highly paid and working in PR, but he'd done various things. There was some evidence that he was on the passport blacklist that Wilfred Burchett was on. I think he had an anti-authoritarian bent, and his politics were complex. He wasn't a member of the Communist Party but he had an affinity with the left. Incredibly, he'd run an English-language newspaper under Franco, he'd covered the civil rights movement in South America, he'd worked in South Africa and covered apartheid. I found Roger East's story a fascinating juxtaposition with the story of the Balibo Five because the Balibo Five were all in their twenties . . .

In terms of finding the inherent truth in a work of fiction, Jane [Norris, casting agent] and I made a decision to cast men that age because I thought that cinema has an ability to conceal the truth in subtle ways.

That worked. There was a vulnerability to them because they were young. It also made you forgive their naivety. I'm thinking of that extraordinary scene where the Fretilin say, 'Hey, do you want to come on duty with us?' and they're half-pissed and staggering around in the bush in their shorts.

That's right, and it speaks of that time. I wanted to speak of their youth and to also look at the idea of the responsibility journalists were given at that point in history. It's interesting, you talk to Tony Maniaty, he goes there as a 26-year-old, he pulls himself out. There's no satellite phones to talk . . . there's no Fox News telling them what to do. Once they're there, they have complete editorial control. So the expectation is that these journalists get the story, film it, record it.

I think one thing we learned is they were very good journalists. You look at the material they did get out: they did scrutinise what was happening and get to the crux of things. But set against that Roger East, who's fifty-two. That scene where he's looking at the photos is there because I wanted to create the idea that he saw in them himself as a much younger man and he knew the predicament they were in because he'd been there himself.

Wiser but also more cynical?

That's right, and I hope that the Horta character stirred something in him and pulled him out of that.

Age is important in the film, isn't it?

That's right. East Timor is a young country. José Ramos Horta was twenty-six. And Anthony [LaPaglia] was really interested in that and how men respond to men. Horta seduces East, basically. In those early scenes he's seducing this older man. He's cast his spell and Anthony was very interested in that, not in terms of dealing with any issues of sexuality but . . . That meeting really happened. Horta had been in Canberra trying to meet Whitlam. Whitlam refused to meet him and he was coming back through Darwin. As we know now, ASIO was spying on him.

Did Oscar Isaac spend time with the real José Ramos Horta?

Yes, met up with him in Dili. They got on very well. Horta said, 'Well, I guess as George Clooney wasn't available, you'll do.' But they liked each other a lot. I needed to find an actor who you could believe would one day lead this country to freedom and win the Nobel Prize, so you've got to find an actor of such strong intellect and a little bit of mischief, as Horta had.

The fight scene by the pool between East and Horta is terrific. Was it a construction?

Horta said something interesting about that when he read the script: he said it didn't happen as it did in the script but it could have. Camus once said a similar thing about works of fiction based on fact, this idea that often the question is not whether something happened as it did but whether it could have. I don't make documentaries but I think that works of fiction can consider history in a way that is liberated from the nuts and bolts and is able to really get into the heart of the human experience.

Is it to do with the word 'immersion', which you have used?

Yes, I think with fiction you are trying to take the audience into that point in history and allow them to journey through it.

You very deliberately avoid the notion of the hero. Roger East is, at moments, slightly pathetic. I was really struck by the lack of vanity in LaPaglia's performance. The only thing I was unconvinced by was that his shirts seemed to be better ironed than the other characters'.

We thought about that detail! Roger East was in the navy. He was in Singapore Harbour as a 19-year-old when it was invaded by the Japanese. He saw great tragedy, he saw boats being destroyed. We got out his military records and saw he was discharged for a psychotic disorder. We discovered that meant he had post-traumatic stress syndrome, something now we're compassionate about. Anthony was very interested in the idea that there lay in him a fear of his own inability to cope. But on a practical level—there's a scene where he's got everything ordered to pack to go. He tried to keep principles he learned in the military. You fold your shirt. I thought the costuming in the film was just great.

The shorts!

That Shackleton did those famous pieces to camera in footy shorts that look like undies now!

Was the murder scene very difficult for the actors, was it difficult for you?

I did the film in chronological order, so I shot their murders as the actors' last scene. When they got on a plane, arrived in Dili, I got them in costume and shot within twenty minutes the scenes of the actual journalists arriving in Dili, so that I could get a sense of . . .

. . . that freshness and that sense of amazement?

That's right. So I cast actors the same age, I took them there, I took them on the journey and I took them to the point where their character was killed. They fell in love with these men they played.

You could see that.

Damon Gameau had Greg Shackleton's real diaries of his trip, so we were in these places and he's reading about thirty, forty years before. It was very moving for them. And Damon after the scene where he was garrotted he had a quiet moment. I went over to him and then I left him there because he was weeping. He'd been to Balibo, he'd stood where Greg Shackleton had stood to film the footage that he was murdered for.

I was very struck by the performance of Mark Winter, who played Tony Stewart. He was a very still character—a more spiritual figure. In the final scene he's sitting there thinking, well, this is it, what do I do now? Do I make it happen quicker or do I just sit here and wait? That's a very beautiful piece of acting.

Yes, he had a photo on the wall when we were filming that of Tony's real mum and his brothers and sisters, so he was really trying to . . .

. . . speak to them.

That's right. How do you contemplate those final moments? His death was the loneliest death, the last. The fact that he stands up and opens the door and goes out to his death knowing that it's impossible to avoid.

And the performance of the East Timorese actors is wonderful too. Particularly Anamaria Barreto as Juliana.

Yes, she lives in Darwin. Her grandfather was in the resistance with Xanana.

Is Juliana an actual character or a construction?

She's based on a whole heap of the CAVR [The Commission for Reception, Truth and Reconciliation in East Timor] interviews, one in particular with a woman in her forties who described being nine and witnessing the invasion and the parachutes coming down. I'm so indebted to the CAVR, who did the 8000 interviews, but also Jill Jolliffe's Living Memory Project, who have interviewed all these women who were tortured under Indonesian rule. These interviews are profoundly upsetting. The film didn't originally have the book-ends of the Juliana story, that came quite late.

I thought she was important because she connects the story of the Balibo Five more broadly to the East Timorese.

There are a lot of people who say, 'Yeah, yeah, five men died, but what about the 200,000 Timorese who died?' The Timorese don't feel that because they feel that the Balibo Five dying kept the story alive in the Australian psyche and that helped them to become independent. They talk about the Balibo Five as their own, it's part of their national story. You talk to Paul Stewart [Tony Stewart's brother], he says when he goes there, Timorese come up to him and say, 'We're so sorry for the loss of your brother in '75.' And he says, 'How many family did you lose?' The answer is often ten or twelve, and yet they still have this compassion. But it was a challenge for us. I hate this Hollywood genre of white men saving the Third World.

A certain cluelessness comes through . . . Tony Maniaty talks about that in Shooting Balibo: *that he wouldn't want to advocate that young journalists be so inspired by the Balibo Five's story that they fling themselves into these situations.*

What I hope is that the film puts their journey in the context of the greater tragedy of this nation . . . but that ultimately the film speaks of this country's ability to demand that its story be told.

It was such a small country.

In 1975, 600,000 people lived there and 183,000 died as a result of the conflict. An hour from Darwin. As a percentage the death toll is up there with the Holocaust. Thirty years on, 50 per cent of the population are under eighteen. The average number of children per woman is 7.2. They're trying to rebuild their population.

Xanana Gusmão is in trouble at the moment.

Yes, I read that. I think it's the fledgling stages in a new nation. It wasn't helped by Indonesia destroying 90 per cent of the buildings when they left in 1999. Indonesia made sure that it would be generations before East Timor could get up off its knees. They wanted it to fail.

I can only assume that the film shoot was much less controlled than other shoots you've done. There's no way you could have controlled exactly how scenes played out, given that you had so many non-actors, that you're in a very particular place . . .

Yes, Timorese army playing the soldiers.

Was that stressful or did you just become Zen?

Yes, I did try and get in a Zen-like state, which was a challenge for me as the way I work is usually very analytical and structured. In a film like The Bank my work is very precise in terms of the shots and storytelling and tracking and so forth. But with Balibo I knew I couldn't do that.

It's all a bit more method-like, isn't it?

I gave lots of thought about this in advance of making the film. I had this approach with the cinematographer, which is that I would set up the drama and we would explore it with the camera—I had two cameras—not construct it. There were lots of times when I'd call 'action' and I had no idea what was going to happen. I'd have five actors filming, I'd have 100 soldiers running up here, in a remote part of East Timor with a crew of ten, and I'd literally have the two cameras and call 'action' and it would be, like, okay . . .

I found that really effective—that sense of chaos as soldiers are running up the hill and the journalists start to run away. I liked the fact it's not a finely tuned battle scene.

Great. And with the pool fight you talked about earlier I didn't have stunt guys . . .

That was almost amusing, you could just see them like two schoolboys, they were pathetic.

That's what happens when people fight, that's right. I just stood back with the cameras and the actors decided that if they didn't get to a point where they were that angry with each other they wouldn't fight. So I let them go and they got really mean towards each other, and then Anthony went and threw Oscar in the water and then he jumped in after him and he put him under the water, then put him under the water again. I'm watching it and we're just filming it, and I'm thinking, did he let him get a breath?

It was hard but I knew that I needed to approach it in that way in order to pull it off, and I just didn't have the resources to make a conventional, huge piece of cinema. We're used to Hollywood making things dynamic for a visceral effect. I think maybe audiences are so used to such structured storytelling in film now that it's become predictable. I tried to avoid that. Take the scene in which the five are killed—there's no music over that scene, there's no slow-mo, there's no tracking shots, it happens in real time. It's brutal.

How many drafts and how many years did it take to write the screenplay?

About five years. There was all the early phase with David Williamson, then I came in for the later phase.

If you think that the characters in the film go on a journey from caring about themselves or, in Roger East's case, caring about the Balibo Five, to ultimately caring about this nation—that's what I've tried to plot. So with Greg Shackleton in his famous piece to camera, you see that he actually cares about East Timor. He might have issues of ambition and ego but in that moment you know the country has cast its spell, and the same for Anthony LaPaglia, for Roger East. When he says 'I'm staying', he knows what's happened to the Balibo Five, he's staying for this country. And the Balibo Five's families talk about the same thing, they all say that the tragic loss of their father, their son, their husband transformed into a passionate concern for the plight of this nation. I think the screenplay parallels that. It was all about the Balibo Five early on but the writing was profoundly affected by my journeys to East Timor. The screenplay shifted from being about the Balibo Five to being about East Timor.

FICTION

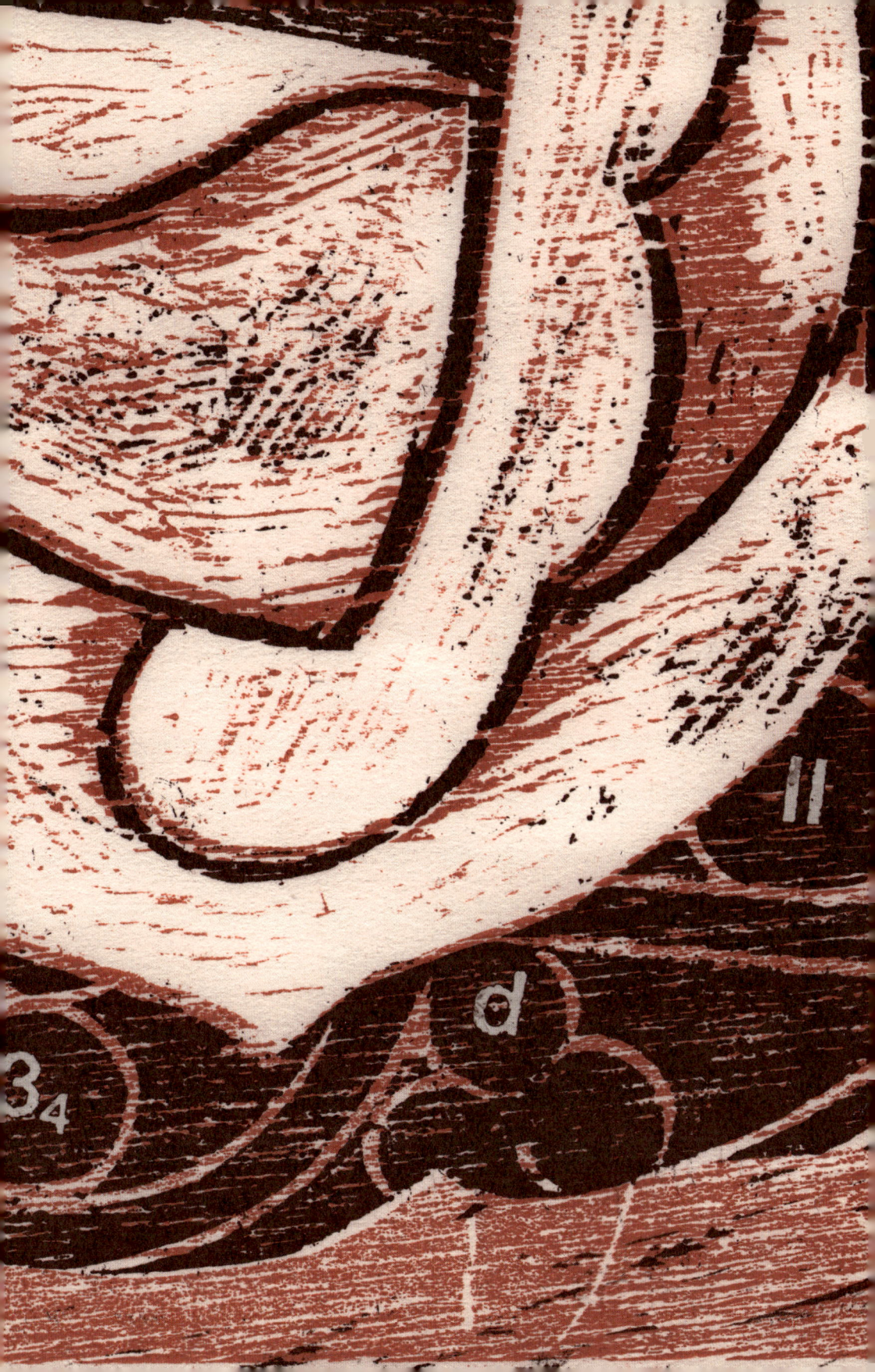

How to Cook a Family

by

SUSAN JOHNSON

WHEN ELIZABETH BARTON was a child she liked to dig in the earth with her fingers. She liked the cool of it, the tickle of falling soil against her palm, the way the black dirt sometimes left a graceful residue beneath her fingernails that formed a clean sharp line and looked as if it had been drawn with a pencil. She did not know that millions of years before she was born the great southern continents of the Earth were joined and that ice sheets had to melt in order for lakes and oceans to form and then recede so that the earth could rise up. The separated continent that eventually formed the part of Australia where Elizabeth came from was made up of the crushed bones of long-dead sea creatures, of earlier peoples, of Aborigines and forgotten whites, of Chinese men whose perished skulls had once been thick with hair. The earth kept many secrets from Elizabeth: lost maps and chips of hand-painted china teacups, the teeth of slaughtered marsupials, and the discarded rings of broken-hearted girls. But as well as these lost things the earth housed worms as fat as arterial veins, centipedes and ants, and Elizabeth had latterly discovered that soil possessed its own muffled weather. Elizabeth knew that grass and plants and flowers took oxygen from the ground but she had yet to hear the earth draw breath. Nevertheless she expected to hear the sound of the earth's sigh at any moment so she kept her ears open, idly picking up any rocks embedded in the soil while she waited. Sometimes she found beneath a rock a tiny grey crustacean, armoured like a crab, which appeared to have crawled from some vanished sea. When she picked it up and tried to play with it, the tiny sea creature acrobatically curled itself up into a locked ball. Elizabeth reluctantly returned the creature to the earth, where it presumably continued its endless search for its evaporated home. The earth in the northern suburb of Sydney where Elizabeth lived was a rich clay soil but beneath it was layer upon layer of Hawkesbury sandstone, a geological skeleton left over from a prehistoric age.

Stealing a cup from the kitchen and filling it with water from the tap, Elizabeth fashioned tiny mud people from this clay soil. She mixed in the water carefully as she worked, building up a thick mud paste. Elizabeth built a human constellation: a daddy, a mummy and a child. She felt herself to be at the end of a long unbroken chain of people that reached deep down into the earth and far across the ocean, right up into the farthest sweep of the sky. Her ancestors made up the stars in the night and the sun in the day, forming the light that enabled her to see.

In those moments with her hands in the earth, Elizabeth Barton first learnt that she could be alive in two places at once. She was both in the world but she was also alive in her representation of the world. There was life but there was also something else, some intimation of a faraway fragmented dream, and it was as if the very essence of that other place was distilled in those tiny clay figures. They were form imposed upon matter, dream given breath, as expressive of something as fundamental to human existence as water or bread. If the tiny figures told some essential truth that Elizabeth could as yet only dimly discern, she instinctively knew enough to treat them with reverence. On sunny days she left them to bake on the back step in the sun where they sometimes hardened enough so that she could gently play with them until an arm fell off, or a leg, or a head.

Now she is a grown woman Elizabeth understands that it is not without reason that the important parts of a ceramic pot are known as foot, belly, shoulder, neck and lip. Sitting at the antediluvian wheel in her studio day after day Elizabeth pushes the whole of herself into the clay: palm, finger, belly, muscle, head and heart. When did the process of turning mud into rock come to mean so much to her? In the beginning she remembers using only her hands, her ten squat fingers with their strong nails cut down as far as they could be cut, with her many rings perpetually covered in white, hardening clay so that they resembled ancient things rescued from Pompeii. Now Elizabeth uses the force of her will, her single gold wedding band off, bearing down upon the wheel with every muscle and fibre and thought in her head bent upon whatever it is that is growing and forming and twisting and turning in her hands. Her whole body is engaged in a kind of dance with the clay so that she can feel the shape of her spine, which holds her up, the fluid lean of it, the tender partnership between her bones and the ever-turning wheel. Elizabeth registers the weight of her skull, the ceaseless workings of her ordinary and yet miraculous brain, the feel of her bare feet against the cold tiled floor. The soles of her feet have recently developed cracks, great gaping splits that are aiming for her ankles. She believes herself to resemble one of her own tentative creations, fired too fiercely, a vessel that no longer stands firm. The more the world doubts the value and relevance of her handmade things, believing them passé and sentimental and utterly lacking in commercial appeal or sense, the more Elizabeth is forced to rely on her own best intentions. She once loved the way clay, like flesh, responds to touch, and she used to marvel at its capacity to acknowledge the passing of human fingers across its surface by holding forever the shape of those fingers like so many captured ghosts. But lately she has found herself asking along with the rest of the world why she is making pots this way in the twenty-first century.

If God fashioned the first man from earth, what is it Elizabeth thinks she is doing? And can it be true that what she sometimes most longs for is to become the moist soft clay itself, to lie ready and waiting and full of potential, already possessing every single quality necessary for form and beauty and life? Is Elizabeth the maker, or the made?

In the pulsating silence of her studio on these warm December days Elizabeth finds herself once again fashioning tiny clay figures. As the day approaches for her to leave Sydney and travel north to the family that made her, Elizabeth begins to mould figures. There is her father, Bob, cradled and condensed in her palm. There is her mother, Nance, reduced and at one with the silence. There are her brothers Robbo and Nick, holding hands as if they still could. And there is Elizabeth herself, small and unbroken.

The clay figures summon up wistfulness in Elizabeth, a yearning for some distant lost moment when goodness still seemed possible. She thinks of her own flesh-and-blood family—the little family that she built herself, made up of Isaac, Raphael, Madeleine and her mutinous husband Neil—but they do not exert the same painful pull on her heart that these figures do.

The silence in the studio is loud in her ears, like a noise itself, a silence full of pregnant space, charged and alive. When Elizabeth is not at work over the electric wheel the only sounds come from the far-off rhythmic beat of traffic and from a cheap plastic clock counting time as it falls away. As she holds her mute family in her hands, the tiny figures are part of that silence. She imagines firing them, putting them in the kiln and showing them exactly what it is she does; how she wastes her time in a world in its eleventh hour, self-indulgently spending her days spinning the wheel, attempting to give form to something only half-imagined. She knows that cooking her family will bind their eyes, and that firing them will seal their lips for good. What she knowingly craves is the absence of sound, for some lasting final obliterating silence that will shut them up and extinguish their incessant familial roar for good. But she never fires them, never once makes a single move towards the hot and unforgiving oven. How hard can it be to cook a family?

How difficult to still the raging noise?

Loud Bones

by

RUBY MURRAY

IT'S BEEN THREE years since Roxanne had sex. For the first six months, it had been funny. Sitting with Rita and Linda in cafés on Brunswick Street, in the city, in Collingwood, she'd thrown her arms up in the air and said things like 'Six months, I mean, what the fuck is that, right?' And they'd all laughed, as if there was something exciting and even naughty about not having sex in six whole months.

By that August, she was shocked to realise that she'd been making the 'six months' joke for a whole year. 'Twelve months' just didn't have the same sound as 'six months'. At the end of eighteen months, she stopped talking about it altogether. When the topic of sex came up, as it invariably did, she sidestepped, laughed, said 'not as frequently as I'd like' or something equally inane, and moved the conversation away from herself.

Toyshop

She wanted to buy something perfect. Something meaningful. Something that would be looked at and admired years down the track for its artistry and its thoughtfulness. But it was hard to choose, surrounded by that orgy of colour. Toys didn't look the way she remembered them. She felt as if she hardly knew what they were supposed to do. Boxes full of angular wood, stretched and turned so that each piece slid into the other, devouring one another, making something out of nothing.

Raucous plastic farm animals assumed regiments along one shelf, straining against each other to escape across the narrow wooden floors. Jagged Lego inside boxes touting the possibility of building new worlds. Lost, she walked up and down the shop, touching things blindly: cheap synthetics, expensive German wood, spindly fairy wings and cold plastic.

The middle-aged woman behind the counter wound up a tin carousel for her and sent its tiny, green and red carriages spinning wildly through the still air. The movement made her nauseous, and she turned away. It wasn't enough. It wasn't expensive enough, for a start. But the slowing staccato clicks of the carriages pulled her back to the counter again and again. The shop was too hot, and Roxanne could feel sweat leaking through the wool of her jumper and turning it soggy against her skin. In the end she just snatched up the carousel's box, jammed her credit card carelessly through the machine, and escaped into the street.

Adult

Linda and Jack lived in a rented terrace in Carlton, their back yard awash with broken plastic, makeshift sandpits and the mouldering rugs of last summer's picnics. Two red balloons were tied to their letterbox, bucking madly in the wind as the taxi drove away.

Inside, everything was muted, as if the close, living smells of the house masked what was actually a place of worship. A couple of Jack's friends sat in the living room, drinking beer and talking in low voices, out of respect. She walked on through the house, stopping to say hello to people, her sweating fingers starting to soak into the tissue paper around her carousel. Before the kitchen, she turned left into a dim room where Linda sat on a couch, holding a tightly spooled bundle of cotton. The baby's face, when Linda turned it towards her for inspection, was horribly disfigured, the mashed-up-late-night-cheap-Japanese-horror-film-on-SBS version of what babies should look like.

'He's amazing,' she told Linda in the same low voice of awe that had infected everyone in the house. 'So amazing.'

Linda smiled beatifically.

Roxanne carried the carousel on into the kitchen, to where her friend Rita was trying to control the madcap capering of Linda and Jack's other kid, four-year-old Matilda.

'Put it down, Matilda, it's sharp,' Rita was commanding in her best adult voice.

'Why?'

'Because it's sharp.'

'It's not sharp.'

'Yes it is. Put it down.'

Matilda, provocative, waved the butter knife, which wasn't sharp at all, spinning it ineptly like a baton twirler, flicking up her bare heels as she careered around the close kitchen.

'Put it down or I'll get your mum.'

'Mum doesn't mind, she lets me do this all the time.'

Rita, losing interest, turned and air-kissed Roxanne's cheek.

'Promise me you're never going to procreate,' she whispered. 'I couldn't stand it if I lost you too. I couldn't stand it if you had one of these.'

Roxanne put the carousel down on the kitchen table in its saggy, splotched paper, where it was instantly lost in the clutter of half-empty trays of sandwiches, torn sheets of wrapping paper and dirty wineglasses.

'I don't think there's much chance of that,' said Roxanne. Rita patted her back, misunderstanding her.

Rita didn't know. 'Good girl,' she said.

Cacophony

After three years, her body aches. At night she has trouble sleeping, feeling that her bones are tightening, that they won't stop clenching, ever so slowly, inside her skin. Her bones are noisy, their aching a cacophony of need. During the day the loudness of her bones is there too, but it's easier to ignore if she just keeps on going, keeps on working, stays out of the house and the quiet and away from the still and silence of her bed. At night she is alone with it and it becomes harder to ignore. She turns over and over. Masturbating, which used to act as such a release, gives her no relief at all. It's become a reminder, a hollow imitation of what it felt like to have someone else press up against you, run their fingers down the small of your back.

She starts taking sleeping pills, which make her fuzzy in the morning when she wakes back up to her clenching body. But at least she doesn't dream of being touched.

Even television has become painful. A week ago, sitting on the floor of her house in North Fitzroy after work, she ate dinner and channel-surfed through the soapies. In one of them, a couple lay on the beach, the camera panning across their warm flesh, light grains of sand sticking to the hairs on their shoulders and the fine creases of their joints as they rubbed their skins over each other. Roxanne sat, soup dripping from the spoon that rested in the air somewhere, forgotten on the end of her arm as the bodies moved in front of her.

The sound of their panting over the canned strings became unbearable, and she muted it, putting the spoon down and pushing her dinner away, suddenly nauseated even though minutes before she'd been ravenously hungry. In silence, the two skins pressed and melded against each other, an orgy of touch, almost orange in their brightness but so beautiful and so heart-wrenching that Roxanne felt like screaming. The *Home and Away* logo scribbled itself across the bottom of the screen, and the entwined bodies disappeared. Roxanne was left in the silent living room with her cooling soup and the blazing red of an advertisement for bargain-basement furniture.

Apologise

'You want a drink?' asked Rita, waving at the bottles lining the kitchen bench.

'Sure.'

'Beer, wine, tequila, what's your booze of choice, Madame? Let's get fucked up.'

Roxanne laughed, the idea of tequila striking her as funny, sacrilegious almost, and the sound was out of place in the muted house. Some people on the other side of the kitchen looked over quizzically, and Roxanne caught Jack's eye as he stood, leaning against the fridge, a bottle of Heineken in one slender hand. He raised it in salute, and Roxanne waved back half-heartedly.

'Oops,' said Rita. 'I actually did bring tequila. Should I be sorry? Is that bad?'

'I don't know if we're supposed to drink tequila in the afternoon now that we're having babies and stuff. It's irresponsible.'

'Linda's having babies, not us,' said Rita. 'Come on, don't make me feel like I have to apologise for being an alcoholic now, too. I thought that was cultural or something, we're Aussie, right? Have one too, come outside, and we can have a naughty cigarette.'

Assumptions

Just before this latest kid of Linda's was born, the three women—Roxanne, Rita, and Linda, huge and unwieldy—sat out the front of Tiamo's on a still afternoon talking about all the things that had changed in what they wanted from life, about all the things they'd been expecting to happen before they were thirty, and which hadn't. It was a conversation they had often, as if they could hardly believe they were there, could hardly believe in their own adulthood. As if it was all just a joke, and they were going home to their parents after lunch, not home to their own houses and mortgages and children and studies. Matilda sat under the table, eating the ends of the garlic bread and yanking frequently on the women's legs.

'I just thought I'd be more successful by now,' Roxanne said, shrugging and twirling her napolitana on the end of her fork.

'You are successful,' countered Linda, shifting her daughter under the table with one hand, the other one resting on her straining belly. 'You're really successful, considering your age and everything. You run a small business. You're a fashion designer, I mean, isn't that cool? We would have thought that was so cool when we were twenty. Fashion, design, ooh-ahh.'

'Exactly, I run a small business. Small.'

'It takes time,' said Rita in her singsong voice, a cigarette clenched in her lips and ash hovering over her carbonara. 'I mean, everything takes longer than you think it will when you're twenty. When I was twenty I thought I'd have finished my PhD by the time I was twenty-five. I'm nearly thirty now and I'm still only halfway through the fucker. Am I even allowed to say that?' Rita gestured at the centre of the table, the flick of her bitten fingernails at the dented wood meant to signify the presence of the four-year-old underneath it.

'Whatever,' shrugged Linda. 'I don't think she really notices the difference if you use it like a normal word. It's only when you tell her that she's not allowed to do things that she gets really interested in them.'

'What about you, Lind?' asked Roxanne.

'What do you mean, like, what did I think I'd be doing?'

'Yeah.'

'I don't know. I didn't think I'd spend so much time worrying about money. I guess that's weird. I didn't expect to depend so much on Jack, you know?'

'He's your husband. Dependence is sort of expected.'

'Partner. But it's not the dependence . . . it's sort of like his career has turned into mine, you know? No, not that really, it's more like I want it, I want his stuff. I want to do it, I keep on trying to give him advice, because I want him to be successful, and I think I know how he can do it so I get really frustrated when he doesn't do the things I think he should, when he doesn't take on the work I think he should. I feel like if I could just make him understand what I see . . .' Linda shrugs. 'Whatever. It doesn't really matter.'

While Linda talked, Matilda crawled out from under the table and into Roxanne's lap. She twined her fingers around the back of Roxanne's neck, her small, hot hands, sticky with butter from the garlic bread, sending shivers across Roxanne's skin, her bones all of a sudden reacting, singing. The weight of the child against her thighs, the heat of the solid kilos of her body, made Roxanne's lunch drop heavily down to the base of her spine, pressing against her bowels like longing, like pain. Shocked at her arousal, at the sudden loss of control over her breathing, Roxanne heaved the kid off, setting her heavily down on the seat to her side, then shying away as Matilda, oblivious, reached out again.

'Don't annoy Roxanne, Matilda,' said Linda absently. 'Don't be annoying.'

'It's okay,' said Roxanne, 'I just need to go to the loo.'

Roxanne set her fork and spoon down in the congealing red sauce, slid off the bench, and forced her way through the crowded restaurant and upstairs to the bathroom. Closing the door behind her, she crouched against the toilet bowl and tried to control her breathing. Her mouth was salivating wildly, like it does just before you throw up, and she spat out a stream of clear saliva into the bowl. She hiked up her thick winter skirt. Shitting was a relief, emptying, calm. As if it gave her back control, restored to her a body she could be sure she still owned.

Hills Hoist

Rita and Roxanne sat on seats under the Hills Hoist in the falling afternoon light of Linda and Jack's back yard, smoking.

'I hate children,' said Rita.

'Come on . . .'

'No, it's true, I really do.'

'You were a kid once.'

'I never felt like one though.'

'Well they probably don't either.'

'I can't relate to them. I don't get them.'

'I'm sure you will when you have your own.'

'I'm not going to have my own.'

'Yes, you will.'

'I'm not that woman.'

'Okay.'

'I'm not.'

'Okay, Rita.'

They were silent for a moment, looking at the lilting back of Jack and Linda's house and the wet sheen of evening dew settling on the rusting bike frames leaning against the flywire screen door.

Then Rita said, 'I'm fucking a Scientologist.'

'But you hate religious people.'

'I know. The contempt makes the sex even better. It's awesome. Sometimes, I make him talk about how the human spirit exists and how you have to fix your spirit up and shit before we go to bed, just to warm us up. He's going to have me take one of those personality tests.'

'No.'

'Yes.'

'God.'

'No, just spirit. What bollocks. But I want to know what it says anyway. Hopefully it's real serious so he can fix me some more.'

'You're gross.'

'I know. But I'm happy with it.'

Castle

It had started because of the Lego. Barefoot, tipsy in the warm summer night, Roxanne had stepped down hard on a piece of Lego out of a princess castle construction box that someone had—inappropriately—given Matilda earlier that day in celebration of her very first birthday.

Through the raucous crowd, the barbecue smoke, the fading light, Jack had seen her bending and cursing, kicking the piece away. He'd made his way over to her, led her into the quiet bathroom inside, taken some ice from the esky beside the back door and wrapped it in a ragged, pale blue facewasher. She sat on the closed lid of the toilet. He sat opposite, bringing her foot to the warm denim of his thigh. She yelled because of the cold ice and he laughed and said she would wake Matilda up and then she closed the bathroom door and in that moment, as the door clicked closed on the world outside, something changed between them. Or maybe it was something that had always been there, but which chose that moment to reveal itself, for no particular reason at all. His hand on her ankle. All her body existing in that stretch of fingers and in the cold point, rapidly numbing, where he held the ice to her skin. For long seconds, neither of them spoke, just sat there in the half-light. And every moment that passed one of them could have gotten up, could have said something, anything, could have walked back out into the party and the evening and the rest of the world. They didn't. They just sat, and the longer they sat the more inevitable it became, and then Jack slid his hand further up her ankle, to her calf, his long hands under her thighs and they were pulling towards each other, and the moment when they could have stopped was behind them.

Arrogance

Slightly tipsy, Rita and Roxanne cleared the kitchen as people left. Without the adult bodies, the smell of babies and children and mess in the house was clearer, a persistent, acrid tinge under the lingering wine, beer and sausage rolls.

'What should I do with all the unopened presents?' Rita asked Jack as he came into the kitchen with two fists full of empties, which he deposited in a cardboard box with a crash. Roxanne flinched, glancing down the hallway to the dim silence coming out of the room where Linda sat with the baby.

'Just put them in a box, or maybe give them to Linda,' said Jack absently, wandering back down the hall to the living room where a few of his illustrator friends still lingered. 'Thanks, guys.'

'Why do people even bother with presents for newborns?' Rita asked the kitchen as she piled up the presents. 'What's the kid going to do with it? How many do-dads and jiggety-bobs does a barely functioning blob of flesh with no motor skills and no concept of self really need? I mean, you're really giving the presents to the parents, aren't you? It's a big competition to see who can give the most extravagant, meaningless gift. Wouldn't giving them nappies be better?'

Since it was obscured by a vase full of lopsided chrysanthemums, Rita couldn't see the wilting tissue-wrapped box with the carousel inside it. When she left the room, Roxanne scooped it off the table, wrapped it hurriedly in a plastic bag, and put it back in her handbag.

Railway

Roxanne walks home.

The night is cold and clear, cars begin to frost over in the stillness. The streetlights are orange beacons in the darkness, drawing her on and on. The carousel rattles in her bag, and in her head its little carriages spin out and out. In each one sit two tiny tin people, a man and a woman, welded to their carriage seats. Two people per carriage: red man, green woman.

Before going home she walks under the railway and down to where the bike bridge crosses the Merri Creek. A late train out of the city pulls in behind her, its empty windows glowing. No-one gets off. After it's gone, Roxanne is alone with the cacophony of her bones and the wet, dank smell rising off the Merri far below. Unwrapping the carousel she puts the empty box and the damp tissue back in her bag, and then she flings the carousel out into the darkness. After a moment she hears a subdued splash, and in her head she sees the carriages sinking to the bottom of the creek, the perpetual smiles of their occupants coming to rest against the claggy silt.

Her bones are needy, loud in the cold Melbourne night, and she takes them home and closes the front door, tight, to keep them from waking up the whole town with their howling.

Suburban Mystery

by

PIERZ NEWTON-JOHN

WHEN HE WAS sixteen, my best friend Adrian ran away from home. It must have been 1983, the year of the fires, because I remember standing in the heat of the back yard in that eerie roseate light, as a fine fleck of ash, white as a snowflake, drifted down to settle on my hair. The sun was a bronze coin smoking in the acrid sky, and the world was tinted a stained-glass cerise, as if it had been tainted by the possibility of destruction.

Adrian's pale face surfaced in the black of my bedroom window one midnight. He was hungry so I stole food for him from the pantry: apples, dried apricots, Salada biscuits and peanut butter. I stuffed them up my jumper and brought them out to him where he was sheltering in the shell of the half-built house next door. It was exciting, a clandestine mission like in the days when we'd gone on unauthorised adventures in grade six, our 'iron rations' wrapped in a tea towel on a stick, the cartoon-approved and only way to go AWOL.

We sat up on the second storey and he crouched there like some kind of bird, his bony knees poking through the holes in his jeans, while he wolfed down the food. He had an Adidas bag in which he carried his worldly possessions: a change of clothes, a copy of *Catch-22*, his Bauhaus and Joy Division records, a packet of Peter Jackson super mild, and two bottles of red wine. I went back into enemy territory to fetch a corkscrew and a blanket.

I got drunk for the first time up there in that empty space full of echoes and moonlight and scraps of electrical wiring. I suggested an experiment. We would see to what extent it was possible to mentally resist the effects of alcohol. I'd read books and I believed the mind could do anything. I forced down gulp after gulp of the cold wine until my face went numb and my words slurred. The moonlight sloshed over us and I sprawled out on the bare floor and watched the trees through the window spin without ever completing a rotation. The wine bottle got knocked over and glugged out a great purple stain.

'Where will you go?' I asked him.

'I dunno, I don't care,' he said. His cigarette end dived and darted like a firefly. He'd been saying that a lot, about not caring. He didn't care about school, about the future, about his mum and dad. Anyway, what was to care about? Nuclear war was bound to come sooner or later. We'd been expecting it for years. When we were younger we'd made plans to bury tins of food up on the Black Spur. We'd have mountain bikes and leave food on the doorsteps of people with less foresight than ourselves. Even at sixteen we still thought a little wistfully about the possibility of nuclear holocaust. At least it would be dramatic.

He opened the second bottle and I guzzled straight from the neck. Yes, hell, who cared? Through the window I could see the house I'd grown up in. It was as familiar as a face, like a big square head with windows for eyes, a head full of memories. But the last lights had gone out, its lids were drawn down. It slept unaware that I was out in the construction site next door, watching it with cold, unsympathetic eyes.

Adrian held up his hand, fingers outstretched. 'How many fingers am I holding up?' That was our ritual *Catch-22* gag—I see everything twice—a sort of comic antiphony in which the response was always 'two'. But I really was seeing double, and trying to focus on his hand caused a swell of nausea that sent me reeling down into the garden to barf a fumy, mulberry slurry into the grass outside my bedroom window. I rolled out on my back on the lawn, the world heaving under me like an anchorless ship and the trees surging in the wind like seaweed. Adrian came down and we vomited together in solidarity, our messes mingling in the grass.

Oh that long, boring year! Bob Hawke's larrikin drawl on the radio after the America's Cup win, having a go at the wowser bosses, and Men at Work's vegemite sandwich song on every bloody radio. We despised it all. We slouched about outside the milk bar—archetypal teenagers with cigarettes and Samboy chips, slagging off parents, teachers and the world we didn't understand. We nicked gin from over the neighbour's fence and drank it at lunchtime. 'Fucking revolting!' we agreed. 'Like drinking perfume!' we protested. And passed the bottle again.

That summer I bought my first record, *The Blurred Crusade* by The Church. As I slipped it out of its sleeve onto the turntable for the first time, the light caught a line of handwriting—some impenetrable in-joke—inscribed in the smooth black vinyl inside the last song. That opaque, mystic scribble fascinated me: Steve Kilbey's last elliptical utterance before the stylus spiralled into the black hole at the centre of the record. 'Almost with You' was my anthem. Its lush, anguished paisley-poetry made my soul bleed. When Steve Kilbey asked *Can you taste their lonely arrogance?* I wanted to shout: 'Yes! Yes! I can!' I understood nothing he said, but I could almost not bear the sorrow and longing when he sang, *I'm almost with you, I can sense it, wait for me. I'm almost with you. Is this the taste of victory?*

Adrian was sleeping rough, in concrete dust and bent nails, or in beds in youth homeless shelters, or under bridges, his own half-asleep dreams of approaching gangs, of boots and fists, pulling him back again and again to the interminable passage of the night. I watched him slip quietly into the under-society of lost kids with white, white skin and unwashed clothes and mouths foul with cigarettes and swear words. They taught him how to inhale Preen from a plastic bag and break into a school by dismantling the slatted windows on the roof. I was afraid that he was slipping out of my orbit, heading for places I would be unable to follow. But I wasn't sure I could grow up on my own. He'd been my best friend since kindergarten.

Adrian was a smart kid, always top of the class in maths. But he'd started failing and then he dropped out of school altogether. Still, I used to see him at lunchtimes quite a bit. He was bored shitless, so he used to come down to the park near the school with his girlfriend Kelly who, it turned out, was doing twenty Valium a day. She liked to share them around like Smarties. If Adrian didn't care any more, she cared even less. She chromed Mortein.

Tony Dawes used to hang out there too, a small twitchy kid we'd known since primary school. We'd watch him pashing his size-16 girlfriend against the fence, their mismatched pelvises pulsing together in a sort of obscene peristalsis. There was something going wrong in his head, though we didn't think too much about it at the time. When he wasn't having dry sex with his girlfriend, he was raving haywired about the monos and how they were coming. He never explained who they were, those awful monos, but we could see his terror of them. His eyes would rove randomly as he spoke, sliding again and again to the alley across the street, as if at any moment it would fill with Daleks. When life was particularly dull, and we felt like passing the kicks down the pecking order, we'd stuff grass clippings down his shirt or punch his skinny shoulders. Time oozed by, Tony's muted shouts of protest falling dead in the heat.

Adrian smoked and rocked idly on the swings. He had adopted a certain way of crossing his thin, stovepipe legs, his forearm resting on his thigh in an arty manner he'd picked up from a Bauhaus album cover. In his all-black outfits, his threadbare jeans, he was both crow and scarecrow. He smoked his nervous cigarettes and picked at people with the beak of his words until the stuffing began to come out of them. We all did. That was the thing we did, the way we were. It was peck or be pecked. We were miserable, inured, bonded by the gravitational collapse of our self-esteems.

Adrian pinched a shopping trolley from Safeway and we rode about in the thing like six-year-olds. Then he took it to the top of the infamous Melaleuca Street hill and jumped in. 'Don't be an idiot,' I told him, but he pushed off and it rolled away down the hill. Its trajectory was doomed from the start, anyone could see that. It wasn't made for those speeds, and halfway down the hill one front wheel buckled and it crashed onto its side and sent him flailing across the tarmac. Just then a car turned into the street at the bottom of the hill. Adrian limped off the road and it went slowly past, the driver pausing to wind down the window and say something, to which he responded with a barked, hurting obscenity. But by the time he got to the top of the hill he was laughing again, though his sleeve was sticky with blood and his wrist was swollen up like a balloon.

Sometimes those suburban streets took on a surreal aspect to me. All those damn orange houses, all those driveways: evidence of some kind of life, but more often than not you saw nobody at all. Maybe some old guy in a singlet watering his roses with a hose, nameless faces like that guy in the car on Melaleuca Street. The thud of a football kicked on an oval, coming late over the distance. There was something weird and mysterious about all this, it seemed to me. Who were the people all this belonged to? Were we happy here or not? Nobody was saying. Everything was sealed up inside those silent brick boxes, like the energy in plutonium, $e=mc^2$. We couldn't puzzle out the equation of our own hearts let alone of so many other atomic units, nuclear families. So can you blame us for carrying textas in our pockets, for making some kind of mark, however crass or banal, on that sealed-up surface?

We sought out high places, places that gave us some kind of perspective, like the overpass over the freeway where the wind blew hot on our faces, stinking of exhaust. It was a good place to watch the night come in. The city in the distance glittered and took on a sci-fi aspect: crystalline towers, and the lights speeding below us, red and white, shaking the concrete pillars of the bridge. The air cooled and there was a softness about the violet sky, a beauty even in that hard, noisy place.

One night Adrian climbed up on the railing, and standing up there on a high wire above the city's streaming artery, closed his eyes and held out his arms as if trying to capture everything, the whole incomprehensible thing, in his embrace. I was terrified. I wrapped my arms around his shins and pleaded with him, my face pressed into the denim. 'Please no, please stop it, come down.' He teetered, then his legs folded in my arms and he slid down my chest onto the concrete walkway. I broke down and wept, filled with shame but unable to hold in the great tearing sobs. My eyes shut tight against the hot flood, my hands over my face, I don't know what I saw there in the dark of myself.

'It's so strange,' he said.

I looked at his fierce face shining in the hard freeway lights. 'What is?'

He clenched his fist and then opened it as if letting something small fall to the ground. 'It's so strange and so . . . fucking banal.'

Tony Dawes cut his wrists in the senior-school corridor, leaning against the wall with a Stanley knife. Afterwards he stood there so quietly, unobtrusive as ever, that it took a while before anyone noticed his crimson gloves and the drip drip drip on the lino, the bloody footprint smear as kids rushed to class. The monos had arrived and he cut his wrists to get away from those crazy fuckers, but they came and got him anyway, poor bastard.

And one evening Adrian and I threw a coathanger across the powerlines on the street that bordered the school, shorting out a substation with a deafening bang and a fireball so bright we were temporarily blinded. For a few seconds we staggered about in darkness, hands groping in front of us, terrified that we had finally done something irrevocable, had lured the demons of brilliance and power from their hiding place and been struck blind for our hubris. Then the swimming blackness cleared to reveal the grass of the nature strip where I had fallen on my knees. The substation was on fire and half the suburb was blacked out. We got up and ran for it, awe and terror beating in our ears, but the houses stayed quiet as ever, nobody gave chase. I cannot remember where we ran or what we did afterwards. Outside the illumination of that fireball, everything is dark now. I watch us run down the street, the sound of our footfalls fading in the humid twilight, while the substation buzzes and sparks and finally burns out cold.

Adrian went back to school and finished his HSC two years after me, got a job in IT, and now he works for a hedge fund, working on an automated share trading system. We met just the other day after work, got blind drunk, and made extravagant promises to chuck in our ethically suspect jobs the following Monday. For just a moment I really believed I could find the courage to do it. 'It's resignation, or resignation!' I shouted at the woman next to me, who moved away to another table.

I'm married and live in a nice brick veneer house not all that far from where I grew up. We're extending this spring to make room for our third child—we're hoping for a girl this time. I drink too much, it's true, but other than that I've got a grip, you know? I've *settled*. I love and worry about my boys and I drink and I try to keep my marriage going, not that it's so bad, no worse than anyone's for all I know. I don't find any mystery in the houses on my street, or, to tell the truth, in anything much. I have, like most people, an almost evangelical belief in the ordinary.

But sometimes I wake at 4 a.m. with the resonance of a frightening dream ringing in the silent bedroom. I am sinking in the harbour in concrete shoes, or I reach a black river and soldiers come to demand my fare, but my pockets are empty. My heart pounds but I cannot puzzle out the meaning, or is it just impossible to allow it in, as one cannot hold on to a burning coin? I get up and pad through the house to the bathroom and splash my face with cold water to drive away the dread. In the unforgiving glare I am shocked at the fine cobweb of age spreading over the face in the mirror, and wonder how the answers always seem to run ahead of me. Nothing has been solved, I realise, and the times I think it has been are an illusion, the lie of the banal that covers over an unknowable truth. I remember Adrian standing on the overpass and shaking his fist. So strange, and so fucking banal. And then I go back shivering to my bed and slide in next to my wife, sleeping sound and untroubled in the breathing envelope of her skin.

Intelligence Quotient

by

GEORGIA BLAIN

JUST BEFORE I turned forty, my mother, who was the only other member of my family still alive, died from a stroke. She left me a small amount of money, enough for a deposit on a semi in a suburb that was not too far from the city, a place where the streets were hilly and treeless, and the houses that hadn't been knocked down to build huge brick villas remained unrenovated.

I'd never had my own place, nor had I lived by myself, and when I first received the key, I held it tight, hesitant for a moment about putting it on the ring with the others. And then I slotted it through the steel loop, its bright, shiny newness marking it out as different from the rest.

I had no work at the time, and so I stacked most of the little furniture I owned into one room and began slowly to remove the remnants of the lives that had lived here before me. I lifted carpets weighed down by years of dust; I pulled back linoleum, finding faded patterns of flowers on tiles that were cracked with age. I scrubbed down walls and painted. I listened to the radio as I worked, hours of music and talk that wafted over me as the days passed.

One morning, when I was out on the street putting undercoat on the front fence, a car pulled over, the engine rattling as it idled. A woman leant across the passenger seat, winding down the window.

'I heard you were in the neighbourhood.' Her blonde hair was pulled back in a scrappy ponytail and her tanned skin was lined. As she pushed her sunglasses up on her head, I could see that her eyes were pale green, a startling colour beneath lashes that were brittle with clumps of mascara. She smiled at me; her front tooth was slightly chipped. 'You don't remember me.'

Balancing the paintbrush on the edge of the can, I took a step towards the car, shaking my head as I did so. 'I'm sorry.' At first I'd thought she might have recognised me from one of the occasional ads I'd done. Most of these were now old repeats that rarely aired, but I'd recently played a teller in a bank commercial and I'd seen it only the other night. Commercials brought in money, a lot more than I managed to make from directing, and I took them when I got them.

'It's Juliette.' She rested her hand on the top of the open window, a ring on each of her fingers, three or four heavy silver bangles jangling on her wrist. 'Juliette Acott.'

I wiped my hair from my forehead, breathing in the acrid paint on my skin.

'I used to babysit you.'

I smiled. 'Really?' And I leant a little closer.

'The Acott sisters. There were five of us. You sometimes played with Susie, the youngest.'

I could sense something tugging at the thick shroud that always cloaked the past: a house on the corner, the sandstone wall covered in jasmine, and Juliette— was it her sunbaking in our garden and smoking cigarettes, while she supposedly looked after us?

'How strange,' I shook my head. 'Do you live around here too?'

She did. Up the road and next to Alison, the only person I knew in the neighbourhood.

'No, I didn't just recognise you,' she explained as I began to ask how she'd known it was me. 'Although I read about that film you made, and told people that I used to babysit you.' Her voice was husky, deep and cracked.

I asked her how Susie was, and she told me she was living in New York. 'An investment banker, earning a shitload of money.'

'And the others?'

'All doing their thing,' she said, and then, inevitably: 'Your brother? Eddie?'

'He died,' and, because I thought she would probably ask me how, I had to expand. 'Killed himself, actually.'

'Jesus,' she shook her head. 'Wouldn't have picked it.' She looked at me with those pale, green eyes. 'You always seemed the one headed for trouble.'

I was uncertain how to respond. 'I'd ask you in,' I eventually said, glancing down at the paint tin and the half-finished fence.

She had already pulled the car over and switched off the engine. 'I'll make us a cup of tea.' As she stepped out into the bright glare of the day, I searched for something familiar, a reminder of the girl she'd once been. She was tall and lean, her jeans close-fitting, and her cotton shirt a delicate print of soft blues and crimsons. The fine bones in her face and the remarkable colour of her eyes marked her out as a one-time beauty. Close up, she smelt of cigarette smoke, the stale odour faintly masked by a lemony perfume.

'Milk in yours?' she asked as she made her way through the open front door.

I watched her disappear down the cool darkness of the hallway and then put the brush in a bucket of water and closed the lid on the paint tin.

When I bought my house, Jono had assumed he was coming with me. I guess I did too. But as he began to talk about building a studio out the back for home recording, I looked at him, standing in my kitchen, surveying it all with plans in his eyes, and I wasn't so sure. I was tired of waiting for him to agree to having a child, of waking in the middle of the night, hollowed out by the heaviness of realising I was kidding myself when I thought he would change his mind. I would look at him sleeping, peaceful, and I would hate him.

He was shocked when I told him I was going to live on my own. He didn't want me to go. We could work it out.

It was hard breaking the habit of trying to believe in him, I confessed to Juliette, surprised at how readily I was talking to her about my life.

She leant back against the wall of the house, stretching her legs out in front of her, her bangles clanking as she lit a cigarette. 'I've met the type.'

Jono never gave much to the people he supposedly loved. He was the kind of man who's closer to his ex-partners than his current girlfriend, I explained.

'I saw him the other day.' I reached for the milk, smelling it to check it hadn't gone sour. 'He wanted to see a movie together. Afterwards we had dinner. He told me he was with a woman called Sally. Just a casual thing, he said. She wanted a lot more, but he wasn't ready.'

I looked out across the street at the neighbour's cat lying in the warmth of the sun, her sleek body stretched out on top of the wall. 'I suddenly realised that was probably how he'd described our relationship to each of his old girlfriends when we were together.' I pinched my teabag between my thumb and forefinger, wanting to wring the last moisture from it before I let it fall into the old paint tin lid now filled with cigarette ash.

Juliette was squinting in the brightness of the day. 'Never known a man who was worth it. Sounds like you're better off without him.'

Maybe, I agreed, although I wasn't entirely sure. My desire for a child crippled me at times, particularly now I was completely alone. At least with Jono there'd been some hope, no matter how false. Now I spent a lot of time trying to face the strong likelihood it wouldn't be fulfilled.

'But I like it here,' I said, looking at my house behind me. And I did. After years of drifting from place to place, I felt comfort and relief at this sense of ownership. I am home, I would tell myself, at last I am home.

Juliette was a painter. Before that she'd been a cook, a nurse and a childcare worker. There'd been a few men, but none had really stayed around. She'd lived for the last ten years by herself in a semi not that dissimilar to mine. 'I'm better off that way,' she laughed throatily. 'People like us,' and I was surprised at how readily she grouped us together, 'we never really learnt how to play the game. You know, not like them.' She waved her arm in a sweeping gesture that took in the rows of streets and houses in a suburb peopled by families. 'But it's not all bad,' she tightened the knot in her hair as it threatened to come loose. 'Swimming against the tide.'

A few days later I saw her again, out on the street. She was walking briskly down the hill towards the station, one hand clutching a cigarette, the other pressing a phone to her ear. As I raised an arm in greeting she stopped for a moment. 'I never said I'd be ready by then,' she told the caller, and then she held the phone away as she mouthed the words: 'Beer, my place tonight?' I could only nod as she returned to her conversation. 'Listen. It's not possible.' She kept walking, without even looking to see whether I'd agreed to the invitation, dropping her cigarette on the pavement and leaving it smouldering behind her.

That night, Juliette told me she had a great idea for a film.

We were sitting in her courtyard, slapping at mosquitoes as they whined close to our ankles and arms before alighting for the kill. I was only on my second beer but I felt drunk.

'Five sisters.' She tilted her head back, blowing out a thin plume of smoke that was swallowed by the darkness and then, resting her cigarette on the edge of the ashtray, she took the last swig of ale. 'Arsehole father. Starts with each one of them on her twelfth birthday, until finally, when he gets to the youngest, the other four are all there hiding in her room that night, ready to stop him.'

I didn't know what to say. Looking at her illuminated in the glow from the inside lights, I was about to open my mouth and express some puny form of sympathy, when she laughed again.

'It's not my family,' and then she began to cough. 'Jesus. You remember what my dad was like. Mr Meek and Mild. Wouldn't hurt a fly.'

I didn't. I remembered very little.

I asked her if she had some photos.

'Somewhere,' she replied. Was I interested in her film idea?

I tried to explain that I didn't really work like that. I only ever wrote when it was my own idea; otherwise, I was a director for hire on other people's scripts. If she had written something, I could look at it. Alternatively, if she wanted someone to write the story, she'd need to find a scriptwriter; they'd have to raise money. As my words amassed she got up to go to the kitchen.

She brought a couple more beers out, along with half a frozen pizza that had been reheated. I took a slice. She didn't touch it.

'I told Suze about bumping into you again,' and she prised the top from the bottle, letting it clatter to the ground. 'She remembered you and Eddie doing Mum's IQ test.'

I smiled as the first clear memory slotted into place, casting light on others that clung to the edges of our conversation: Susie, Juliette, all the sisters, and that house on the corner, the one I had vaguely recalled with the high stone wall that stopped you from seeing into the garden, although you could still make out the top storey and the slate roof from the street. The bedrooms had been upstairs. Camille and Juliette shared, and then there was Deborah (who had been in Eddie's year at school) and Amanda and lastly Susie, in a room on her own.

It was Camille who'd looked after us most often. She, too, had long blonde hair, loose and silky smooth. When she babysat us during the day, she'd strip down to a string bikini and sunbake lying on her back, and then her side, and then her front, lifting the edges of the crochet to check on the progress of her tan. Sometimes her boyfriend came with her, and Eddie and I would spy on them as their bodies tangled around each other, his hands working their way into her bikini bottoms, until she pushed him off and sat up again, leaning across him to grope for her pack of St Moritz cigarettes in the grass.

He would roll joints, carefully spreading a fine line of tobacco and dope along one edge of the paper, rolling it between his thumb and first two fingers of one hand.

'Want some?' he once asked Eddie, who, at a couple of years older than me, was just twelve—almost too old for a babysitter really, but because he and I had a tendency to argue, our parents didn't like to leave us alone.

Cross-legged on the emerald green lawn, Eddie tried to measure up to the adult status that was being offered. Voice cracking slightly as he reached out a hand and told the boyfriend (whose name I couldn't remember) that yeah, sure, a toke'd be good, Eddie didn't dare look at me watching him. Breathing deep, he held the smoke in, holding it, holding it, until unable to bear it any longer, he bent forward, coughing out a choking cloud, while the joint kept burning.

'Don't waste it,' the boyfriend scolded and I could see Eddie was mortified.

'What about me?' I asked, sure I could do a better job than my brother.

'Like this,' and pinching the end of the joint between his thumb and forefinger, Camille's boyfriend drew back, a sharp intake of breath, holding it for a moment, before finally letting the air out.

Eddie watched.

'I wouldn't give him any more,' Camille half-protested, standing slowly. 'And I definitely wouldn't give her any.' She looked at me. We all kept our eyes on her as she walked, languorous, long-limbed and lazy, across the brilliant expanse of grass and down to the house, the sunlight cutting through the slender poplars that marked the border between us and next door.

She was the ideal woman, Eddie told me later. He drew pictures of her, sketches on the back of school notes and in exercise books, line drawings that never quite caught the perfect symmetry of her features. He wrote her name over and over again, scribbling it out as soon as he completed it. He even took a photograph of her, keeping it, crumpled, under his pillow.

Once, he and his friends had followed her and the other fourth-formers to the dank marshy ground under the Gladesville bridge, where magic mushrooms grew in the clotted dirt near the concrete pylons. It was Camille who discovered Eddie hiding in the sticky asthma weed and her boyfriend who gave him a mushroom to try.

'You didn't,' I said.

Eddie just rolled his eyes, and although I didn't want to ask him what it was like, I wanted to know.

'Amazing.' His long hair fell across his face, and he pushed it aside. 'We took it in turns to kiss her.'

'Who?'

'Camille.'

I knew then he was lying.

'Ask her.'

I told him I would. Then he'd look like an idiot. Then he'd be embarrassed. As I went to pick up the phone, he finally confessed. He hadn't kissed her after all. But he had taken the mushrooms, and he grabbed my arm in a final attempt to convince me.

Sitting out in Juliette's courtyard, the last piece of reheated pizza cold between us, and me now feeling well and truly drunk on my fourth beer, I asked how Camille was.

'Married money,' Juliette told me.

'Eddie was in love with her,' I smiled.

'Everyone was in love with Camille,' Juliette grinned, picking at a fleck of tobacco caught near her chipped front tooth. 'All my own boyfriends included.'

She looked at me, pale eyes narrowing as she leant forward. 'So when did he do it?' she asked and I knew she was referring to Eddie.

It was when he was seventeen. A couple of years after my father lost all his money and we moved away from our stone house by the river to a red brick flat on the other side of the overpass.

'But it wasn't that,' I told her. 'When you're a kid you don't care about money, or your house, or any of that. It wasn't even the fights between my parents. He was just one of those people.' I could see her looking at me. 'He never fitted in and because he wanted to be liked so badly, other kids were cruel.'

I remembered one of them taking Eddie's school shorts and leaving him, knees together, hands trying to cover himself as he walked home. And then there was the time he was bashed, nose broken and bloody, weeping as my mother asked him who had done this to him.

'And then later on there were the drugs. We all took them. But they messed with him.'

It was easy now to provide a list of possible reasons, all I should have seen at the time, and probably did see, but I always felt that somehow, in the tangle of isolated incidents, I had never really grasped the larger whole, the truth of what had taken him further than he should ever have gone.

Juliette shook her head. 'You know he lost his virginity to me.' She leant back in her seat, and looked out at the black limbs of the trees that grew behind the collapsed paling fence. 'One of those times I looked after you, and he came home, later.'

'Well that would have made him happy.' I smiled and looked across at Juliette, who was standing now, beer in one hand.

'Want to see my paintings?' She nodded in the direction of the sunroom at the back of the house.

I had noticed the canvases stacked against the wall when I came in, and I'd been curious, wanting to pull one out, unable to imagine how Juliette would paint. Something unfinished, I thought. I followed her now into the small narrow room, lit only by a single bulb hanging from the ceiling. She turned the first of the paintings around, and then stepped back so that she, too, could have a look.

It was difficult to see it properly, there on the ground, the light too dim to really show the depths of soft darkness. There was a bridge spanning the night and a low cloud, barely visible, pressing down, heavy and sombre on the earth below.

'Can you hold it up?' I asked her.

Resting her cigarette on the window ledge, she obliged, stepping back, head cocked to one side as she watched me, observing.

In the distance I could see a light, only small, illuminating one corner of the canvas a little more brightly than the other. I leant closer and, having drunk too much, almost knocked the painting out of her grasp. She steadied herself, never taking her eyes off me as she waited for my reaction.

'God it's good,' I told her.

She turned another around and then another, and I sat on the floor in the middle of her sunroom as she held them up for me one by one, each a world of darkness, a blackness that made you want to lean right in to see what you felt was there but was never quite discernible.

I was about eight when Sarah Acott gave Eddie and me the IQ test. Sarah was studying psychology at university and she must have asked my mother if she could use us as her subjects. We went, not entirely sure what we were expected to do, just wanting a break in the monotony of a weekend that had entailed more bickering than usual.

We let ourselves in through the tall wooden gate, and walked up the path to the open front door. The Acott house was one of the largest in the neighbourhood, surrounded by an overgrown garden, the grass knee-high, the trees pressing against the windows, and the weeds tall and sticky. In the darkness of the hall, it was quiet. Everyone seemed to be out. Eddie called out, his voice uncertain. I shouted a little louder, and Sarah appeared, her footsteps soft as she came out of the lounge and into the hall. She was a thin woman, her hair streaked with grey, her eyes cloudy and her skin smeared with pale freckles. She was wearing glasses, which made the occasion much more serious than I had thought it was. She pushed them down to the end of her nose.

'Now, who first?' she asked. 'Eddie or Lena?'

I was surprised she knew our names, because although I had been there to play a few times and her daughters had babysat us, she'd never seemed to register who we were. This was a house in which the adults had little presence. The children did as they pleased, helping themselves to the food they wanted, leaving the mess they made, fighting without intervention, turning on the television whenever they desired; it was chaotic and loud. But on that day it was quiet.

'Is Susie home?' I asked, once it had been determined that Eddie would go first and I would be left to wait.

Sarah wasn't really sure where she was, and she looked at me for an instant, uncertain whether she should trouble herself with finding me an amusement.

There was nothing at hand, so she left me to sit on a sofa in the lounge.

With big windows that let in the northern light, it was the only sunny room in the house. The couch was soft, and I stretched out my legs on the cushions, looking at all the cuts and scratches I had accumulated. Then, bored with this, I wandered around: picking up a vase and putting it back, a family photo in a small frame, a soft piece of fruit in a bowl on a table next to one of the armchairs. This was a room for grown-ups, one where there really wasn't much for me to do. I would have gone upstairs to the girls' bedrooms or out to the family room at the back of the house, but I wasn't sure when Sarah would be calling me.

I went to the kitchen instead, and opened the fridge. Dinners had been left in casserole dishes, the food crusty now. Cheese was unwrapped and hard at the edge. There was a glass bowl with jelly and I ran my finger through the middle, cutting a line that wobbled through the raspberry, hastily licking it off when I heard the door to the lounge open, followed by Sarah's voice saying my name.

'There you are.'

I looked around for Eddie and she told me he'd headed home. 'I won't keep you long,' she promised.

The small room off the lounge (which was, I suppose, a breakfast room) had bookshelves around two of the walls, dog-eared paperbacks stuffed into each shelf. The floor was covered with papers, stacked in piles that threatened to topple at any instant. Under the window, there was a round table, with four wooden shapes on top of it: a circle, a square, a triangle and a hexagon.

We were going to play a game, Sarah explained as she pulled out a seat for me. 'It's called: Find the Smartie. I want you to close your eyes when I tell you and then pick the shape that has the Smartie underneath it.'

It seemed both easy and pointless.

'You can eat any Smarties you find,' Sarah said. 'Or save them to take them home.'

I shrugged my shoulders. 'Sure.'

The game must have lasted about fifteen minutes, maybe less. I closed my eyes when I was instructed. Sometimes Sarah asked me questions while I waited for her to choose her hiding place, strange questions that I attempted to answer. When I was allowed to look, I picked shapes randomly, never thinking there could be a pattern. I had mixed success. The few Smarties I won, I ate immediately. I was thirsty, and didn't really want them but didn't know how I was going to carry them home on my bike.

Eventually we finished.

'Thank you, Lena,' and she smiled at me, letting her glasses fall to the tip of her nose again. She scratched at the side of her neck absentmindedly, her skin red and flaky beneath her nails. We stood at the front door together, the day bright outside the gloom of the hallway, and she told me she would see me soon.

At home, Eddie's Smarties were in a bowl. I didn't know how he'd got so many.

'I won them.' He looked at me with an icy triumph that was unfamiliar. 'It was an IQ test.'

I had no idea what he was talking about.

'A test to see how smart we are. How quickly we could figure out the pattern and find the Smarties.'

'No it wasn't.'

Eddie began to count his out—slowly, loudly.

'You're lying.'

He ate one, looking across at me as he did so.

'It was just a game.'

'Was it?'

His smirk made me want to punch him.

'She never said it was a test.'

'Yes she did.' He ate another Smartie. 'Besides, it was obvious. To those of us with high IQs.'

'What a load of crap.' I tried to hit him but I only succeeded in sending all the Smarties scattering to the floor.

Eddie seized me in a headlock and I kicked him. We rolled onto the ground, crushing the Smarties beneath our body weight. When I bit him, he screamed.

In the cool of the late afternoon, I rode my bike along the narrow backstreets that led to Susie's house. It was almost evening and the lights were on in the upstairs windows. The front door was open and I could hear the TV inside and music coming from one of the bedrooms. I had crept out of our house and ridden over there because I had thought I wanted to talk to Sarah. I hadn't envisaged encountering the rest of the family, and now that this seemed possible, I was less certain of my mission.

I stood for a moment at the front door, and then feeling foolish and embarrassed, decided to go home. As I picked up my bike from where I had dropped it at the entrance, Sarah peered out from the light of the house into the oncoming evening.

'It wasn't fair,' I told her, when she realised it was only me standing there, hesitant, eyes still red from crying after being punished for the fight with Eddie.

We sat together on the cold sandstone paving that surrounded the house, our backs against the wall as she tried to understand.

'What were our marks?' I wiped at my nose, smearing grease from my bike across my cheek.

They were both high, she told me.

Was Eddie a genius?

According to the test, he was certainly in the upper levels.

And me? Was I a genius, too?

She looked at me directly, her pale eyes watery and blinking nervously as she tried to explain that the test was just one measure of intelligence.

'It was wrong,' I said.

She waited for me to continue. At only eight years old, it wasn't easy to explain why I felt there had been an injustice.

The garden was in darkness now, only the camellia bushes that grew near the house were visible. At my feet a few bruised heavy heads had fallen onto the sandstone, the petals crushed underfoot, their thick perfume sweet against the smell of mud, dirt and leaves. I picked one up and pulled it apart, the bloom silky to the touch.

She would take me home. My mother would be worried. And she stood slowly, reaching down for me. I didn't take her hand. Lifting my bike up from where I had let it fall, I told her I would be fine.

'It's just around the corner.'

It was too dark. She would get her keys and we could put the bike in the boot. 'I won't be a second,' she told me.

But I didn't wait. Swinging my leg over the crossbar, I rode down the garden path and out onto the street, the coolness of the night soothing as I pedalled faster, the wind in my hair and the rush of air against my skin as I turned down the steep hill that led to the river.

At home, they didn't hear me; my parents, sitting in the kitchen and discussing Eddie's test results, while in the sunroom, Eddie watched television, holding a bloodied piece of meat to the black eye I had given him.

'I worry about Lena,' my mother told my father. 'She is so angry.'

'You worry about Lena?' My father was surprised.

I stayed perfectly quiet.

'Maybe she is jealous of him?'

I could tell my mother didn't really believe her own words.

'Maybe we don't give her enough attention?'

With my ear pressed against the door, I clenched my fingers in the palm of my hand, white-knuckled and silent. They had got it so wrong. But I stayed where I was, listening to them searching, fumbling for an understanding, while I remained unable to explain what it was that had upset me.

As I sat on the edge of my bed, having left Juliette still drinking beer in her sunroom, I could articulate why I felt there had been an injustice with a concise clarity that had eluded me then.

You see, I would say if I could inhabit my eight-year-old self, I thought it was just a matter of random chance. I should have been told that there was a predetermined pattern for me to decipher, and rules to follow.

But at the time, when it had mattered so much, I had been unable to find words for all I felt.

I got into bed. Somewhere, in a suburb nearby, Jono would be lying next to his new girlfriend, one arm half draped across her body. Up and down my street, people slept in pairs, children dreamt, and dogs and cats curled up in baskets. And then there were the others, houses with people like us. At the time, I had backed away from Juliette's casual grouping of the two of us. But perhaps she was right. Like her, I was alone. My work was barely happening, and it was choices and accidents, and my own doings and the doings of others, that had brought me to this place. Sometimes I thought of it as freedom, but I had come to be less sure now that I was here in an empty house I called home, a place where the wind was liable to rush through the gaps under the doors, as sudden and cold as the fear of having once again missed what matters.

Provisional Desire

by

TIM RICHARDS

I.

URING THE FIRST month of the strike, the Players Association ran a series of costly television ads designed to show that its members were highly accomplished entertainers and that, even for the best, their time in the spotlight was short and precarious. At any moment, an individual could suffer a career-ending injury, and the players' portion of the television revenue had to be commensurate with the delight they gave to a huge fan base and with the massive risks they took.

Convinced that an accommodation would soon be reached, and untroubled by the loss of pre-season games, most fans sided with the players. If their heroes were expected to accept a socialistic wage system, to demonstrate unwavering loyalty, to submit to out-of-season drug tests, and behave as perfect role models for youngsters, they deserved serious remuneration. According to media analysts, viewers were touched by the oft-screened images of star players who couldn't bend to lift infant children, and young retirees who needed sticks when walking to the newsagent's. Every survey pointed in the same direction. Players were to be cherished as selfless knights through whom we can project our fantasies of adulation and triumph.

As March tipped into April, and the opening of the season proper was postponed, public sentiment began to shift. With negotiations between the

Commission and the association stalled, the union was seen to be self-serving and intractable by an increasing number of impatient fans. While defending the players' right to swan about like European royals, association spokesmen seemed content to see the grassroots game bled dry. Soon, front-page stories told of drunken players assaulting citizens who'd criticised their strike in the letters pages of the major newspapers. These bullying allegations quickly led to ruptures in the united front, with various star players—golden boys whose contracts were eight times the league average—complaining that the strike was unnecessary, and that their association had been hijacked by radicals with a long-term political agenda.

By the last week of April, with the association now widely perceived to be the cause of this turmoil, and with its members increasingly subject to random acts of violence, the executive warned players to exercise strict caution regarding when and where they appeared in public. More generally, police were recording high levels of violence in the community as small frustrations quickly escalated into dangerous conflict. Though the attendances at minor-league matches trebled, crowd behaviour at those games took sudden brutal turns. One match at Sandringham had to be abandoned when a riot broke out, the result of remarks exchanged between members of the crowd and a player whose brother was prominent among the striking players' representatives.

Then, on 9 May, after three days of discussions that pundits described as promising, the commission shocked the sporting world by announcing that the season would be abandoned. Despite rumours that a secret deal had been struck between the commission and the television rights holders, the general response was not so much outrage as stunned disbelief. Melburnians would have to endure the unthinkable: a bleak winter without warmth from the game they loved.

2.

The game had always been much more than that in the city of its invention. It was a ritual, a quasi-religion, a second language that nearly everyone spoke to some degree. If you had nothing particular to say to someone, but needed to mark their presence, you made idle chat about the outrageous ill-fortune of the Tigers, or the likelihood of an old champion returning to his former glory. Even those who disliked the game, and privately disparaged it, found it easier to nominate a club allegiance and maintain some awareness of that team's fortunes than to be automatically considered alien and deficient by those they did business with. In many large city offices, full-time positions were created for persons who did little more than run the tipping competitions.

The game seemed to define and determine the rhythms of a sprawling metropolis whose growth had run parallel with the growth of its great clubs. Even in a relatively young city, these were among the oldest sporting clubs in the world, and the feel and spirit of many communities was inextricable from the history of the clubs and players who had carried that suburb's colours into battle.

To speak of pervasive grief would be to understate things. Having lost a measure of their identity, many fans became unbalanced. Through May and June in the year that time forgot, one couldn't drive the streets of Melbourne without seeing troubled wanderers who'd been cut loose by history. Nearly everyone said the same, there was danger in the air. In the absence of the game that bound the social fabric, anything was possible.

3.

While this new sense of possibility frightened many citizens, for some it represented a unique opportunity. Not all lost souls were beanie-wearing imbeciles. Among their ranks were scholars and professionals who had, before the strike, no real notion of how much the game, and the continuities it represented, meant to them. In the normal course of events, a diminutive painter like Kylie Petz would have been invisible to a game-worshipping barrister like Chris Wright.

'You're missing it, aren't you?'

When he nodded, she knew she could do whatever she liked with hunky Chris. Gumby wasn't as malleable as fans rendered bereft by the game's absence. But if you gave these people attention, if you looked as if you understood what they were going through, they were grateful.

To friends, Kylie described it as a *Planet of the Apes* situation. Though humans like Chris had brain capacity approaching that of an ape, there were too many situations where they'd never been required to use their intelligence, and, under stress, they reverted to default settings.

She could take Chris to a David Lynch film such as *Mulholland Drive*, and he would appear to be engrossed, clutching her hand tightly while Naomi Watts and Laura Harring got amorous on the couch, but later, in the foyer, he'd be in a daze. When asked what he thought, he said it would've been great if the umpiring hadn't ruined it.

'The actors? You didn't like them?'

'No, they were fine. But the umpires wouldn't let them play.'

'You couldn't follow the story?'

'Umpires should let the game flow, and not be so arbitrary.'

Most likely, Chris had struggled with the editing, or the fractured narrative, but she wouldn't press him further on the matter. Better to ask if he wanted some comfort food, like a pie or a hot dog.

'Can we? That would be great.'

With his excess nervous energy to be burnt off, their lovemaking was frenetic, and if Kylie's man needed to imagine himself with a bone-headed trophy girl when they made love, it didn't bother her. She saw real gratitude in his eyes. And afterwards, he kissed her neck, and thanked her as tenderly as he would the flanker who'd snapped the winning goal in a tight semi-final.

'Do you love me?' she'd ask.

'Mmm.'

'More than anything?'

'Mmm.'

'So, we'd be doing this if there was a game on?'

She only said that to provoke him. There was no game, no winter, no time or time-keepers. The lovers had been beamed to the Planet of Forgetting. One might have expected Chris to spend this non-season reviewing the hundreds of matches he'd recorded, but he feared the staleness of their taste. He was worried it might never be the same again, that the corporate types running the league would seize this chance to snuff out unprofitable clubs and lay waste to the game's great traditions. Best not to think about it. Best to think of anything but.

'If you'd like, we could do that again.'

He gently kissed her breast, grateful that Kylie had come to the aid of a lost soul.

4.

Kylie couldn't be with Chris all the time, and her hunky barrister simply wasn't equipped to make small talk about the Guggenheim exhibition or the DVD re-release of *The Umbrellas of Cherbourg* with persons recently accused of murder or kidnap. Now, when barrister and client ran short of things to say, there was nothing to be said, and this led to crises of confidence that saw good lawyers like Chris sacked for the pettiest reasons. If the strike leaked into a second season, society would crumble. In this city, it wasn't possible for strangers to speak of Giacometti's innovations, or the young Catherine Deneuve's bizarre choice of wallpaper in the way two decent men—a barrister and an accused killer—could discuss players who'd never come good after a whack across the head, or the old-style enforcers who dispensed whacks.

As spring, the season of the glory, arrived with no whistles blown in anger, talk turned to the validity of the players' long-term contracts, and whether some kind of rapprochement could be effected in time for the national draft. Even under constant pressure from politicians whose seats were threatened as a result of new crime and productivity figures, the commission—with the deck stacked in its favour—wanted to teach players a lesson they'd never forget, as if it would be possible for survivors to forget the Plague Year.

Once or twice, Kylie caught Chris straining to initiate something—to suggest a café, or an exhibition that they both might like—and was moved by his efforts to learn her language. Could she introduce such a man to her parents? Would they praise her for winning an unlikely victory over natural selection? Hardly. Soon, both sides would call an end to the power struggle, and she'd have to set her big man free. Maybe he'd remember her twinkling eyes, and her praise of Rothko's spirituality; maybe those things would be forgotten the instant he heard the crowd roar when his team took the field. But in the meantime, they had the bedroom and Chris's deep well of gratitude.

5.

Though nothing would be the same again, soon everything was almost exactly the same. Just 8 per cent richer, the players gave and received big hits, and trains bulged with fans still rubbishing the umpires as they made their way home. People soon learned to speak of the strike year as if life and death had taken a holiday. Events attributed to that year were accorded the same status as legal testimony given under hypnosis.

Some painters like Kylie made it their business to become the memory of that time, and wouldn't fail to see the irony when rich players, acting on their manager's advice, purchased key Absentialist works.

Often, when she was lonely, Kylie thought of Chris and his need of umpires, and whether it could have been possible for someone like her to meet those needs, or for him to more truly meet hers. As a golden autumn turned sullen grey, and the fans' loyalties were tested as they had been for a hundred and fifty years, Kylie wanted to believe that her lost man was truly found, even if he could never know the joy she'd known when ruling the whistle.

Part Six of our serialised novel

Stripped

by

CAROLINE LEE

The story so far

We begin at the end: Lillian's family and friends witness her death. Then we go back in time and meet Sophie, Lillian's sister, at her job table-top dancing in the city; Daniel, Lillian's husband, brushes off the sense that something is looming. Martin, ex-lover of both Lillian and Sophie, out and about in the city, stumbles upon Sophie dancing up a storm; Sophie, under pressure, loses a shoelace and her mojo, and Jack, a customer, watches her slam dance. Lillian goes to the doctor, Daniel plays cards with the boys, and then Lillian, waiting for the news about her health, understands that they are all inexorably setting off into something new.

The screws begin to tighten: Sophie finds it increasingly difficult to ignore both the bad things that have gone on at the club and the bad state of Lillian's health; Lillian starts her treatment: she is coping, Daniel isn't; Martin visits Sophie at the club and cries—about Lillian.

Eighteen: Sophie plays nurses and doctors

LILLIAN IS REALLY ill. Her eyes have puffed up and so has her face, but the rest of her is sunken and shrunk, like someone very old. She has no hair, not one strand anywhere on her body, and of course there's also her bandaged jaw and mouth, the parts messed up by the surgery. I had no idea it had got this bad.

I'm at her house in the suburbs—Rowville. In the ugly house with flat, stark light everywhere. Lillian doesn't care about material possessions. Or something. It's Saturday morning.

I'm dressed in one of Lillian's nighties because there was nothing else. I didn't know that I was going to stay. It's one of those old-fashioned nighties in flannelette, with three buttons at the neck, a little collar, and sleeves that end in an elasticised frill. It made me cringe to put it on but that's all there is and it's chilly and bleak out here. The only heater's in the living room. I have some thick socks on too. Won't stoop to the slippers.

I'm standing at the kitchen bench, laminated in grey, making toast for Lillian. Daniel's gone fishing. His friend rang him last night and asked him and he lit up like a boy but then said he wouldn't. Lillian and I made him ring back and say yes. He needs time out, and I'm here. So he left in an excited rush really early this morning. It's still early now, and everything is very quiet out here.

I spread the first slice with margarine and vegemite. On impulse I slice off the crusts and cut the toast into triangles. It's a little joke and I'm sure Lillian will protest, but anything to make food somehow palatable, manageable. She's eaten hardly anything since I arrived. She has ulcers in her mouth and throat, on top of everything else. As I arrange the triangles on the plain white plate, so utilitarian, I feel my chest tighten again. I thought she'd get over it. After the first shock, of course. I mean, Lillian's a rock, she gets over everything. The little pieces of toast look so frail, so young, sitting there on the solid white plate. My face gets hot but I can't cry, tears aren't so good for Lillian, I've seen that already, when Daniel cries. Tears stop her from eating.

So I work slowly on the next piece, taking the margarine across the regular white slice in careful sweeps, trying to breathe, trying to stay in control,

57

keeping myself whole. But the tears come anyway, just a few before I can stop them . . . drop, drop, drop onto the laminex. I straighten up. Drop, drop, drop onto the flannelette, and a few onto the floor. I watch as one tear slides off my nose and falls onto the bench, glistening despite the harsh fluorescent light in the kitchen. There's so much going on. Things feel different, but maybe it's just the flannelette nightie. The ugliness of the light irritates me all over again, it's so harsh, so uncompromising, so holy in its ugliness.

Holy things don't have to be ugly. There are so many amazing cathedrals, here and all over the world. And the Pietà is not ugly. Made me cry for hours. The love between mother and child, the vulnerability of the naked, dead man.

But Lillian has adopted another way. Has turned her back on the mystical, the religious, the emotional, even the sensuality of the material. Except in her relationship with Daniel. From what I can see, that is the only living thing around her. The rest is hard, bleak, rational, ethical. And suffused with the smell of Pine-o-Clean.

When did it start, Lillian's obsession with Pine-o-Clean? Sometime during adolescence, or maybe earlier, but it has certainly developed further. Perhaps it's the illness. I've already seen five bottles. One on the sink, two under it, one in the laundry and one in the bathroom. All just the regular type, no lemon or ice-breeze or anything, just straight Pine-o-Clean. All hospital grade. It makes me realise that here there's no pretending any more. The house is drawn up for battle.

I should have realised that things had changed from that phone call with Lillian when she went on about the cyclone. She doesn't usually do that—talk about the past, or how she feels. But I hadn't really been listening, hadn't understood much of what was actually happening. It took the conversation with Danny to wake me up.

'Shit, Sophie, it's so good to hear you.'

'So how is she? Is she still home?'

'Yeah, for the most part. She's just finished the second round of chemo.' He paused. 'It's bad, Sophie.'

I started to tremble.

He continued. 'So she did this next round of chemo and she hasn't been handling it, well, her body hasn't. She's been really nauseous, she's had a bad stomach, awful ulcers, lots of pain and then there's her jaw . . . And she's gotta

5⁸

have at least one more cycle, before we find out if it's working.'

If? Trembling. Aching. Lillian. 'Oh Daniel, that's awful.'

'Yeah and—' his voice cracked. 'Look, Soph, I know you're busy and that, but do you reckon you could—'

'What?'

'Well, I know it's a long way . . .'

'Come over?'

'Yeah, come over, Sophie, that would be great.'

After the phone call I left home straightaway and arrived about one in the afternoon. Daniel picked me up from the station and we spent that first day and night together, the three of us. With Maxine, the nurse, appearing intermittently. We cooked and talked, caught up. I hadn't seen Daniel since Christmas and the last time I'd seen Lillian properly had been that difficult lunch at the Syracuse. After that there'd been a few phone calls, her telling me bits and pieces about her diagnosis and treatment. But she hadn't given a lot away about how it really was.

When I first got there Lillian was really tense, kind of angry, which I guess was understandable, but I hadn't seen her like that for years, not since our teens, with that kind of wide, wild rage. In the evening when we fired up the barbecue for dinner, she staggered out to watch us cooking, to feel the warmth. It was fun; I felt necessary, somehow, part of it all. When Daniel asked me if I'd stay the night, there was no question, I stayed. That was a few nights ago. Now she's getting used to me being around, she has relaxed a bit and has even started shouting orders from her new bed, perched up like a princess in the middle of the living room. Well, a bandaged-up, bald princess.

So here I am, feeling pretty ashamed and stupid, playing with triangles of white toast on a grey laminex background. Abstract art at its finest.

The doorbell rings.

'Can you get that, Soph? I'm not expecting anyone.' Lillian from her throne.

'But I'm still in my—'

'Don't worry about it!'

'It's okay for you, you're the one who's ill. *I* have no excuse.'

I open the front door. 'Hello?'

59

The couple outside look startled. The woman is staring at my nightie. 'Oh, hello,' she says, 'we're here—oh, my God! It's Sophie, isn't it? Louise! I'm Louise—well it was Burson, now Maitland, Lillian's friend from school. I work in her chambers now. And this is my husband, Jack.'

'Louise! Hi! God, how long has it been?'

'Who knows? Years. Jack, this is Lillian's little sister, Sophie. We were all at school together in Brisbane.'

'Hi, Jack, forgive the outfit, wasn't expecting visitors.'

Louise continues, 'Sorry it's so early, Sophie, but we've got brunch with some friends out in the Yarra Valley and so we thought we'd drop in. We know these guys are always up at this time. I try to drop in at least once a week. Where's Danny?'

'Fishing.'

'Fantastic! Perfect! Oh, and these are for Lillian.' She hands me some really beautiful flowers, big plump tulips, a deep rose colour. 'How is she?'

Lillian calls out from her bed. 'Lou? Is that you? Come in, I'm in here now, in the living room, come and see my new bed.'

I go back to the kitchen with the flowers Louise has brought and to make tea for everyone. I find a vase for the flowers. The toast is still sitting on the bench. Something is niggling at the edges of my mind. I take the toast in to Lillian. 'Eat it. I don't care if you have visitors.'

They all laugh. These two are like all of Lillian's friends. Nice, decent, pleasant people—although the husband, Jack, seems pretty tense.

When I return to the laminex to make the tea, I realise what it is. Louise's husband is one of the regulars at the club. I can picture him in his preferred spot three-quarters of the way down the table on the left-hand side. Yes, that's it. He comes to the club. And not only that, I remember him eyeballing me, putting money in my bra. I'm pretty sure I'm one of his favourites.

From the kitchen I can hear Louise chatting. They had stopped on the way to get the flowers, she was explaining, from her favourite flower shop. It's in Canterbury and is run by a woman called Little Bird because she knows everything about everyone, 'a little bird told her', and she makes perfect decisions every time on what flowers to give to what people on what occasions.

I come to the conclusion that it is very unlikely that Jack will recognise

60

me, encased as I am in the voluminous folds of flannelette, sans wig, and carrying cups of tea, but as I lift up my cup (coffee for me, any time day or night) I see him looking at me with a shocked expression. Oh God, he does know. Our eyes meet. Louise is still talking. He blushes. Just a little red spot low down on each cheek near his ears. He opens his mouth a little. Looks at Louise. Fiddles with his cup. No, he's not going to confess, now, in front of everyone? Please don't let him feel he has to play the hero. He doesn't need to do that.

I realise there is a pause, a long pause. Even Louise has stopped talking. I take a sip of coffee. Sneak a look at Jack. He's still fiddling with his cup.

But then Lillian starts to talk. A monologue, demanding and authoritative. The sacred province of the ill. And there's still an edge of that anger. 'You know,' she says, 'I should never have given up ballet. I think that was a mistake. If I had held on to ballet, I might not have been ill now.' She smiles. 'No, not really, that's something Mama would say, or the lovely Cathy, I've told you about her, haven't I, but more because I miss it, I really miss it, and I have time to think about those things now.'

Jack relaxes, takes a sip of his tea. And, mercifully, doesn't say a thing. I realise that Lillian is deliberately taking us to another place. She knows! Lillian knows that something is up. It's not so surprising, after all these years, but still . . .

'Do you remember, Lou,' she continues, 'the time we danced across Princess Bridge at four in the morning?'

And a crisis is averted. For now.

Later, after they've gone, Lillian has a sleep and then wakes up with a raging thirst, so I'm again in the kitchen. This time I'm making a cup of raspberry leaf tea.

Looking after someone who's really ill is a bit like camping, one's attention is completely focused on the basics of survival: food, water, defecation, and how to keep clean, warm and dry. You go into another time zone, a time separated from the cares of the ordinary world, a time that is more immediate but also more connected to the larger things, in the present but also in the past and the future. I'm waiting for the kettle to boil and looking at the packet of tea. It's pink, and printed on the packet is a picture

61

of a raspberry, with some leaves and branches. It reminds me of home, home in the stories Grandma told me about Russia. It's reminding me of the story of the expedition to pick raspberries where Grandma was wearing a pink dress and a white cardigan and my grandfather was wearing a plum-coloured shirt with a blue stripe and blue trousers. They were young. And when my grandparents went picking raspberries that time they found each other inside the canes of the raspberries and they started to kiss each other with the taste of the raspberries and that was when they fell in love.

I'm remembering that story of Grandma falling in love when the kettle boils. I pour the water into the cup and take a teabag out of the raspberry-leaf-tea box and put it in the cup to brew. I go into the living room to ask if Lillian wants some honey in her tea and as I enter the room all of a sudden I fancy that Grandma, my grandfather, Mama and our father, as well as myself, are sitting around the bed next to Lillian. We are all much younger. We're not facing in towards Lillian, we are sitting facing out, like in a family portrait, a family portrait that was never taken, and we are all looking towards me because I am also the photographer. I look at my family, look at them looking at me.

The young me is having trouble sitting calmly in her chair, being still for the photograph. The chair is very wobbly. And then I see that the chair I'm sitting on only has one leg. Mama is becoming very irritated with my noise, my agitation, my attempt to sit still and upright on the chair.

'Sshh!' Mama says. 'For heaven's sake, Sophie, for *once,* could you be quiet!'

Then I notice that Grandma's mouth is red: she has been eating raspberries. So is Grandpa's. Mama's chest is red, how it used to go when she got angry. Then I notice that my father's *cheeks* are red, and that he is puffing and panting, as if he has run a long way, and then I see that Lillian's mouth is also red, red and swollen, part of her lip is gone and you can see the redness of her gums.

The young me has very red nipples, they are visible through the white dress I am wearing. My mouth is red too, red where Mama has slapped me, I can see the marks of her fingers on my skin. Then I realise that all of our eyes are red, red because we have been crying.

But now we are trying to smile. We are all trying to smile at Sophie the

62

photographer. Grandma, Grandpa, Mama, Papa, Lillian and little Sophie, all trying to smile for me. And I am the photographer and so I lift up the raspberry-tea box and hold it up to my eye and in the cracks of light I can see them, all smiling bravely at the camera and so I begin to take photos.

'Hold still!' I say. 'That's right! Good!'

I take the shot.

Then I'm looking at the group and I realise Lillian is not in the picture any more, she's gone. I hear myself saying: 'That's right! That one will be just gorgeous. Just look a little bit more this way, that's right. Smile. Smile! You'll be okay. It's all going to be okay. Smile . . .' but I can't continue, not with Lillian gone. I stop, bring down the camera and look at the bed.

Mama says, 'Sophie! Take the photograph! Concentrate! You can't be trusted with *anything*!'

But I just stand there, frozen. Where's Lillian? Where is she, my big sister, who's always been there, has always stood between me and the world?

No, I was mistaken, she's there. She's just tucked down in the blankets and sheets of the hospital bed. It's okay, she's there.

I look down at my hands. I'm still carrying the box of tea, gripping it tightly.

Lillian stirs, among her blankets. 'Is that you, Soph?' she asks croakily.

'Yeah, it's me. Do you want honey in your tea?'

I go back into the kitchen and get the tea. I lean against the bench for a moment. The vision has freaked me. And then I remember the dream about Martin and, finally, stupidly, realise that it was also about Lillian.

As soon as Daniel gets home, I'm going for a walk. I need to clear my head. I need to get ready for what's ahead.

Nineteen: Daniel buries the fish

Finally I get to go fishing with Chicko. I was worried about going, but Lillian and Sophie made me. It's good that Sophie's staying. We need her. And of course, now we've got Maxine, the nurse, coming in every day, things are easier. Lil's had another awful week, still swathed in bandages, and dealing with all the side effects of the chemo. There's lots of pain. Maxine reckons

63

they're all normal side effects, the blistering, the ulcers and the nausea, all part of what goes on for everyone, but Jesus, she should try living with it. And what about the anger? Lil's burning up. What am I s'posed to do about that? At least I'm getting better at doing the laundry. Dad would turn over in his grave. Ma'd be rapt though.

I'm out on the bay, and I'm cleaning the fish. Chicko's driving the boat and I'm cleaning. We haven't done too badly, caught some whiting and some flathead. Pretty good so far. It's a beautiful day, sunny but kind of sharp too. The sea's almost completely green, not that dark, mysterious, wintery green, but a light green, clear, almost like jade; and in lots of places, even though it's deep, you can see the bottom.

So we're moving slowly to another of our favourite spots and I'm cleaning. I work quickly, throwing the guts over the side before we get to the new spot, because otherwise we won't catch jack shit. I start on the biggest fish we've caught and I cut the head off then cut the belly open and start cleaning out the innards and then I see what I've got in my hands and I can't do anything. I can't move, I just stare at the fish in my hands.

I must have made a sound or something because Chicko calls out to me, 'You right, mate?'

I can't reply. I just stare at that fish.

'You cut yourself?' Chicko stops the motor, lets out the anchor and comes over. He's sweaty, I can smell him. He's breathing hard, must be worried.

I still can't say anything. I just stay where I am. On the esky. Holding the fish in my hands. It's Chicko's favourite esky. He's had it for fifteen years. Bought it with his father when they first started going fishing and strictly speaking he doesn't usually let any of us sit on the esky because he's seen too many lids crack that way but this time he lets it go. He lets it go because he can tell that something has happened.

I sit, Chicko stands, and the boat slows its movement and is quiet. We can hear the water against the side of the boat, and feel a tiny breeze. Chicko waits. He can be a patient man when he wants to. He's looking at the water, probably watching the reflection of the clouds; there's some little fluffy ones quite high up, moving across the sky. Might get a bit of a change later on, or they might just drift away. Yeah, they're really high, they're not sticking round. Probably be lovely again tomorrow.

64

'What's up, mate?'

'The fish, this fish. It's fucked . . .'

That's it. I can't push any more words out.

Chicko waits some more. And then he says, 'Yeah, I had one like that once. When I was eleven.'

He waits again, but I'm just stuck on the fish, so he tells me that he was out with his dad, and there was just the two of them. They were cleaning all the fish they'd caught and then all of a sudden Chicko cut a slice up the belly of a fish and inside was this bright orange and yellow growth. He remembers looking down at it. The shock of seeing the fish's body like that, and the confusion. He'd wanted to throw up.

'Yeah,' he says, 'I just wanted to chuck it away.' He pauses. 'But Dad said that it was normal, that things get sick sometimes, that it wasn't a bad thing. He said that it was part of life and that if I just pushed it away I'd never escape the fish and that I'd have bad dreams about it.'

He scratches at his skin, his beard coming through . . . it only takes a few hours after he's shaved and he's already dark again.

'I believed him. Because I'd sometimes had bad dreams, after me mum had left, and I didn't want to have any more dreams like that. So I said to my dad, "Well what am I s'posed to do with it?" And he said the best thing to do is to take it home and bury it. Because that way you're lookin' after it, and you're lookin' after you. And then he said that he thought the fish had probably suffered quite a bit already. So we could just put it in the back yard, under the lemon tree and we'd probably all feel better.'

Chicko stops. He moves to the side of the boat, splashes his hand in the water. He's relaxed, he's not worried about the fish. It's okay for things to be a bit fucked up. I look back at the fish and my shoulders relax, just a little.

'Just chuck it in a bag and we'll fix it up later.'

Chicko looks at me and then walks back and starts up the boat and we go and fish for a few hours in our other spot.

I keep the fish separate and take it home with the others. Later, after we've all had dinner, well, just me and Sophie really since Lil hardly eats any, although at least tonight she has kept what she's eaten inside her, and after I've helped her with her shower and put her back to bed, I bury the fish in the back yard. I can't bury it under a tree because there are no trees in our back

65

yard, but I bury it in a nice corner, a spot that would be good for a lemon tree, perhaps, one day.

Twenty: Sophie and Lillian at home together

It's Monday. The start of another week. It seems I'm staying. We need to talk about how long I'm here for, but we've never been good at those sorts of conversations. And actually, I'm in no rush. Now that I've got a sense of what's really going on I'm reluctant to leave. Even though it's really full on, I feel useful at least and it's also time out from the club.

Lillian takes a sip of yet another cup of tea. 'I'm almost starting to like this,' she says, 'it's so grassy and bitter it feels like it must be doing me good.' She takes the cup and holds it carefully against her chest, her delicate fingers warming themselves up. She looks out at the afternoon sky.

I wander over to the sound system, housed in a long black unit. The tulips Louise brought still look amazing. There's also a clock and there's a couple of photos of Lillian and Daniel, one, in a shiny gold frame, of their wedding, and one of them out in the country somewhere, which is in a silver frame. I touch the silver one and feel my irritation rise. Why couldn't they both just have been gold?

'Do you remember Basho?' I say, don't quite know why.

'Yes.'

'Do you miss him?'

'*Miss* him? No.'

'He's grey and stained now, splitting in a few places . . . but he's still as beautiful as ever.' I'm still looking at the photo of Lillian and Daniel in the silver frame.

'I don't know how you can keep all that old stuff, Sophie. You've always been a hoarder. Old things . . . they smell like old ladies, and mothballs, and dust and—I don't know how you can bear it. But I suppose he was always more yours than mine.'

'No he wasn't. Not at first. Not until you went to high school and got books, and science and knowledge.'

'Oh, is that what I got?'

66

Uh-oh, I hear the steel in her voice. I turn to face her. Retreat. 'No, okay, it's not all you got, no. Sorry.'

But Lillian is already fired up. 'And what did *you* get Sophie?'

'Junk, obviously.'

'No, Sophie, I'd really like to know. What did you get? From *dropping out*? What do you know about? Sex? Men? Money? You obviously know all about Jack. Not to mention Martin.'

I guess this was inevitable. It has been brewing since Christmas at least. So what have I got? I'm besieged by images of Mr Alan and the green glove, but I'm not going to talk about *that*, and as for Martin, where to start? But it's not the whole picture. I feel my own anger and resentment start to rise. I manage to say: 'Well, Lillian, I think I got questions. I got problems. I got ambiguity. And yeah, sure, I think I've still got them, yeah, maybe I'm fucked up, but at least I got the questions.'

'Oh, *questions* . . . and where exactly have your questions got you?'

'So maybe I don't have a house, Lillian, or a car, or a husband, or a barbecue, or a bloody ugly back yard with a bloody ugly view but . . .'

'Yes?'

'But inside it seems—'

'You're thirty-two, Sophie.'

'*Inside* I seem broader, somehow . . .'

'You're smart, you're tough, you're beautiful, you're thirty-two and you work in a strip club. A *strip club*, Sophie! What are you doing there?'

I move to the window and look at the clothes line, closed up like a massive cocoon in the back yard. I hear my voice, flat, hard. 'Yes, Lillian, I work in a strip club. And what would you know about that?'

'What I know is that you are wasting yourself and your life in some sordid, male-dominated fantasy world. I used to buy it, used to buy your line about being in control, this job being useful to serve another purpose, but you've got to wake up to yourself, Soph. It is serving *no* other purpose. You aren't doing anything else with this money that you make, except what? Buying expensive clothing and drinking. It's pathetic. What's more, it's having an effect on you. You are becoming hard, cynical, closed, sarcastic.'

I turn away, move towards the kitchen.

'Don't run away. It's time for you to hear me, Sophie. You have to face

67

this. Where are your friends? Who are they? What's your life? I'm sorry, but it's bullshit Sophie, and it's such a waste.'

I want to kill her. The heat runs through my body. 'Yeah, I know, I know. Little Miss Perfect. Little Miss Perfect Know-All. You are fucking perfect and know everything and judge everything and I'm just fucked, I've always been fucked and I always will be.'

Lillian doesn't miss a beat. 'Oh, for heaven's sake grow up, Sophie. It's time to move on. I don't know how you're going to do it, I don't know what it will take but you have to *move on from all that crap*!'

I don't know what to do. I'm feeling so much anger, rage, shame, grief, all at once. I take a step or two towards the bed. I want to hit her. I feel my arms start to rise up and then I stop, mid movement, confused and horrified. I do want to hit her but there she is, lying there with her bandaged face and her messed-up body.

She watches me, and then it's like it happens in slow motion, I see her face start to crumple, tears seep from the edges of her eyes. 'Oh. Oh no,' she whispers. 'No. I'm sorry, I'm sorry.'

I stand there, suspended, my arm raised, and I feel all my anger dropping out of me. I lower my arm and look at her. Finally I say, 'No, I'm sorry.'

She looks at me, stricken. 'I push people, too much.'

'I think I deserved it.'

'Well, maybe,' she says, brushing away a tear, 'but it's not all.' She takes a breath. 'I saw you.'

'What? Saw me what?'

'I saw you. Strip. At the club.'

'Bullshit.'

'I did. A couple of months ago. Not long after we had that lunch. Not long after I found out . . . how sick I was. And . . .'

'What?'

'What I saw Sophie, what I saw were beautiful women . . .'

'Who did you go with? What night was it?'

'I went with a man from work. And it was a Saturday night. I thought there would be less city men around, that I'd be less likely to run into a client. Or a colleague.'

'Did you tell Daniel?'

68

'No.'

Strange, somehow that makes it feel real. I sit on the side of the bed.

'It *was* different to what I'd expected, Sophie. In lots of ways. I mean it's all so genteel, isn't it? The doormen, the woman at the desk, the cloakroom. And then you go through those doors, and it's like . . . another world. It's so warm, and dark, and cosy. And then there's you, the women, stretched up like naked pillars, holding the roof up. Those incredibly beautiful bodies, on display, but also not on display . . . like art. You can look at it, you can admire it, but you can't touch and you can't have. It's incredible. All this pent-up desire, all this longing. And yes, I saw it, you have power, all of you. You are in control. At least of *that*.'

I think of the club, part of me for so many years, many more than I had planned, and yet the very place which let *that* happen to me.

'Then later I saw you dancing, upstairs, doing a solo; and you were amazing, so confident and free, so beautiful. Your routine was clever, that dialogue you have with your clothes, "don't throw me away, don't get rid of me, I'm good for you . . ." It made me laugh. I loved it. I thought you were incredible.'

I hold my knees, rest my head on them. Hold on tight. Listening, but thinking about the rubber glove. And the lime condoms. And the men who wanted to break me. Wishing I could make it better.

'The only thing was, you know, I couldn't really see *you*, Sophie, my . . . precious . . . little—'

She breaks off, and looks out into the back yard. I can see she's trying not to cry. I want to cry too. Because about that, at least, she's right, there's no room for that part of me at the club. She turns and looks at me, and there's so much love in her face that I think I might implode, right there in front of her. I can't say a thing. I'm stuck. Will she still feel like that when I tell her about the rape? About Mr Alan and his friends? If I could stop time right now, I would.

69

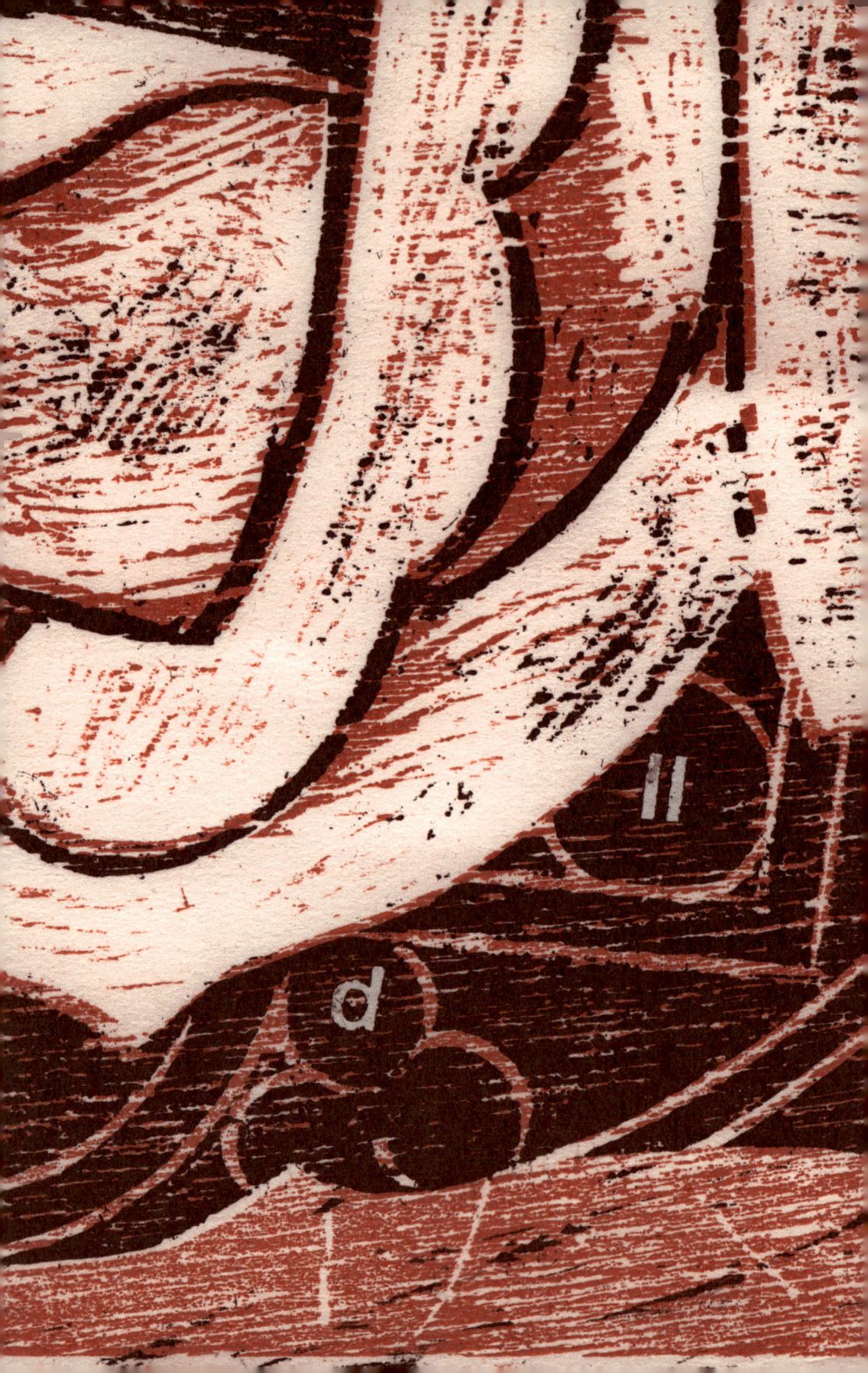

2

c

POETRY

HEAT WAVE, MELBOURNE—
HOTTEST DAY ON RECORD SINCE 1855

Snorkelling a sunken platform three feet deep
    south of Ricketts Point,
        coralline, in various shades of lime

some white with death
    stand out in a field of glow weed
        and sea lettuce.

A transparent shrimp
    treads water—its swimmerets
        on fast-flipper—crunches a piece

of eel grass with maxilliped-snatch,
    does a ninety-degree shift,
        drops the fragment,

then return-butts a dark-mouthed conniwink
    as if mad
        with reckoning.

That's when I notice
    an entire family of conniwinks
        bumping into each other.

A smooth pebble crab, its swollen claws
    embracing the base of clump grass,
        holds tight as a boat's wake

churns sand
    and gusts everything
        sideways. Then an

unidentified mollusc,
    with its own moss garden
        on its back—has learnt

to trust camouflage—manoeuvres
    in strap weed without
        freezing-frame. Easy to

float for hours in this kelp meadow
    — the heat above —
        where

orange winged spider-wasps
    oddly emerge
        from coastal heath

and hover sea-surface
    for anything liquid. Where
        cormorants gather with no need

for wing-drying. Where
    crested terns fly lower
        than yesterday. Where

a fly drops out of the sky
    landing dead
        on my lap.

Michelle Leber

RELIGIOUS EXPERIENCE

Something like a temple has appeared in the hotel lobby
                                        rising up past the mezzanine
huge tarpaulins engulfing extravagant chandeliers
                                        in their diminishing perspectives.
The deep green weight of it pools at corners
                                rough paint spattered
                                        one foot forward.
It makes the workmen with their saws and bolt guns tiny
                                as they step in and out of its tall sides.
Despite the muffled hammering and scrawl of power tools
                                the lobby has gained a kind of quiet.
We sit backs against walls conversations subdued by nothing
                                but size and darkness
while those emerging through glass revolving doors
                                        pause one arm still raised
bemused at having to take the long way around.
Something has arrived
                        that turns this place of occasional impatience
                                        into ceremony
its broad canvas its giant taking up of space
                        like a mountain or a chasm
                                those epiphanies of geography we worship
but moved into another realm of intercourse
                                like seeing through our own eyes by reading
                                        someone else's book.
And then it's gone wrapped up lifted away
                                and out of a mighty sleeve
                                the newly renovated coffee lounge
a bit of glitter some fresh plastic
                        perpetually resurrected altar of cakes and libation.
Together with the one cup one page readers
                                and the low cupped hands bow
                                        of the lighters up of cigarettes
I breathe the deep aroma and read my magazine
                                with a diligence to be aware
                                        as if it's a grain of sand
while the blessed stamped and proven human chant resumes.

Caroline Caddy

UNBORN

1. Morning sickness

I had lost myself in a novel by Marie Darrieussecq
in which a woman grows bacon skin—broken by
hair that claws with its roots, coarser than on her
pudenda—and teats like gelatinous melanomas.
I saw her fretting and muddying the earth until her
rear end let forth a litter of mutant-lets, pink and
coarse as tongues and slippery. Their lids were serene
as if eyes did not exist, and their ears were closed
to the sound of their own not screaming. It was then
I felt the tide come in, bearing silt stirred from the
fetid sea floor, old with starfish and eel bones. The
moon, for nine months, did not care to claim it again.

2. Ultrasound

I had read that some women feed life with scratched
hunks of earth that gravel their teeth, with the residue
of fire that sludges their gums, and with the odourless
powder their grandmothers used to stiffen petticoats
of crinoline. I imagine the starch creaming my throat grey,
and to us you look colourless as if you were made that way.
Still emerging from yourself, the bud of your nose alone
makes the universe less impossible. You do not know
that we are here, but this is how we watch you: on a
black-and-white plasma screen suspended on a wall
—the happy technician flicking us between dimensions
like Dr Who—and as if from an infinite distance.

3. Foetal movement

In my guidebook to pregnancy, a pencil illustration offers me
a profile of myself: armless and headless, legs to mid thigh,
only my reproductive organs and waste channels sketched in.
My abdomen encases an upside-down foetus above the
bulbous and textured outline of my rectal cavity, the muscular,
smudged passage of my vagina and my clear urinary tract.
The caption announces that by the end of the seventh month
the foetus can respond to taste, light and sound, and it can cry.
As I watch you shadow box with sourness, radiance and din,
the sources of which you must fear like a medieval Christian,
you make of my belly a theatre for unseen marionettes and
for pain that has no origin—except for the life I have given.

Maria Takolander

STANDING AMONG THE PHILOSOPHY CLASS
THERE WILL BE SHADOWS, MURMURING

Have courage to use your own understanding!
—Immanuel Kant, 'What is Enlightenment?'

Coats wet, we come
fog-breathed
to hear how we might come to know the world through pure
    reflection without recourse
to experience

rain on our foreheads, little fists from the tremendum,
    we wait
at the doors of an unlocked lecture hall.
Coughing has been falling from a cold girl's mouth. A huddle
    of minds in the dark morning
apprehend. The trees

are wearing the shape of trees.

Dan Disney

PRECIOUS FEW

Not him. You've seen him by a garden bed,
Hard at it on his haunches with a trowel,
Though once the pink dome of his hairless head
Emerged above the fence,
And there with glistening eyes and wobbly jowl
And idle humour to dispense
He left you free to let five minutes lapse,
While somewhere in the grounds his guinea fowl
Made cries like rusty taps.

But that won't do it. Certainly not her,
Above her boyfriend with her knees apart
And ardour which the broad day can't deter,
Sprawled in a public park
Among such seeding grass as Jeffrey Smart
Would paint, and over them that dark
Oppression behind the sky and garish city
He brings to bear. One day. And yet your heart
Is hardened against pity.

Nor even her. You scarcely would believe
Such indurated certainty. But no,
Not even her, met on her final eve,
And with her wasted frame
Depleted even from two months ago,
A rumour then who could not claim
Indulgence of your thoughts through half an hour.
Look how her daughters usher her as though
She held a precious power

The having and the loss of which they'll bear
Like some glass vessel brimming in the hand
Away with them. But you will not go there.
The dead with claim on you
Are elsewhere, and you're shocked to understand
In all the crying world how few.
One day. Then you will bear what must be borne.
And these will not turn back to reprimand
Your impotence to mourn.

Stephen Edgar

GRAPHOLOGY 808: BEETOPIC OR BEETOPIA?

Indifferent to imagery and choreography,
the bee colony intense with the sparseness
of pollen—only wattles and some eucalypts
are in blossom. Near the hamlet, in the hollow
of a York gum—fruits of dead core,
living tree eaten out, dead bone within
living bone, all trace of age digested like ritual—
a message from Rumi, master of the whirling
dervishes, implanted like compassion shaped
as 'hive' amid 'nature', God's exotica,
we are annihilated, forgetting consequences,
disciples threaten, letting the 'wild' be 'wild'
and the farmed be farmed, a cartoon gimmick
in the age of cinematography: Australian
cinematographers famous for their clarity,
preciseness of imagery exported across
the world stage, elevation of local
to a universal chatter, blasphemy
holy and healthy, desirable.
Within the hive, within the nest,
admire warily, as politics
is proximity cross-pollinating
to make food an essential alibi,
performing to be heard, to gain
right of entry, see in and out
of the dark heart
where the queen works
the crisp cold of a valley winter.

John Kinsella

TALKING TO ANGER
after Denise Levertov

Ah, anger, you are a bat,
a serrated shadow
on every pearling dusk.
        You hang blackly overhead,
sleek and folded,
shuddering with growing thunder.

Your silent call
vibrates the great dark bowl cupping us
and creeps into our hidden places,
a tolling bell with no sound.

You have a proper function:
you catch the scuttling rats and sharp-plated
creatures before they grow too big
in their unlit caves.
        Even if we are only white figures disappearing
from the corner of your unwinking eye,
maybe you yearn to put up your black umbrella wings
and shelter us.

But it is against your nature.
        When the friendly hand is extended
you must bite.

Roberta Lowing

BREATH POEM

In at least one Eskimo dialect the same
words mean both 'to make a poem' and
'to breathe'.
—Ruth Finnegan

There is a hole in the ice
and you wait patiently
making clouds with your own
breath.

You draw out with the vapour
such a song, of birth
and hunting, the white intense
depth of the sea, how small
and lonesome it is to be.

Inhale: a great bear
has reached your island.
Exhale: the fish has accepted
your hook.

A seal twists into shadows
of ice. Stars tumble
over the snow. Each breath
enlarges the sky.

Gather your joy into
stanzas, chant. Feel songs
like bubbles in your blood
rise up and overwhelm you
in their ecstatic flood.

Shane McCauley

LURE

Cold in the river, his finger
let fall the ring, his life
unravelling in a coil of light.

Later, it seems the ring itself
sought resolution, deliverance.

At the time, all he could do
was follow the spinning
glint of it, like a fish to a lure.

Jillian Pattinson

VOCALISE IN THE HEATED WORLD

Clearly the song will have to wait
Until the time when everything is serious.
—John Ashbery, 'A Pact with Sullen Death'

Outside—spookily,
all that posturing,
repetition. Everything falls away
as it was encouraged to do,
traffic, orthography,
language of the unattributable dead.
    Leaving us with what?
Schoolyards without a cause,
the children grown up and off
at their rackety wars. Men
crisp enough to knot a noose
burst from foreign cars—
extras of the underworld,
    demanding,
but what is it they want,
whom do they importune?

Carmen is more like a man, don't you think?
says the devilish diva in her Eiffeled apartment.
    She should know,
extending her tapered fingers,
running them up her arms like spiders
that trill for her alone.
She may live to play the Don,
seduce the aristo opposite,
jilt herself in the only act set in paradise.
But no repeats, she insists. No repeats.

    Distant,
an old gate creaks open, shut,
still as the mandated night.
Late sirens moon above the city.
This is Hollywood—ever
and only Hollywood.
    But there is no gate,
not where we live now.
Never was.

Peter Rose

MERE COGS

Walking wide autumn on Old Quarry Hill
z-running dog deranged on potent scents
a painted sign: *Attention Bees At Work*
arresting rows of hives, a sudden chill.

Deja wooden barracks whose order stamps
through florid sun-and-hum to black-and-white
to documentary skin, the hollow eyes
of ill-starred fellow beings culled in camps.

Work really is freedom the troops insist
as their million volts arc the loquat trees.
Sick-smelling flowers give up in silence
meticulous the purge, not one heart missed.

Beelines don't deviate for man or dog
it's always thus for all the thousand years
down chains of command the click to obey
cool shibboleth of acting as mere cog.

Trudge home, hugged loads of wood to fiercely axe
for day has fallen deathly cold at six.
On the hill the barracks will be guarded
no eyes peer inside, dark silence of wax.

Firelight fakes ripples on this glass of wine
no gay gypsy jew heartbeating my door
or need to front the question bunkered here:
Open . . . or deafly bolt? Think: mine! Or mein?

THE MOUTH OF BABE

In the beginning, of the end,
was the word
fishlippery she blurted it
he, oh yes, he heard.

Athlete, adagio, neighbour-knocking
the mutual lust they'd slaked
decades of climactic slide and grip
she'd Oscar-winning *faked*!

It flew her lips at breakfast
never the time or place
for once to fold the peacock's tail
now ego all over his face.

Her o-shaped mouth cannot unsay
the zero before *gasm*
their stripped-pine kitchen table
now two sides of a chasm.

'Don't let it come between us'
(a pun she'd not meant to utter)
but as the toaster popped its load
both knew they were out of butter.

Rod Usher

SPRANTO LOST

Once on a time
    Time was a language
Once on a time
Old everybody spoke
In god's esperanto

Once in the language
They made a lot of bricks
A bric-a-brac of bricks
To stack and stick and stack
Way up to heaven

A tower in clouds
Aloud in the cloud
Stack rattle pop
And they all could speak
    In god's esperanto

Not happy, little men,
Said the god like thunder
Booming broadly
Against that babble
Of people from Babel

So he broke their language
    Like bits of firewood
And blew them all away
Across the desert
Of differing tongues

Off now they scattered
Camelback muleback
    Misunderstanding
But yearning still for
The language umbrella

Chris Wallace-Crabbe

ON BECOMING A BUDDHIST

On becoming a Buddhist you were not seen,
busy with yourself in another country, anointing the Dalai Lama's feet,
rearranging Jesus on your memory's mantle.

This is what you knew: someone made you, added the eggs
and beat into stiff peaks. Yes, surely that was God,
surely that was Him and Her tearing their robes in the back seat.

You divine baby, you holy child, swinging teenage salvation arms.
The nuns forewent you with their sextants to heaven
trained on the perils ahead. Perhaps it was the yoga

that gave you the ability to flex beyond your old beliefs.
Now you woo deities with perfumes and glances, sure the arc
of an ecstatic pose will get you into somebody's heaven.

Maria Zajkowski

TANK WATER

After each winter we felt we had plenty,
like a year's worth of words, waiting to speak.

Given by drizzles, showers and floods,
the rainwater mellowed for months
in the tank, till we washed some, drank

some, returned some, as steam, to the sky.
To measure the depth, we'd strike with
a spade, translating the answer by ear,

or slice off bamboo and jiggle it down
to show us where low tide began.
If summer rains fell, we saved

every drop, but I wished I could
waste just a little, to roll back
the lid, when the days got too hot,

and dangle my feet, where the sky
swam. To ease myself in, and float
on my back, cradled by decades of storms.

Marita Hastings

DOROTHY SARGENT ROSENBERG ANNUAL POETRY PRIZES, 2009

PRIZES ranging from $1,000 up to as much as $25,000 will be awarded for the finest lyric poems celebrating the human spirit. The contest is open to all writers, published or unpublished, who will be under the age of 40 on 6 November 2009. Entries must be postmarked on or before the third Saturday in October (17 October 2009). Only previously unpublished poems are eligible for prizes. Names of prize winners will be published on our website on 5 February 2010, together with a selection of the winning poems. Please visit our website www.DorothyPrizes.org for further information and to read poems by previous winners.

Checklist of Contest Guidelines

- Entries must be postmarked on or before 17 October 2009.
- Past winners may re-enter until their prizes total in excess of $25,000.
- All entrants must be under the age of 40 on 6 November 2009.
- Submissions must be original, previously unpublished, and in English: no translations, please.
- Each entrant may submit one to three separate poems.
- Only one of the poems may be more than thirty lines in length.
- Each poem must be printed on a separate sheet.
- Submit two copies of each entry with your name, address, phone number and email address clearly marked on each page of one copy only.
- Include an index card with your name, address, phone number and email address and the titles of each of your submitted poems.
- Include a $10 entry fee payable to the Dorothy Sargent Rosenberg Memorial Fund. (This fee is not required for entries mailed from outside the USA.)
- Poems will not be returned. Include a stamped addressed envelope if you wish us to acknowledge receipt of your entry.

Mail entries to:
Dorothy Sargent Rosenberg Poetry Prizes, PO Box 2306, Orinda, California 94563.

MEANJIN.COM.AU

Articles · Essays · Stories · Poetry · Spike

Designed by The Golden Grouse
www.goldengrouse.com

Developed by Inventive Labs
www.inventivelabs.com.au

INFORMATION
~ ABOUT ~
SUBSCRIPTIONS

Please check out website for online subscriptions, which should become available by September. Also check out the joint *Meanjin/ Overland* subscription deal. Two journals for only $110 a year. *Meanjin*'s subscription rates are set out below.

To subscribe, contact the *Meanjin* office on (03) 9342 0317 or visit our website at www.meanjin.com.au.

SUBSCRIPTIONS RATES

WITHIN AUSTRALIA
Individual—full: $80
Individual—concession: $60
Schools: $80
Other institutions: $125

OVERSEAS
Individual: $105
Schools/Institutions: $150

MORE THAN ONE YEAR
8 issues: (individuals only)
Regular: $145
Concession: $120
Overseas: $180

12 issues: (individuals only)
Regular: $190
Concession: $165
Overseas: $240